Accounting for Taste

PRISCILLA PARKHURST FERGUSON

Accounting for Taste

The Triumph of French Cuisine

The University of Chicago Press
Chicago & London

PRISCILLA PARKHURST FERGUSON
is professor of sociology at
Columbia University. Her previous books include *Paris as Revolution* (1994) and *Literary France* (1987).

The University of Chicago Press, Chicago 60637
The University of Chicago Press, Ltd., London
© 2004 by The University of Chicago
All rights reserved. Published 2004
Printed in the United States of America

13 12 11 10 09 08 07 06 05 04   1 2 3 4 5

ISBN: 0-226-24323-0 (cloth)

Library of Congress Cataloging-in-Publication Data

Ferguson, Priscilla Parkhurst.
Accounting for taste : the triumph of French cuisine / Priscilla
Parkhurst Ferguson.
p. cm.
Includes bibliographical references and index.
ISBN 0-226-24323-0 (hardcover : alk. paper)
1. Cookery, French. I. Title.
TX719.F423 2004
641.5944—dc22
2003020876

♾ The paper used in this publication meets the
minimum requirements of the American National Standard
for Information Sciences—Permanence of Paper for
Printed Library Materials, ANSI Z39.48-1992.

For Robert A. Ferguson, once again and always

Quoi! dira-t-on peut-être, encore un ouvrage sur la Cuisine? Depuis quelques années le Public est inondé d'un déluge d'écrits en ce genre. J'en conviens: mais c'est précisément cette multiplicité d'Ouvrages qui donne naissance à celui-ci.

[What! perhaps someone will say, another work on cooking? For the past few years the public has been deluged with writings of this sort. I agree. But it is precisely all these works that give birth to this one.]

—Menon, *Le Manuel des Officiers de bouche* (1759)

My definition of man is, "a Cooking Animal."
The beasts have memory, judgment, and all the faculties and passions of our mind, in a certain degree; but no beast is a cook.

—James Boswell,
The Journal of a Tour to the Hebrides with Samuel Johnson, LL.D. (3d ed., 1786)

Contents

Illustrations

Acknowledgments

Every book is also a collective endeavor, one that calls on a great range of institutions and individuals. Since *Accounting for Taste* has been in the making for some time, my debts are great, first to the institutions and groups that invited me to share my research and to the journals in which some aspects of this research appeared: the *American Journal of Sociology* for a version of chapter 3, *Gastronomica* for part of chapter 2, and *The French Review* for sections of chapter 4. In these days of dire budget cuts in New York City, I mark special appreciation for the New York Public Library, an immense resource to every scholar and a great pleasure for every reader. Then, too, the Feast and Famine seminar at New York University extended my culinary purview considerably.

The National Humanities Center provided a wonderful retreat from academic cares in 1994–95 and for short visits since. I am extremely grateful to The National Endowment for the Humanities, whose award of a fellowship in 2001–2 allowed me the uninterrupted time to complete the manuscript.

My greatest debts, however, are to the *gourmandes* and *gourmands,* the chefs and the cooks, the friends and acquaintances, who have shown such interest in my work, passed on anecdotes as well as references, who have dined with me and debated my ideas, pushed me to look beyond what was on my (and sometimes their) plate to the complexities of many eating orders in which we all participate. Finally, to Robert A. Ferguson, who wined, dined, and sustained the author, read and refined the book: as always, the thanks go beyond words.

The Culinary Pantheon

Consider the power of culinary nationalism in this revision of the Panthéon in Paris.
A giant oven-chef bestrides the frieze in place of the usual classical dome, and the
motto now reads, "To Cuisine, the Grateful Country" in place of "To Great Men, the
Grateful Country." Illustration by Bertall in Briffault, *Paris à table* (1846). Courtesy of
Columbia University Libraries.

Eating Orders

I.

The destiny of nations depends how they feed themselves.

—J. A. Brillat-Savarin, *Physiology of Taste* (1826)

The art of eating and drinking, is one of those on which more depends, perhaps, than on any other, since health, activity of mind, constitutional enjoyments, even learning, refinement, and, to a certain degree, morals, are all, more or less, connected with our diet.

—James Fenimore Cooper, "On Civilization" (1838)

"Mann ist, was er ißt"—We are what we eat, the German adage tells us, and it has never been truer. In a veritable explosion of critical work on food over the past decade or so, literary critics and sociologists, historians and anthropologists, not to mention nutritionists and organic farmers, have repeated, claimed, and examined this truism from every conceivable angle. Some reverse the dictum, starting from, rather than ending with, identity. But whether practitioners take the culturalist tack—we are what we eat—or the materialist notion—we eat what we are—virtually every discipline now understands that food presents us with what Marcel Mauss called a "total social phenomenon," that is, behavior and products so tightly woven into the fabric of the social order that society cannot be imagined without them.

Recently critics have begun to explore how and why and under what conditions this work of cultural weaving occurs. The same interest has prompted a proliferation of journals and conferences, series at university presses, articles and textbooks, degree programs, literary works, investigations in a great number of fields, and finally, organizations that range from the Association for the Study of Food and Society to a cosmic answer to fast food—namely, "Slow

1

Food." The sudden intense scholarly and cultural interest in food must be looked upon as a fin-de-siècle phenomenon, one that deserves close consideration as we move into the new century.

Accounting for Taste takes up this enthusiasm through a French version of the German axiom: "Tell me what you eat, and I'll tell you who you are." The aphorism, from Jean Anthelme Brillat-Savarin's totemic culinary text, the *Physiology of Taste* (1826), reminds us that food practices are constructed within a social relationship. Like Brillat-Savarin, I listen to what people say about food, most especially what they write about food; and I do so to discover what, in a very fundamental sense, they, and we, are. I take France as the template for thinking about food because, now as in the nineteenth century, France and its culinary customs, or foodways, are emblematic of a distinctive, highly constructed, and sophisticated conception of food with a special emphasis on its role in cultural understandings.

The first problem in such an investigation is a fundamental one. How do we get a handle on "food," the physiological need that is always more than nutriments? Where does one start to follow the many transformations and metamorphoses of food; what concepts do we use; what analytic perspective do we adopt; and, for that matter, how do we define *food* in the first place? Do we follow the farmer and the cook or the diner and the chef, the dietician and the doctor or the customs officer and the restaurant owner? Each will have different and possibly conflicting agendas and idiosyncratic definitions of what food is, what it does, what it should do, and how to talk about it. The physiologist and the biologist look at the foodstuff itself: how and where it is grown, and its place in the food chain. Others focus on the symbolic manifestations and meaning of food: the writers who describe food in their work, the painters who dote on representations of it, and the critics who try to address both the writings and the paintings. Economists will likely track the production of food, while historians work to reconstruct patterns of its consumption from the past. The anthropologist typically examines the foodways of a given group, while the sociologist will focus on institutions such as the meal or the restaurant, on occupations, on concepts. Still—and however convenient in the disposition of the intellectual and even the "real" world—these divisions are largely artificial, the by-products of disciplinary and occupational boundaries that are themselves constantly challenged.

Accounting for Taste examines the scene of "culinarity," or what the French would call *le culinaire*, "the culinary." It seeks to circumscribe, to explore, and to elaborate some of the ways in which food structures and expresses the worlds in which it is found. If, as Claude Lévi-Strauss famously put it, food is "good to think with," it requires a form that makes such thinking possible. For Lévi-Strauss that form is myth. For me it is cuisine—the code that brings food into the social order. As dining socializes eating, so cuisine formalizes cooking, and it does so by reworking the fundamentally private act of consumption. We cannot share the food we actually eat, but food as subject and scene creates a collective experience that we can and indeed must share.

There is a larger theoretical point to stress here that turns on linguistic categories. It is all too easy to conflate food and cooking, gastronomy and cuisine. They are, after all, closely related phenomena, each impinging on the other in ways both expected and unexpected. But beyond the fact of the relations, translation and conversion govern the connections. To understand the larger cultural system in which these conversions operate, we must work to keep the terms distinct in a more finely tuned awareness of their mutability. *Food* refers to the material substances we humans consume to meet the physiological requirements for sustenance; food is what we eat to live. *Cooking* begins the primary transformative process that puts food in a state ready to be consumed. But if *cooking* involves chiefly the producer of the dish, *gastronomy* (a new term in nineteenth-century Paris) points to the sophisticated diner, to the embodiment of Brillat-Savarin's ideal consumer: "Animals fill themselves, people eat, intelligent people alone know how to eat." From eating simply to live, *gastronomy* moves us into the realm of living to eat. Comprehending producer and consumer, cook and diner, *cuisine* refers to the properly cultural construct that systematizes culinary practices and transmutes the spontaneous culinary gesture into a stable cultural code. Cuisine, like dining, turns the private into the public, the singular into the collective, the material into the cultural. It supplies the cultural code that enables societies to think with and about the food they consume. As cooking makes food fit to eat, so cuisine, with its formal and symbolic ordering of culinary practices, turns that act of nourishment into an object fit for intellectual consumption and aesthetic appreciation.

I propose this book as both a geography and genealogy of culinary culture. Taking cuisine as a privileged agent for the elaboration of a collective identity, I focus on culinary texts ranging from cookbooks and menus to poems, novels, essays, and latterly film and television, to track French culinary identity from its beginnings in the seventeenth century through its elaboration over the nineteenth century and into the twentieth. Today, in the opening years of the twenty-first century, as my last chapters suggest, this conception of culinarity continues to counter the ephemeral nature of food and to dominate the transitory culinary gesture, both in France and abroad. For it is the tour de force of French cuisine to be defined as at once national and cosmopolitan. National identity is invariably constructed from without as well as from within, and French cuisine offers a case in point, playing as it has these three hundred years and more both abroad and at home. Today, French cuisine has competitors that it did not have a quarter century ago. Diners everywhere have discovered tastes of which they had no inkling just a few years ago. Long gone is the unquestioned superiority that allowed a French restaurant guide to judge Japanese cuisine as neither good nor bad but simply "astonishing." Other cuisines today lay claim to culinary precedence. Even so, and however assertively its ascendancy is contested, French cuisine retains its power as the ideal of culinarity. Today as in the nineteenth century, though differently, French cuisine supplies a point of reference and a standard. It is that identification of cuisine, country, and excellence that *Accounting for Taste* seeks to understand and, indeed, account for.

II.

And so one can hope to discover, for each particular case, how cuisine is a language in which a society unconsciously translates its structure, unless, equally unconsciously, it agrees to reveal its contradictions.

—Claude Lévi-Strauss, *L'Origine des manières de table* (1968)

The French, as we all "know," are culinary masters—so much so that to modern ears, *gastronomy* sounds far more like a French enterprise than the original Greek word on which it is based. The etymology of the term—the law *(nomos)* of the stomach *(gastro)*—presumably refers to a biological fact, but the law of the stomach in France legislates much more than what actually enters the digestive tract. It bespeaks the normative nature of French foodways that so strikes foreigners. At some level, everyone acknowledges the rules, regulations, and hierarchies that make eating in France at its best a distinctive experience. However much culinary dissidents may flout these rules, few can afford to ignore the laws of gastronomy. As an emblem of French civilization, cuisine ranks right up there with cathedrals and châteaux, recognized by citizen and visitor alike as somehow intrinsically French. Not without reason did that superlatively French writer, Marcel Proust, identify his great novel with a cathedral on the one hand and a sculptural beef in aspic on the other. Moreover, the recognition obtains whether or not the cathedral is actually visited or the great meal consumed. Each belongs to the national heritage.

But what makes Proust's beef dish French? How did it get to be part of that heritage? How does it differ from the boiled beef that is a staple all over the world? Why does food loom larger in the cultural landscape of the French, if in fact it does? True, French elites have invested heavily in culinary affairs at least since the seventeenth century; to what extent have these official resources moved down the social scale and out to the country as a whole? What does French cuisine "do" for France? Why has this tradition not become just another vestige of the Ancien Régime, such as Versailles or the châteaux of the Loire Valley, visited for their distance from life today? Finally, what future does our assertively postmodern era hold in store for distinctive cuisines, French along with many others? How do the cooks and chefs, these artisans of the everyday, cope with contemporary pressures of globalization, internationalization, rationalization, democratization?

These questions led to this book. The ensuing answers have turned up less in the particulars of French culinary history than in an ideal that accounts for the extraordinary vitality of this cultural product and its position in French culture. As anthropologists have long known, foodways set societies apart from one another. The French can invoke a vast number of regional specialties, from Roquefort cheese to foie gras, but they are hardly alone. Americans, too, can turn out a sizable list of culinary products defined by place—from New York bagels to North Carolina barbecue, New England clam chowder to southern fried chicken, scrapple from Philadelphia, and on and on. These foods, anchored in place, lay the foundations of regional cuisines—the culinary practices defined and enriched, and also limited, by local products and producers. A truly national cuisine is something else again. A modern phenomenon, a national cuisine is part and parcel of the nation-state that emerged in the West during the nineteenth century. As a culinary system both different from and greater than the sum of its regional parts, French cuisine materialized across a tumultuous century of political, social, and cultural revolutions. Cuisine supplied one building block—a crucial one—for a national identity in the making, for it encouraged the French to see themselves through this distinctive lens as both different and superior. Moreover, this form of Frenchness compelled all the more because, unlike Bastille Day or "La Marseillaise," it was not an artifact of official decree. The power of French culinarity comes from its reach into daily life. Not that regional cuisines disappeared. On the contrary, the late nineteenth and early twentieth centuries saw their integration in a French culinary landscape where they became what they still are: vital components in the intellectual and cultural construct of French cuisine, a lively type for the relationship of the regional parts to the national whole.

An illustration from a guidebook of the mid-nineteenth century cleverly captures the status of cuisine as national cultural good. The tour of Parisian dining in Eugène Briffault's jocular *Paris à table* (1846) takes us to a familiar Parisian monument, the Panthéon. Begun as a church in the mid-eighteenth century, this imposing edifice served the French Revolution as a final resting place for its great men, Voltaire and Rousseau most notable among them. *Paris à table* shifted these priorities. In place of the imposing classical dome, a giant oven-chef bestrides the frieze. With a kitchen knife stuck in his apron and two sauté pans dangling in front, the monumental chef sports two forks as arms, one of which brandishes a giant skimming ladle. A steaming stew pot–face grins under the pot-cover hat, from which stringy vegetable tops stick out like unruly hair. The inscription on the monument conveys the redirected expression of patriotic gratitude: replacing the "Aux Grands Hommes la Patrie reconnaissante" of the original—To Great Men the Grateful Country—this version of the Panthéon proclaims "À la Cuisine la Patrie reconnaissante"—To Cuisine, the Grateful Country.

France had every reason to be grateful. At least from the mid-seventeenth century, French chefs had journeyed to foreign courts as culinary missionaries. In the expanding economy of the nineteenth century, as Briffault and many others incessantly rhapsodized, the production and consumption of food kept the commerce spinning and the culture lively. All of the many regimes that followed the storming of the Bastille—three republics, three monarchies, and two empires from 1789 to 1870—relied on culinary practices to further their own ends. All of them operated from the urban center of Paris and its definition of country. In this domain as in so many others, it was the bourgeoisie that legislated in the name of France, and it legislated from Paris. Hence the culinary pantheon could stand nowhere else. Like any other cuisine with claims to a national audience, French cuisine negotiates the shifting space between the center and its peripheries, between the capital and the provinces, between the ties to geographical place and those, no less real, to an inclusive cultural space. As the culinary pantheon makes abundantly clear, French cuisine conveyed, promoted, and inspired Frenchness—no small contribution in a country where regional divisions ran deep enough to compromise a fledgling national unity more than once over the century.

Rhetoric notwithstanding, neither the revolution of 1789 that overthrew the monarchy nor the new century of Napoleonic conquest and nation building wiped the slate of cultural legacy clean. Indeed, the purposeful melding of antithetical traditions with contemporary concerns constitutes one of the enduring paradoxes of French society. The new century only strengthened the centralizing forces inherited from the Ancien Régime. "Since 1789," a critic on the Far Right groused in 1870 as Paris was besieged by the Prussians, "there has always been a king of France, and only one: Paris."[1] Others greeted this Paris-centric society with joy. It was, after all, the immense concentration of cultural institutions as well as economic assets in this city that led Walter Benjamin to his celebrated characterization of Paris as the Capital of the nineteenth century.

And one great resource of this kingdom, as *Paris à table* impresses upon us again and again, was the range of public dining it offered the wealthy and (relatively) impecunious alike. Although restaurants first appeared in Paris in the late eighteenth century, they did not dominate public space until the nineteenth, when they became one of the most visible and distinctive of modern urban institutions. In contrast with the Ancien Régime, which coupled cuisine and class, nineteenth-century France tied cuisine to country. It urbanized and then nationalized the haute cuisine once sustained by the court and the aristocracy. It translated largely class-oriented culinary practices into a national culinary code. The elites that supported the haute cuisine of the new century shifted as well. Most of them were new to their entitlement, which originated more from wealth than from birth. (Until the Second Republic in 1848, postrevolutionary regimes restricted the right to vote to men of a given tax bracket.) Consequently, the ostensibly apolitical nature of French cuisine was a great advantage in promoting national goals over partisan interests. Culinary practices served political objectives all the more effectively in that the fellowship of the table seemingly transcended political divisions to draw groups together.

In connections that are more than incidental, the French language took a similar path from the old regime to the new. The fetishizing of the French language has its parallel in the adoration of French cuisine; both presumed not simply excellence but also superiority and order. The cuisine of France, like its national language, is greater than the sum of its parts. Each illustrates the relationship between language and speech, between grammar and rhetoric, between code and usage, between collectivity and creator. During the Ancien Régime the use of the French language characterized a specific group—the king and court, the administration and elites more generally—and a particular place—Paris. The events that followed upon 1789 turned that language into the language of the Revolution, loosening the connections to place by extending the collective identification beyond elites and beyond Paris. Of course, the "frenchification" of France required a century. It began with the dismissal of the many other languages spoken in French territory as dialect or patois, neither of which had any place in the new and, it was hoped, unified country. How to decide? In the oft-cited definition of the great twentieth-century linguist Ferdinand Brunot, a language has an army and a navy. So it was with French cuisine. It could call upon an external, incontrovertible authority. As the great chef Auguste Escoffier would observe with pride, it could call on a cadre of missionaries to spread the culinary good news. French cuisine was, he boasted, one of the most effective forms of diplomacy.

These examples raise central concerns of cultural construction and survival. How do cultures work to reconcile past and present? How do they resolve the constraints of tradition with the imperatives of innovation? Studying any culture in isolation skews perspective and compromises every conclusion. *Accounting for Taste* therefore invokes multiple frameworks of comparison. Although my focus is squarely on cuisine in France during the formative years of the nineteenth century, I set culinary culture against other subcultures within French society. I consider French cuisine and French food-ways in terms of other cuisines and other foodways, and I look at the nineteenth century against the eighteenth and the twentieth, and the twentieth century against the fledgling twenty-first. These many perspectives allow a clearer sense of the myriad ways that modern cultures evolve and function in different places at different times and with different agendas. Issues of cultural survival warrant our concern. Yet the pressures of rationalization, globalization, and internationalization, although identified with contemporary society, do not begin with it. People of the nineteenth century, too, had to deal with the costs of modernization, with the losses as well as the benefits of an industrializing, urbanizing world. French culinary matters hold lessons that reach well beyond either France or culinarity. They touch on issues that should carry great weight for us all—the opportunities for cultural construction and the possibilities of resistance, survival and demise, and, perhaps, revival. Our place in the future depends on understanding our relationship to the past.

The cluster of activities that surround cooking and eating stakes out culinarity as a privileged entry into the social order. Food and foodways afford a singular insight into any culture—into the worlds of women, the empires of men, the realms of children. Cuisine shifts agriculture into culture and inserts physiology into society. Whether taken as product or practice, chef or consumer, or everyone and everything in between, cuisine acts as a vital agent of socialization. It translates the corporeal, "natural," uncooked, and unprocessed into a social actor. By fixing the individual gestures that would otherwise remain buried among the pots and pans, cuisine pushes culinary practice out of the kitchen into the culture beyond. There, in that larger culture, cuisine reaches beyond the food that supplies its raw materials; it outperforms the cooks by whom it is produced; it outshines even the consumers who justify the cycle of production. All this is possible because cuisine is not merely a culinary code that anchors custom. It is as well a panoply of narratives that sustain praxis. Cuisine constructs and upholds a community of discourse, a collectivity held together by words, by language, by interpretations of the world in which we live.

III.

Modern myths are even less understood than classical myths, even though we are consumed by myths. Myths press on us from everywhere, they serve for everything, they explain everything.

—Honoré de Balzac, *La Vieille Fille* (1836)

> Myth is a term chosen by history; it cannot come from the "nature" of things.
>
> —Roland Barthes, *Mythologies* (1957)

Every culture has its myths. Neither right nor wrong, neither truthful nor mendacious, myths *are*. Above all, they are useful. Products of a collective imagination, these understandings of the everyday serve individuals as they work for societies. Whether we are aware of these stories or not, every one of us needs them to make sense of the world that we inhabit, and that need is no less pressing today than in the past. As the exuberantly modernizing Paris of the early nineteenth century impressed upon Honoré de Balzac, myths surround us on all sides, all the more powerful because they are seldom recognized as the outsize narratives that they are. A century later, Roland Barthes located the power of modern myths in just that misrecognition. Putting myths back into history, discovering how, when, and why they took hold, revealing how they work—this is the task that Barthes set for the critical "mythologist."

Accounting for Taste considers one modern myth and the community of discourse in which it operates: the collective understanding that French cuisine offers French culture. Why France? Surely, all cultures have more or less distinct foodways, and many, perhaps most, can lay claim to distinctive foods. Yet few will deny that culinary matters are not everywhere equally present and are not equally valued. Not many cultures look as far as the French beyond the immediate, material consumption of food or cast culinary practice as a general social good. Just why this should be so is by no means self-evident. "Of course," one eats better in France; gastronomy is "unmistakably," "unquestionably" French; and it has "always" been so. That we encounter frankly bad meals under the guise of French cooking only means that the French are not living up to the standards that we accept and believe in. Our acceptance of this "naturalness" and our reluctance to imagine otherwise allow Barthes to identify a myth. Like every other myth, that of French cuisine appeared in particular historical circumstances and continues in others, equally specific, equally discrete, equally compelled by social change.

French cuisine also stands apart not simply as a set of culinary practices, but as a grammar, a rhetoric of that practice, a discursive space. Although every cuisine is a code, some cuisines—and French cuisine has long supplied the paradigmatic example in the West—are considerably more codified than others. If, as commonly alleged, there is no American cuisine, it is because for all kinds of obvious and not-so-obvious reasons, cooking in the United States ranks low on the scale of formalization and codification.

The importance and significance to cuisine of language, texts, and representations can hardly be overstated. As much as the foodways by which it is shaped or the actual foods consumed, words sustain cuisine. These words, the narratives and the texts shaped by them, are what translate cooking and food into cuisine. They redefine the individual act of eating into the collective act of dining. In explaining these modifications in French cuisine and its culinary culture, I have also endeavored to keep in mind what this particular cultural phenomenon might imply for processes of cultural formation generally. It is not just a question of finding out about cuisine and food in a given social setting but of exploring culture itself—how it works, how particular phenomena create and sustain a collective cultural consciousness. French cuisine offers one means to this larger end of understanding how discourse identifies a collectivity.

Chapter 1, "Culinary Configurations," places "cooking" against "cuisine." It sets the analytic logic of the culinary code against the diversity of culinary practices, thereby allowing me not to trace a history of French cuisine—vast numbers exist—but to pinpoint some of the culinary narratives that the French have told about themselves and their food at least since the seventeenth century. Written up, written down, and published, these stories make the text the primary vehicle for the distinct, and distinctive, cuisine of France.

In a close study of the career and the culinary system of Marie-Antoine Carême (1783–1833), chapter 2, "Inventing French Cuisine," focuses on contemporary French cuisine. For it is to Carême that we owe the reconfiguration of the aristocratic cuisine of the Ancien Régime into the elite and assertively national cuisine of the nineteenth century. Analyzing his career and the culinary system that he perfected tracks the emergence of both modern French cuisine and the modern French chef. The portability of Carême's resolutely rationalized culinary code enabled the subsequent professionalization of cooking within France as well as its diffusion abroad; the nationalization and internationalization of French cuisine proceeded apace. A predictably emphatic culinary nationalism in turn made this cuisine integral to a newly identified national patrimony even as it traveled around the world.

Chapter 3, "Readings in a Culinary Culture," moves from the producers and production of cuisine to its consumers and consumption. Here I situate the emergent gastronomic field in the new production site of the restaurant, in newly utilitarian attitudes toward pleasure, and above all, in the gastronomic writings that were published in such numbers beginning in the early nineteenth century. The expanding publishing industry was a boon for food writing of every sort. Here we also shift methodological gears from a historical to a more properly sociological perspective in order to ask what social structures apply to cultural change. The gastronomic field that took shape in the decades following the French Revolution represents a modern cultural formation that grounds a highly developed, particularly acute culinary consciousness in France. These writings—Carême's culinary treatises, the gastro-nomic journalism of A. B. L. Grimod de la Reynière, the protosociological es-says of Jean Anthelme Brillat-Savarin, the "gastrosophy" of the utopian phi-losopher Charles Fourier, and finally, the novels of Balzac—signaled the metamorphosis of the consumption of material foodstuffs and corporeal satis-faction into an intellectual and aesthetic pursuit. French cuisine is French at least in part, this chapter argues, because so many have written so much to insist upon the connection.

Chapter 4, "Food Nostalgia," examines some of the texts that marked French cuisine as a dominant trope of French national identity and reflects on some of the consequences of that dominance. The culinary paradigm evolved in the dialogue between city and country, capital and provinces, nation and region, (male) chef and (female) cook, tradition and innovation. Coming at the juncture of the nineteenth and twentieth centuries, Marcel Proust's *À la recherche du temps perdu* (1913–27) illuminates wonderfully well the dynamics of this nationalizing culinary culture. In a country where the written word has long dominated public discourse, literary connections enhance any cultural enterprise. Although "gastro-literature" is hardly a French monopoly—some of the greatest examples date from antiquity—the salience of the connection between matters literary and culinary is a distinctive feature of French culture generally.

The last chapter, "Consuming Passions," reflects on the place of French cui-sine within the culinary order of a postwar, postmodern, postindustrial soci-ety marked by both globalization, which markets uniformity of production and product, and internationalization, which promotes difference and "au-thenticity." French cuisine in the twenty-first century works off both registers in telling ways. I draw on intensive interviews with leading chefs and restau-rateurs in the United States and France to highlight the striking changes of the twentieth century and the skillful adjustments that French culinary leaders have made as a consequence. These postmodern chefs are masters of the art of the everyday as well as cultural heroes in the public eye. In an almost im-possibly intense world of competition and change, they are bound by a culi-nary contract that constrains consumer and chef with reciprocal obligations, shared ideals, and a common history. As these chefs testify so eloquently, the continuing presence of French cuisine is one of its unmitigated triumphs in the twentieth century.

An epilogue focuses on the quasi-cult film *Babette's Feast* as a modern fable of French culinary culture. That a film should supply an iconic culinary text for the twentieth century is surely appropriate for a food culture that has be-come at once more cosmopolitan and more local. A celebration of the senses, *Babette's Feast* invests cuisine—very pointedly French cuisine—with incom-parable powers of conversion. The spectacular repast that caps the film summons up a vision of sensual and spiritual well-being created by the transcendent artistry of a chef who, through her art, recreates her country. Babette makes the vital link in the culinary chain that converts the raw to the cooked and the material to the spiritual. This film takes French cuisine as emblematic of the community that the culinary creates, sustains, and restores.

Cuisine, then, for me, is both a structure and an action, a set of principles as well as practices. Following Pierre Bourdieu's injunction to keep contraries in play at all times, we need to think dynamically of a structuring structure and a structured action, a changing structure and a fixed action. This dual perspective leads me to consider the many ways that eating structures society, how individual acts of consumption create and become part of the collective order that we usually term *culture*. The significance of the claims made by Brillat-Savarin, Cooper, and Lévi-Strauss in the epigraphs of this prologue lies in their insistence on just this connection between eating and the social order.

Accounting for Taste deals with the many explanations that French cuisine gives of taste. I consider the characteristic stories about food and the people who tell them, the ideas no less than the products that sustain a distinctively French culinary order. And since French cuisine has long played in an international arena as well as on a French stage, this culinary world has shaped the experiences of food around the world, often in unexpected and even unlikely venues. Taking a cue from Norbert Elias, who famously claimed that "civilization" constituted the self-consciousness of the West, I suggest that cuisine in France, French cuisine, has acted as the culinary consciousness of the West and, at times, its conscience as well.

Culinary conscience? The claim is a large one, but it applies. Individuals and groups always coordinate in the making of a decision, whether it is personal or public. We are shaped by the arrangements that society sometimes allows, sometimes gives, sometimes enforces. What we decide, then, is a mixture of choice and cultural formation. The development of French cuisine offers a wonderful example of how this process can achieve unprecedented heights in common understanding and celebration. As such, it is an exciting story that carries beyond itself in what might be called the sociology of cultural agreement. Taste is intensely personal and simultaneously a matter of collective conception. Just as we see only what we allow ourselves to see, so we taste what experience has taught us to accept. No one ever sees quite the same thing, and there is no taste on which everyone will agree. French ideas about food rose to dominance through an extraordinary collaboration of the general and the idiosyncratic. In a remarkably short period of time, a handful of striking figures put their stamp on the way food should be prepared, consumed, and, even more important, thought of. That said, they were able to conceive better than they knew only because of the social institutions within and against which they acted. The centralization of individual initiatives through institutional affiliations and codifications is a very characteristic French behavior pattern. That this phenomenon came to rest so powerfully and permanently on food, its preparation and its consumption, is the mystery that this book seeks to explain. And the answer will lie in another collaboration. For whatever the difficulties of the enterprise, the pleasures in the accounting for taste won the day—a day that extends from the eighteenth century to the twenty-first.

CHAPTER ONE

Culinary Configurations

I. Culinary Identities

"If you are what you eat, this is one strange-looking salmon."

—Caption on a photograph of a brown bear in an
advertisement for the Bronx Zoo in the New York City subway, summer 1997

Food, Cooking, and Cuisine

That we are what we eat explains why so many of us expend so much effort to control what we do—and do not—eat. From allergies to aversions, the dangers of the palate lurk behind the anticipated pleasures, and both preoccupy us precisely because food plays so central a role in constructions of the self. Thinking rather more like our premodern ancestors than the postmoderns that we often fancy ourselves to be, we alternate between the hope and the fear that we will somehow come to resemble what we eat. Apprehension of the unknown invariably colors the hope of bliss. Inescapably, fear of pain colors our expectations of delight. At the same time, as the Bronx Zoo poster reminds us, we do a lot with what we eat, and on all levels. Transformation, not addition, supplies a more appropriate model for what humans do with food, from digestion and defecation to symbolization, which is why food has so much to do with constructing our identities. Individually and collectively, though in a very complicated way, we are indeed what we eat.

We are also how, where, when, and why we eat. Humans eat many different foods in different venues, on different occasions, and for different reasons. Our most fundamental physiological needs convey relatively little about our social selves. Fully as much as standard analytical variables such as work, education, ethnicity, or class, our delights tell us and others what we are. The

15

pleasures that we practice offer signs to the ways in which we construct our selves and how we connect to the worlds around us. Pleasures loom all the larger in our readings of the social world because they limit fully as much as they liberate. More than any other single factor, this fundamental duality, and the ensuing ambiguity, transforms our pleasures into a privileged setting for the production of social identity. Put another way, our needs and constraints force us to think about our pleasures as one definition of well-being. Making and remaking social worlds with every bite we take, we eat what we are and to become what we'd like to be.

A fundamental element of social as well as psychic construction, no pleasure more than our encounters with food defines us more, offering as it does great opportunities for conflict and communion. As a literally incorporated foreign substance, food offers up an emblem of the individual's relationship to the outside world. At once intensely individual and vividly social, our often-convoluted relationships with the food that we consume allow, even invite, us to reflect on the dynamic interrelation of the private and the public, the individual and the communal. A total social phenomenon, food is also a "total sensory phenomenon." It addresses the baser senses—the tongue, the nose, and the palate—along with the traditionally nobler eye and ear. The two totalities are intimately connected. To survive, every individual, every society must discipline that sensory experience and put it to social account. The production, enactment, and expression of that discipline inscribe this totalizing pleasure in an evolving economy of both use and power.

What we do with food, therefore, how we think about it and use it, inheres in what we are, as societies and as individuals. To understand how food operates in an economy of use and power means understanding food as a source of pleasures as various as they are complex, passionately experienced, and ambiguous. The many roles food plays in society reflect as they reproduce this complexity and this ambiguity. A material product that engages the senses and appeases appetites, food is at the same time a symbolic creation tied to the intellect and the spirit, as an end in itself and a means to any number of other ends. Like sex, to which it is insistently compared and invariably linked, eating grounds us in the terrestrial and points us to the divine. We taste the beloved and also the fruits of divine love. The closer edibles come to the volatile, mysterious realms of desire, the more they identify us, individually and collectively. To reach beyond the singular to the collective, beyond the individual to the social order, these antitheses have to be negotiated. Or, rather, we must negotiate. The ephemeral, irremediably private nature of the material culinary product confines actual consumption to the individual. After all, food must be destroyed to be consumed, and in rigorously alimentary terms, consumption is strictly individual. To gain cultural currency, to circulate in society, the material artifact has to be recast in an intellectual mold.

The distinctive properties of food dictate both a need for collective control and a desire for collective experience. If every product implies a consumer, food requires the consumer with an insistence that sets food apart from other goods. Moreover, the consumption of a culinary product requires its destruction. Once presented to the consumer, the culinary product itself, meal or dish, cannot be saved, stored, or otherwise secured in the long term. As with the performing arts, cuisine offers less a product than an occasion for a particular kind of consumption experience. Like music, to which cuisine is so often compared, the culinary experience is ephemeral.

The sensual, corporeal urgency of the culinary experience offers both opportunities and constraints—opportunity in the very immediacy of that experience and in the direct, palpable connection to the individual; constraint in that same direct connection. The more immediate the experience, the more individual, the more private, and the less amenable that experience is to control or to collective construction. The materiality and ephemerality that make eating the ultimate private, fleeting experience demand strategies of a different order to reach the necessary public. Those strategies lead to formalization: first, the imposition of form to regulate the individual appetite, and second, the intellectualization and aestheticization that counter the materiality and ephemerality of food and make a private experience part of a public order. Whereas food calls for eaters, a culinary culture contends with a different sort of consumer, the reader-diners whose consumption of texts rivals their ingestion of food. Reading and evaluating, like eating and cooking, are so many "taste acts" by which individuals "perform" their connections to a taste community. That participation in turn—the culinary practices, norms, and values that derive from and support the cuisine in question—sets us in a culinary culture.

The social survival of food in any given form depends entirely upon the critical discourse that translates the cultural presuppositions about food for the reader-diner. Just as the written word fixes speech, so culinary discourse secures the transitory experiences of taste. It figures the material as intellectual, imaginative, symbolic, aesthetic. These representations socialize food, not the dishes and meals of culinary practice. The texts of culinary discourse convert culinary production into a truly cultural phenomenon. Where cooking humanizes food by making it fit for human consumption, cuisine socializes cooking. The culinary text reconfigures an individual activity as a collective enterprise. The texts themselves include cookbooks and gastronomic journalism, philosophical treatises and literary works. Each of these genres sustains a critical culinary discourse by providing an idiom capable of communicating and generalizing individual sense experience and specific culinary practices. Together, these works make up an archive of culinary attitudes and ideas, techniques and usages. It is to these culinary texts, then, that we must look to investigate the special role that food plays in constructing both the cultures in which we live and our places in them.

The most obvious social objective of culinary discourse has to do with the control of individual and collective relationships to food. The individual no less than society has a strong interest in controlling sensuality—even when that interest is to eliminate all apparent control. Where the individual looks to control pleasure and pain by seeking or avoiding given foods, any group concerned with collective behavior regulates food as an important means of social control. From the parental promise of dessert in exchange for vegetables dutifully consumed to sumptuary laws and religious dietary interdictions, the manipulation of food orders the lives of individuals and institutions. These maneuvers prove all the more necessary, and all the more effective, to the degree that food carries negative as well as positive connotations. Whether "forbidden fruit" is taken literally or symbolically, no collective order exists without alimentary injunctions and interdictions. Foods give pleasure, and they bring pain; they bring health and life, and they bear disease and death. Food poisoning is an omnipresent fear—whether it is a question of eating unfamiliar foods in strange surroundings or anxiety about food allergies. And when *poison* is understood more broadly as "pollution," it is evident that anyone subject to dietary injunctions of any sort for whatever reason is equally concerned with avoiding foods deemed improper, inappropriate, or unacceptable.

Appearance offers no more than clues to acceptability. As Proust's emblematic encounter with his memorable cookie impressed upon the Western literary imagination, we easily miss what is right in front of our eyes. The sight of the madeleine that late winter afternoon told the Proustian narrator nothing; it triggered no memory. Not until he actually tasted the cookie dipped in tea could he fix the gustatory experience and connect it to his life. It is just this discrepancy between external appearance and internal reaction that turns eating into such an intense enterprise. Again, as the Proustian example reminds us, the discordance between seeing, tasting, and memory is one of the reasons sensory experience needs translation into an idiom that encompasses rather than separates.

The cornerstone of culinary discourse and the discipline that it represents is cuisine—the code that structures the practice of food and allows us to discuss and to represent taste. Cuisine places culinary practices in a social context by sharing the experience of taste in an idiom that allows articulation of the present and reproduction in the future. Because they allow us to conceptualize cuisine theoretically as a code and to analyze it empirically as a set of practices, gastronomic words matter as much as culinary deeds. Cuisine specifies the conditions between the general and the particular as it negotiates the gap between collective taste and idiosyncratic tastes. Above all, by socializing appetite and taste, cuisine turns the individual relationship with food into a collective bond. *Accounting for Taste* argues that the central place of French cuisine in the West for some three hundred years is very much a function of the extent and depth, the prestige and authority, of the culinary discourse that it sustains and by which it is amplified, magnified, glorified, and spread.

The ambiguity of the term *taste* and the general impoverishment of our vocabulary regarding taste make collectivization all the more necessary insofar as the simultaneous reference to a sensorial faculty and an intellectual capacity exacerbates the disparity between the general and the particular. Incertitude of reference lies behind the ritual rationalizations of discordant experiences of taste—"Chacun a son goût," "Tutti i gusti son giusti," "There's no accounting for taste." All this despite clear evidence that none of us has a wholly singular taste and that, from chefs to sociologists, many of us in fact spend a good deal of time accounting for taste. In any meaningful sociological sense, moreover, the radical relativism of these aphorisms—which suppose that all tastes are equal—is patently false. Hierarchies govern taste. Every social setting prizes certain tastes and disdains others, and food is no exception. Georg Simmel long ago pointed out the distinctive and paradoxical situation in which the activity that supplies the lowest common denominator for all humans—eating—gives rise to such extensive and elaborate social differentiation. These many hierarchies remind us that the foodways of any collectivity concern not just behavior and practices but also the values that sustain those practices.

Certainly, cuisine cannot exist without food; nor can it survive without words. A more or less coherent repertory of culinary preparations, usually structured by the products at hand, becomes a true cuisine only when its status as a repertory becomes apparent. That is, culinary preparations become a cuisine when, and only when, the preparations are articulated and formalized, and enter the public domain. Although the preparation of food easily accommodates, even necessitates groups as well as individuals, when it is confined to a specific place—say, the kitchen—the group in question will remain small because its foodways and beliefs are dependent upon personal transmission of techniques and practices. Such dependence on connections between individuals renders the cultural status of any practice highly precarious. Thus for any cuisine to reach beyond the originating group, its culinary practices need to be fixed. The written text and the image put cuisine into general circulation by turning culinary practices into cultural phenomena.

Its dual nature as a material and intellectual product distinguishes cuisine as a cultural and artistic product. The element that distinguishes cuisine from other cultural products similarly divided between the material and the intellectual is the utter insistence upon that materiality. Consequently, the intellectualization of culinary discourse necessarily confronts the limits of the material. However much cuisine has to get out of the kitchen to circulate in society, its place, still and all, is in that same kitchen. The comprehensive culinary space of the larger society cannot afford to lose contact with the originating culinary place. Cuisine cannot live by food alone, and neither can it live only by words.

This dependence of the primary cultural product on a secondary intellectual discourse situates cuisine at the opposite end of the production-criticism spectrum from literature, where the original literary work and the critical interpretation make use of the same medium—language. In this respect, cuisine belongs with the performative arts, and as for other such arts, the social survival of the culinary performance depends on words. Recipes make it possible to reproduce the original, or a reasonable approximation thereof. On this continuum, the plastic arts lie somewhere between the literary and the performing arts because although there is a disjuncture between the medium of creation-production and the idiom of criticism, there is a palpable, more or less permanent product. In a paradigm of what cooking is all about, culinary discourse transforms the material into the intellectual, the imaginative, the symbolic, and the aesthetic. This encompassing rhetoric has much to do with shaping the larger culture that envelops every cuisine.

There are probably as many ways to talk about food and cuisine as there are to cook and eat. Whatever the definitions invoked, one cannot fail to be struck by how many of them come in pairs. Rather as if any given culinary mode must be thought of as what it is *not* as much as what it actually *is,* each term works off one or more contraries. So we talk about cuisine as fancy or plain, creative or routine, daily grub or festive fare. Regular rhetorical skirmishes these days pit organic foodstuffs against industrialized dishes; homemade dishes against store-bought, canned, or frozen; local, "authentic" products against exotica; oral against written culinary traditions. Then, the charismatic authority of the (customarily and most frequently still male) chef, reinforced by a plethora of military metaphors, sets up against the domestic authority of the (archetypically female) cook, dominated by comforting images of nurturing and the home. Thus, *home cooking* can be either a term of limitation or an advertisement of authenticity, between the mundane evening supper and the roadside sign enticing the weary traveler to the comforts of home. Plainly, the categories of cuisine are themselves highly heterogeneous. Some refer to the sources or the food served, some to the sites of consumption, others to the occasion, and still others to the producers or consumers.

Virtually all of these differences can be traced to the fundamental opposition between *cooking* (or *cookery*), with its German roots, and *cuisine,* with its French flair. The material transformation of food into a culinary product parallels its intellectual mutation into the kind of culinary discourse that we call cuisine. For the latter, even though the imported term entered the English language in the fifteenth century, it retains a certain air of otherness, of distance from familiar indigenous foodways.[1] Whereas the practice of *cooking* supplies a basic template for material transformation, *cuisine* codifies that practice. The intellectual and cultural metamorphosis of cuisine takes food beyond the strictly culinary and the patently instrumental. Cooking gives us food for thought; cuisine offers thoughts for food. The larger question turns on the relationship between these two kinds of culinary connections. Where does the dividing line fall? Or are we instead dealing with a continuum rather than a dichotomy?

The mutual dependence of cooking and cuisine emerges in the ever-shifting relationship between *place* and *space*. Material culinary production and consumption occur in a circumscribed place—the kitchen and the dining room. By contrast, the production and consumption of cuisine—the writing, reading, talking, and thinking about the intellectualized, aestheticized culinary product—happen anywhere. Here the culinary good consumed is not the food, however transformed, but representations of those transformations. Liberated from culinary place into a broader cultural space, the culinary text circulates freely, subject only to the constraints of writing, not those of cooking and eating. This cultural circulation brings us to modern times where, like texts and images generally, cuisine circulates through complex systems of publication and distribution.

The distinction between culinary place and cultural space helps to delineate the many connections in the culinary worlds that we inhabit, the terms of each equation as well as their constantly shifting relationship. To take one obvious example, the cook and the chef are located at opposite ends of the spectrum running from physical place to cultural space. The cook participates in a largely oral culinary culture circumscribed by physical place. He, but more usually, she, is the quintessential amateur who works alone in a kitchen, relies on products at hand, and reproduces familiar recipes. The connections to other culinary worlds may be direct—my mother's favorite recipes—or indirect—my neighbor's grandmother's recipes; yet they all work through personal connections, however attenuated. The exemplary *chef*, by contrast, works not with friends and relatives but with other professionals who are engaged in innovative culinary preparation and who draw on products from all over. In that professional context the chef acquires systematized techniques, which he hones through extensive practice and research. In contrast with the local public of the domestic cook, the modern chef addresses the anonymous, heterogeneous, and constantly shifting consumers of the restaurant. For cooks, "cutting edge" most likely elicits images of a sharp knife on a chopping board. Top chefs, however, would tend to understand it much as ambitious researchers in other disciplines would, as a metaphor of the innovativeness driving their enterprise.

These portraits, of course, present ideal types and, to a certain extent, idealized ones as well. "Chefs" will have less to do with actual cooking, more with creation, organization, and systematization; the equation is reversed for the "cook" (a distinction formalized in contemporary restaurant kitchens in the United States in the division of labor between the "executive chef" and "line cooks"). Real chefs working in real kitchens do not perfectly fit the mold of the highly professionalized creatures that this model of the chef supposes. As a cursory glance through contemporary culinary magazines will show, the affective, nurturing aspects of food preparation, traditionally associated with the homemaker cooking for her family, show up as well in the world of the professional chef.

That the professional plays in a larger culinary arena than the amateur is largely the work of the culinary text, which extends the private into the public, raises the individual to the collective, and removes food from culinary place to cultural space. Cooking turns the raw into the cooked, and writing transforms the cooked into the cultural. By enunciating cultural practices, values, and norms, culinary texts instill the consciousness that turns cuisine into a full-fledged cultural product.

Cuisine/Cuisines?

At one end of the cooking-cuisine continuum, individual or community styles of cooking work off local products and associated dishes; at the other, a highly formalized and typically normative culinary system sustains a cohesive and coherent cuisine. The pertinent distinctions are more geographical than intellectual or social: the more local or idiosyncratic a style of cooking and the more dependent upon strictly local produce, the less likely that cooking will "travel." In addition to means of transporting products, culinary diffusion needs texts to translate styles of cooking into a general cultural medium. Then, too, there is the vexatious question of *authenticity*. Is a localized, product-based cuisine "authentic" when reproduced elsewhere? Since at least the nineteenth century, when increasingly rapid transportation began to allow defiance of local strictures, culinary conservatives and progressives have been at a perpetual standoff. Conservatives argue that, transportation of foodstuffs notwithstanding, local cuisines should not travel because they have neither culinary nor cultural logic away from their point of origin. These localists assume the indissolubility of a cultural configuration, of foodstuffs, producers, and consumers, and they conclude that, although food can travel, the community cannot. On the other side, whether considering an immigrant group's recreation of a familiar culinary pattern or a traveler's importation of exotic tastes, culinary progressives tend to make use of every new opportunity in their search for culinary creativity and/or "authenticity."

Because every cuisine continually negotiates indigenous and imported foodstuffs, it is far more useful to replace *authenticity* with *integrity* or *identity.* Does the cuisine hold together? Is the whole somehow greater than the sum of the changing parts that it never ceases to incorporate? How strong is the power of assimilation? With time, imported elements—say, any of the foodstuffs brought to Europe from the Americas—become an integral part of the cuisine in question. If one looks far enough back in the culinary history of any country, the most "authentic" foodstuffs are apt to be a good deal less traditional than alleged. Can we imagine any European cuisine without potatoes? Yet the potato came from South America in the early sixteenth century and was first regarded by Europeans as an ornamental plant! Acceptance as a foodstuff took a couple of centuries. (The wary French preferred bread.)

If we look closely at cuisines to determine their governing principles, it becomes clear that the term covers widely, and often wildly, divergent referents. Many of the comparisons made with such alacrity concern culinary configurations that are not at all comparable. At best, *cuisine* is a sliding concept, one that encompasses the nostalgia of "peasant cuisine" or "home cooking" but also the glamour dispensed by the celebrated chef. Subtly or not, these culinary connections imperfectly render practice. They play off the confusion between the social or geographical location of culinary preparations (peasant, bourgeoise, home, restaurant, regional . . .) and the assumed quality of the food. In truth, each of these cuisines sets its own standards. Each has its own hierarchy, which responds to the question implicit in all of these locations in space: *whose* home, *which* peasants, *what* restaurant, *which* region, and so on.

When we look to the actual culinary orientation and content of these many cuisines, we find two basic configurations: *traditional cuisines* and *modern cuisines*. Geography largely controls the former. Self-sufficient and self-contained, the archetypal traditional cuisine neither imports nor exports either people or products. Production and consumption occur in the same place and involve the same agents. However, even the specific meaning of *local* varies considerably, which is why traditional cuisines have been identified with everything from a single community to a region and even a mega-region such as the Mediterranean. Insofar as the locality coheres around products and a lifestyle, communities throughout the region share similar, simple modes of preparation. For staunch culinary conservatives, this fidelity to the land, this rootedness—what the French call *terroir*—makes these local or regional cuisines the only true cuisines.[2] Their assessment favors the material ingredient (the food) over the cultural product (the dish or the cuisine), on the implied assumption that the less transformation undergone by those raw materials, the better and the more authentic the cuisine.

Its origins in subsistence preparations and its development restrained by a necessary frugality explain the fundamental conservatism of traditional cuisine. For the long centuries when famine was an ever-present possibility and wherever resources have to be carefully husbanded, traditional cuisine dictates culinary practices. In precarious circumstances, it is the only culinary mode that makes sense. Even as traditional cuisine entertains a close relationship to the land, it is also tied to the community on that land. Culinary creativity is a luxury, not only because of material concerns but also because experimentation would damage the connections that traditional cuisine makes within the communities from which it came.[3] Of course, this connection, too, becomes part of a cosmopolitan marketing of the local: "Tuscan food," *Saveur* peremptorily decrees, "is about clarity of flavor and a sense of the earth. Not innovation or complexity." Practitioners take pride in the preservation of recipes handed down for generations. The larger culinary culture remains importantly an oral culture, and recipes, when they exist in written form, tend to be imprecise, serving more to jog memory than offer instruction. In the same issue of *Saveur*, the author of an article on Vermont chicken pie enthuses about her "surge of pride" that she is "now one of the custodians of such a rich tradition."[4] *Saveur* works hard to justify the promise it proclaims on its cover, to have us "Savor a World of Authentic Cuisine."

Modern cuisines counter these traditions even as they draw upon them. Their modernity lies, first of all, in simple chronology: historically, they come after traditional cuisines. For that matter, modern cuisines suppose traditional cuisines as a base both from and against which to work. This logic of succession does not entail a unilinear development. The elaborately prepared and highly refined cuisine of Sung China of the twelfth and thirteenth centuries proves every bit as modern as the haute cuisine that emerged in seventeenth- or nineteenth-century France. These cuisines are modern as well by virtue of their willed, highly self-conscious complexity—a self-consciousness that makes the very notion of simplicity exceedingly complex. If place grounds traditional cuisines, freedom from that same place liberates modern cuisine— freedom to experiment and recast the material, freedom from the community, freedom to make cuisine an intellectual and aesthetic as well as a material and sensual experience. Where traditional cuisines must deal with scarcity, culinary invention requires abundance just as it supposes transportation of goods, services, producers, and consumers; a broad geographical arena; and the psychic space to innovate.

Above all, because modern cuisines depend upon extensive communication with a heterogeneous and anonymous public, they must be written. Recipes are published, no longer handed down from one generation to the next or shared among neighbors. Paradoxically, this textuality of modern cuisine fixes food as traditional cuisines never can. Writing stabilizes culinary practices while publication significantly increases the chances for social survival. The work is fixed not in a culinary place—the recipe box on the kitchen counter—but in cultural space.

It should be obvious that these models of cuisine are just that—the possibilities of practice. Nevertheless, they have the advantage of clarifying various constellations of culinary practices and explaining the persistence of certain associations—those, for example, that identify culinary creativity with men and routine cooking with women. The models also help us to understand the principles behind some of the culinary labels so often used indiscriminately. Thus, *peasant cuisine* is constrained less by the social class of its practitioners than by the context of that practice—the oral tradition of transmission, the products particular to a given place, the unformalized and unsystematized culinary practices. Peasant cuisine is the ultimate traditional cuisine defined by place, and regional cuisine is not far behind. Which term is used depends on the social and rhetorical context, whether the emphasis falls on the social class of the producer or the geographical source of the products.

What, then, do we place against peasant cuisine? Presumably, *aristocratic cuisine* would afford the greatest contrast. But with its aura of exclusivity and overt class privilege, *aristocratic cuisine* is not an appropriate designation in contemporary societies. Moreover, consumers alone classify aristocratic cuisine, whereas peasant cuisine connects to a community of producers and consumers. From a strictly culinary point of view, then, traditional cuisine should stand against modern cuisine, with its luxury, formalization, intellectualization, invention, and experimentation; its reliance on advanced technology; and its alignment with diverse urban publics.

Despite the principles that set the two cuisines apart, contemporary foodways draw on both. As with the similarly slippery categories of *popular* and *high culture,* culinary types are subject to continual redefinition. Local cuisines are no longer so local as they presumably once were, since they, too, now circulate in a general cultural space, propelled by texts and representations, even films. By the same token, broad communication, rapid transportation, geographical mobility on a national, continental, and international scale, generalization of technological advances in the preparation and preservation of food—these and other developments mean that most contemporary cuisines blend the traditional with the modern. Even when presented as such, traditional cuisines today constantly move away from the culinary place of origin. Local cuisines import ingredients and techniques as insiders move out and outsiders settle in.

Chowder(s) and the Culinary Civilizing Process

The complexity of culinary action, reaction, and interaction finds a wonderfully vivid illustration in the annual Chowder Contest held on the island of Martha's Vineyard off the southern coast of Cape Cod (Massachusetts). The chowder served on the Vineyard is a variant of the fish soups found in virtually every community close to a source of fresh fish—thus, France has *bouillabaisse* from Marseilles, garlic-laden *bourride* from Provence, *chaudrée normande*, and the *matelotes, meurettes,* and *pachouses* made from freshwater fish in a number of regions. This contemporary chowder of Martha's Vineyard is associated with the North Atlantic coast of Canada and the United States and now usually features clams in a flour-based cream broth.

The *Oxford English Dictionary* first cites *chowder* in 1762. The claim that Native Americans were already making chowder before the Europeans arrived points to the inevitable imprecision in dating a "traditional" dish. Native Americans did not have salt pork, a key ingredient in chowder making; in what sense, then, did they have chowder? The act of naming has the advantage of fixing a dish in that the more specific the name, the closer the definition of the dish comes to a recipe. In this sense *chowder* is generic, while *Manhattan clam chowder* is not.[5] The name most likely comes from *chaudière*, the old French word for *cooking pot* or *cauldron*, and from the custom whereby fishermen would contribute part of their catch to a communal pot and receive a portion of the cooked dish in return. *Chaudrée* was the original French word for *chowder*. From Brittany fishermen carried the custom to Newfoundland, whence it spread south to Nova Scotia, New Brunswick, and New England. Clam chowder is already a variation on the basic chowder, which tended toward the cod fished in abundance in the Atlantic, sometimes in its salted form. Today, as this trajectory and history would lead us to believe, there are any number of local variations, including two that make use of neither flour nor milk: Rhode Island clam chowder, with its clear clam broth, and Manhattan clam chowder, which adds vegetables to a tomato-based broth. Martha's Vineyard "Island chowder" retains the flour-milk base and the potatoes but substitutes mixed seafood for the clams.

If chowder is, then, a traditional, "authentic" regional dish, crossing regions means changing chowders. At different times and in different contexts it may designate the North Atlantic fishing communities on both sides of the ocean, the northeastern American coast from Newfoundland to New York, coastal New England from Maine to Connecticut, or particular communities within each. The Chowder Contest on Martha's Vineyard draws the boundaries of the relevant region, and if we knew when and under what circumstances this particular version became "Island chowder," or, for that matter, when clam chowder became "New England clam chowder," we would have a vital, if undoubtedly ambiguous, indicator of Islander and regional identity. Certainly, in the most famous literary celebration of the dish, the chapter entitled "Chowder" in Melville's *Moby-Dick* (1851), there are two varieties, clam and cod. Melville's nineteenth-century Nantucket, the island to the east of Martha's Vineyard, esteems the two types of chowder equally. Because he is from New York, Ishmael does not realize that the dining choice he is peremptorily given by the hostess of the Try Pots Inn, "Clam or Cod?", refers to chowder, and momentarily fears that he and Queequeg will dine on a single clam.

> But when that smoking chowder came in, the mystery was delightfully explained. Oh, sweet friends! hearken to me. It was made of small juicy clams, scarcely bigger than hazel nuts, mixed with pounded ship biscuit, and salted pork cut up into little flakes; the whole enriched with butter, and plentifully seasoned with pepper and salt.[6]

Chowder fanciers will note in this passage the differences from contemporary chowders. As dishes become less tied to a single source of supply, the ingredients more generally available, the preparation becomes more refined. In addition to the milk and potatoes added in the nineteenth century, bacon now usually replaces the salt pork, and flour thickens the broth instead of ship biscuit. Ishmael solves his culinary and existential dilemma by ordering a cod chowder in quick succession, but even that seems to contain eel as well as cod. As Melville's semi-mock evocation of the Try Pots makes clear, chowder was a way of life, served for breakfast, lunch, and dinner. Chowder pots were always on the boil. Within the novel, chowder serves as sign and portent of the civilization created around the ocean, in stark contrast with the great white whale, the figure of the undomesticated, unknowable, uncivilized ocean.

Traveling from the "Clam or Cod?" of nineteenth-century Nantucket to the Island chowder of twentieth-century Martha's Vineyard takes us on a short but decisive culinary voyage from a highly traditional, very local dish (the outsiders have a hard time finding the Try Pots Inn even with directions from the owner's cousin) to one in which that tradition has assimilated outside influences and has become, in the process, both less local and more self-conscious. Even the ingredients have changed and become more "civilized," since Ishmael's chowder contains neither the potatoes nor the milk that today characterize New England clam chowder. The Chowder Contest—a food event centered on a local specialty that can be duplicated in innumerable variations across the country—articulates these complex connections between, and continual redefinitions of, traditional and modern cuisines. Such an organized competition to valorize a local specialty is likely to come into being precisely when those traditions are felt to be imperiled. With the consciousness of impending eradication on the part of natives or outsiders, the "natural" bond between product and place that Melville makes so significant an indicator of civilization becomes an intellectual, highly self-conscious enterprise of cultural preservation.

An island, Martha's Vineyard would seem to present a textbook example of isolation and all the conditions for an authentic, that is, self-contained, local cuisine. But local cuisines cannot remain wholly local as people and products move and mix. Not only has the Vineyard, like seafaring communities the world over, always communicated extensively with the outside world: for the better part of half a century it has also been a vacation site for thousands of "off-islanders," some of whom possess considerable wealth along with sophisticated culinary habits refined in elite restaurants worldwide. The Islanders must cater to this public even as they work to preserve their identity, and the comments of those in attendance at the Chowder Contest make it clear that chowder presents one means of just this sort of culinary-cultural negotiation. The reporter of the local newspaper and many of the four hundred attendees of the December 1997 contest remarked on the many variations of this one, simple dish, each with its "own unique personality." Devotees and experts divided into two distinct camps: those who swore by the "conservative" chowders made with the sanctioned ingredients of Idaho potatoes and celery, and those who pleaded the case for "radical" chowders. "On the cutting edge of chowder culinary trends," as the reporter put it with only the barest hint of irony, these chowder experimentalists employed variously a sweet potato and carrot base, smoked oysters or mussels as the seafood, sherry, or unorthodox spices (spicing rejected by at least one "chowder traditionalist" as acceptable in a soup but certainly not in a chowder).[7] The expression of folkways and the affirmation of tradition identify the modern culinary consciousness that turns practitioners into traditionalists and modernists, that is, advocates in opposing cultural camps.

Then again, the divisions between the two camps are considerably fuzzier than some of the foregoing statements might suggest. The 1997 winner in the Island chowder category offered a paradigmatic union of new, exogenous ingredients and the tried and true. On the one hand, she made use of cumin, an herb prominent in Mexican, Indian, and Middle Eastern cuisines, among others, but definitely exotic as far as New England is concerned; and on the other, this restaurant chef proudly laid claim to the very traditional prize ingredient of the family cook—"a lot of love." Modern cuisine, however "avant-garde," however professional, however elaborate, is never entirely divorced from this traditional culinary context of the family kitchen, where feelings and emotions are reputed to be such important ingredients in food preparation.

The stark divisions between cooking and cuisine, between traditionalist and modernist, between chef and cook, cannot capture the complexity of their interdependence. Where cuisine calls attention to structure and order,

cooking highlights process, movement, transformation. As for all social practices, we are dealing concurrently and yet discretely with movement within
structure. The idiosyncratic rhythms of cooking counter the rationalized codes
of cuisine. Custom counters creativity, consciousness opposes habit. Should
the spotlight be trained on the cook as guardian of traditions rooted in a community? Or should it instead concentrate on the chef and on individual innovation and creativity? How should one approach the modern artist, whom the
chef resembles in more ways than one? How can we do justice to the movement, the rhythms of culinary process without losing track of the structuring
elements that direct those rhythms? We could do worse than follow Norbert
Elias's invocation of dance to characterize a properly sociological analysis, one
that maneuvers deftly between all-determining structure and utterly free
individuals. Patterned movement, dance is neither a rigid system nor free-
associative action. The configuration—or figuration, to use Elias's preferred
terminology—captures both structured change and the changing structure,
and especially the nature of the relationship between the two. Like Yeats, Elias
knew full well that the dancer cannot be separated from the dance. He also
knew that this impossible synthesis is precisely what the sociologist must endeavor to disentangle.

Elias's concept of the "civilizing process" offers a further entry into understanding the culinary in the modern world. Since the Middle Ages, culinary
practices in the West, particularly consumption practices, support Elias's hy-
pothesis of an increasing social control dependent on an acute consciousness
of others and our dependence on them for a sense of self. Table behavior provides Elias with a great many telling examples of the increasing constraint on
the public exhibition of the body at work. Like other specialized instruments
such as the handkerchief or a dedicated space such as the aptly named privy,
the fork constrains body behavior and distances the physical action from the
social activity. Simultaneously extending, obscuring, and protecting the hand,
the fork picks up the food, rather than the fingers that its tines resemble. (In
contrast, the multitask knife recalls precisely the kinds of aggressive conduct
that refined table manners are designed to repress.) Turning up in Europe in
the thirteenth century (although it took several more centuries to become
standard cutlery), the fork offered Western societies a sophisticated dining instrument to "dematerialize" the patently material and "decorporealize" the
manifestly corporeal. The fork at once connected and dissociated food and the
body. Along with this advance in the division of dining labor and the formalization of the individual act of ingestion, the fork transformed commensality—eating together—into dining—eating together in accordance with pre-
scribed forms.

Working from Elias's characterization of "civilization" as the "self-consciousness of the West," I would like to suggest that this consciousness-raising

29

extends to the production and consumption of food.[8] Cuisine bespeaks culinary self-consciousness. It points to a typically modern critical apprehension of food and foodways and their connections to the other lives that we lead. How and why did French cuisine become the culinary consciousness of the West and, at times, its conscience as well? This is the question that *Accounting for Taste* seeks to answer.

Brillat-Savarin

Jean Anthelme Brillat-Savarin (1755– 1826) wrote his wonderfully quirky *Physiology of Taste* in 1826, and it marks the launch of many gastronomic voyages in culinary France. A provincial lawyer elected to the National Assembly in 1789, mayor of his hometown in 1793, a musician in America during the Terror, and later a judge in Paris, Brillat-Savarin made dining the supreme social setting in France. He understood better than any other that tastes must be communicated in words to be fully understood. "Tell me what you eat," he advised, "and I'll tell you who you are." From *Les Classiques de la table* (1845). Courtesy of Columbia University Libraries.

II. French Cuisines

The *Physiology of Taste* and French Exceptionalism

Nowhere is culinary self-consciousness more finely tuned than in France. There may be cultures of equally intense culinary commitment—China comes to mind—but for the West and for reasons that I shall explain, France long supplied the standard against which other modern cuisines have been measured. A key element sustaining this acute consciousness of the culinary self has to do with the stories the French tell about food. Of the stories that every culture tells about itself, some achieve emblematic status, told and retold from one generation to the next because they are felt to say something fundamental about that culture and what it is all about. In France culinary stories tend to be emblematic in just this way, and surely one explanation for the culinary exceptionalism commonly attributed to French cuisine lies in the number and variety of "culinary stories" that have circulated in France and about France for the past three centuries, stories circulated by foreigners as well as the French.

For the spirit of these stories, and of the larger culinary discourse to which they contribute, we can scarcely do better than consult Jean Anthelme Brillat-Savarin's *Physiology of Taste*.[9] For the French and outsiders alike, this work early attained the status of an exemplary culinary text, perhaps *the* exemplary text. So far as I can tell, the book has never been out of print in French since its original publication, and there have been an astonishing number of editions in English. In large measure the *Physiology* owes its popularity to Brillat-Savarin's ability to convey so succinctly and so engagingly what I have called the "culinary civilizing process." Its semimedical title notwithstanding, the *Physiology of Taste* civilizes eating. Moreover, it socializes food, and it does so by recounting in story after story our social relations with food. Brillat-Savarin works from the premise that taste varies across social groups. For all his old-fashioned mixture of genial anecdote and semi-mock instruction, he steadfastly fixes the reader's attention on the social settings of food, particularly its consumption. Far from the frivolous work that some commentators have dismissed as unworthy of serious consideration, the *Physiology of Taste* appears to us today as something of a sociology of taste ahead of its time.

The obvious comparison is the well-known German adage "Mann ist, was er ißt," which Americans personalize as "You are what you eat."[10] Brillat's French take on this truth, however, makes an altogether different assertion, one that bespeaks a distinctly French perspective on food in its social setting. He will not shrink, he tells us, from tackling the putative aphrodisiacal qualities of truffles, and does so by interviewing a lady of a certain age and considerable experience. He recounts his culinary adventures in America, spending much time on the roast wild turkey served by his host in Hartford. As these anecdotes indicate, Brillat-Savarin takes food and eating beyond the individual to the social. Without fail he reaches for a broader understanding of food and its place in the social world. Where the German saying makes a sweeping statement about eating as a physiological process, the French writer locates his claim within a particular social and linguistic circumstance. The title page of the *Physiology of Taste* proffers "the professor's aphorism"—"Tell me what you eat, and I'll tell you what you are"—and sets up the book that follows not as individual ingestion or digestion but as collective appropriation. Brillat-Savarin imagines a standard narrative situation constructed around a speaker and a listener—a *you* and a *me* in a classic context of communication. He elicits information from one party in return for a promise of analysis from the other.

The patent inequality of the professorial speaker (whose status is enhanced by identification on the title page as a "member of several learned societies") and the nameless listener endows this particular communication with especial intensity. The assumed professorial authority substitutes for the implied power of the otherwise unidentified author. The *Physiology of Taste* inextricably ties analysis to prescription. The off-hand, humorous tone belies the numerous quasi-dictatorial precepts and principles embedded in the stories. The dichotomy is intentional: the use of "I" and "me," Brillat-Savarin explains, supposes a "confabulation" with the reader, who is free to "examine, discuss, and even laugh." But when the author comes armed with the "redoubtable *we*," it is a lecture, and the reader must submit. "I am, Sir, oracle," he declares in a half-teasing and yet earnest directive lifted from *The Merchant of Venice*, "And, when I open my lips, let no dog bark!" (preface, p. 36). The individual exhorted to culinary confessions—the *you*—stands in for the readers, who, Brillat-Savarin assures us, need only turn the pages before them to find out what they are and what others are as well.

A close reading of the *Physiology of Taste* shows off a Brillat-Savarin who is far more interesting than the genre of genial food writing allows. From an admittedly quirky amalgam of anecdote and commandment, science and philosophy, medicine and morals, he lay the foundation of a French culinary code and a taste community that was at once French and cosmopolitan. Brillat's culinary code is rooted not in the haute cuisine of the Ancien Régime but in the more mobile, confusing, visibly urbanizing world of postrevolutionary Paris. Its public is not the wealthy aristocrats and financiers of the Ancien Régime but the more fluid, cosmopolitan taste community of connoisseurs that, as Brillat-Savarin takes care to point out, can be found in every social station. This democratization of culinarity is what Brillat refers to as the spread of "a general spirit of conviviality" into "all classes of society" (meditation 27). In principle, gastronomy, the pursuit of culinary excellence, concerns every station in society; in practice, in the first quarter of the nineteenth century, the pleasures of the table had become far more readily available to a broader, and broadening, range of individuals.

It is Brillat-Savarin's tour de force to have used the engaging personal anecdotes of the *Physiology of Taste* to initiate something that is much more. This eighteenth-century philosophe—born right at midcentury—makes an accounting of the new worlds of food that came to the fore in nineteenth-century France, and he does so by analyzing the "pleasure of the table" in terms of its ever-changing social contexts. Cookbooks focused on production, he assures us, cannot possibly do justice to the ramifications of the pleasure of the table in society. Confronting the culinary as well as the social uncertainty of postrevolutionary France, the *Physiology* asserts the norms, values, and practices of French culinary culture. The elevation of gastronomy to the rank of a science justifies the exceptional social utility that Brillat ascribes to "social gourmandise" (meditation 11). He tracks the emergent taste community of French cuisine—the Parisian gastronomes, to whom the book is dedicated— and, finally, offers precepts to guide those who aspire to gastronomic excellence. His inventory of the principles of gastronomy and examination of social gourmandise set French cuisine on course for a century and more.

The authority typically assumed in this culinary discourse gets us to the "Frenchness" of French cuisine. Although every cuisine relies on texts to carry food from its originary place into cultural space, cuisine in France is carried, and reinforced, by an especially far-reaching discourse about food. The sheer number and variety of stories, along with the cultural narrative to which they link, testify to the privileged position that cuisine occupies in singling out things French. To understand how, why, and when cuisine acquired the cultural credit that it enjoys in France and how that cuisine acquired a cosmopolitan cachet as well, we need to look at the culinary stories and the cultural narrative that they weave. How the requisite culinary connections come about, and how a national culinary identity emerged from local foodways over all of France—for this we turn to the culinary discourse and the culture that it defends.

When we reflect on how food is talked about in France, we cannot fail to be struck by the degree to which cuisine is assimilated into intellectual rather than material culture; by its systematic, aestheticized, and insistently normative disposition; and, finally, by the way this discourse aids and abets a decidedly national enterprise. The discourse itself, in its modern form, flourished particularly in the nineteenth century. As it developed over that period in France, cuisine worked off and with the expanding world of restaurants and the professionalizing world of cooking. Still, institutional support is necessary but not sufficient to explain the extraordinary presence of cuisine within French culture and its prestige abroad. Such a marked cultural presence absolutely requires the printed word—from the most instrumental recipe, political directive, or religious interdiction to the essay and memoir, the restaurant review, the ethnography and travelogue, the literary work and scientific treatise, and not forgetting the philosophical disquisition. Such were the most prominent manifestations of an expanding, and aggressively expansionist, culinary discourse based on a stridently presented claim of authority. It was this discourse that transformed the class cuisine of the Ancien Régime, associated with the court and the aristocracy, into a national cuisine, that is, a culi-

33

nary configuration taken as a sign and symbol of the nation itself. French cuisine became French not so much from the food eaten as through the texts written and then avidly read. The nationalization of French cuisine, in short, came through its textualization, and it depended on the readers of culinary texts as much as on the cooks or the consumers of the material preparation.

The crucial period of culinary textualization began in the early nineteenth century, when the growing market for all kinds of writing initiated a notable, even spectacular growth that lasted until the end of the century. Given that modern cuisines are written cuisines, the national status of any cuisine that would make such a claim for itself hinges on a set of writings that penetrate the culture at large. The publishing market provided just such a vehicle. One long-term consequence was the linguistic integration of the disparate geographical and cultural entities into a national whole. At the end of the eighteenth century, according to a study undertaken by the revolutionary government, French was a foreign language for the vast majority of the 20 million or so inhabitants of metropolitan France. From Brittany and Normandy to Languedoc and Provence, from Picardy and Flanders to Touraine and Burgundy, most of the inhabitants of French territory continued to speak the language, dialect, or patois of their native province well into the nineteenth century. Only after a full century of fervent educational investment on the part of the central government did the situation change appreciably; even as late as 1870, French was not the first language for fully half the population.[11]

It is not unreasonable to suppose that culinary texts contributed to the spread of French linguistic and cultural norms, although the middle-class public for these texts stood at some remove from the urban proletariat and the peasantry, neither of which had the time, the pecuniary or intellectual resources, or the incentive for culinary innovation. National though it may have been, what came to be perceived as French cuisine nonetheless remained profoundly class based. This particular cuisine—an amalgam of haute and bourgeoise cuisines—could claim identification with country over class only because the class in question—the bourgeoisie—aligned its interests with those of the nation. The legacy of the universalizing rhetoric of the French Revolutionaries meant that almost any discussion of particulars inevitably found itself thrown into the arena of the universal. As a result, the relations between the particular and the general in France tend to be framed as a contest between the idiosyncratic and the universal, with the universal taken as national and the national taken as universal. Ongoing culinary dialogues and disputes offer no exception to the rule.

It has long been a commonplace of French culinary discourse that France has "always" been the favored land of fine food with eaters as knowledgeable as they are enthusiastic. *Savoir-manger* subsists as a highly prized branch of *savoir-faire,* a supposedly indigenous flair whenever food comes into question. Culinary excellence is routinely ascribed to a centuries-old cultural patrimony. So it is only to be expected, for example, to find French Jews in the Middle Ages distinguished by their love of food—a love that on occasion overrode religious dietary prescriptions. Mediaeval rabbinic commentators cite over twenty different kinds of cake eaten by Jewish contemporaries, some in the fanciful shape of birds and trees. Even the admonitions reinforce the association of France and food. One disapproving account from the thirteenth century noted that French Jews "study the Talmud with their stomachs full of meat, vegetables and wine!" Certain French rabbis were so lax as to allow servants to reheat dishes on the Sabbath or require only an hour between eating meat and dairy products instead of the six hours fixed by Maimonides.[12]

Much of this activity engaged Paris, the most populous city in mediaeval Europe and one where the business of cooking and eating occupied a prominent place in the urban landscape. In 1577 the Venetian ambassador remarked upon the extraordinary abundance of foods available in Paris and the propensity of the French to spend their money on fine food. A century later the chronicler Brantôme weighed in with his own opinion that "in France one always eats well."[13]

Examples of such intense appreciation abound early and late. Let me jump ahead several centuries to one of the most egregious modern instances of culinary chauvinism. In the aftermath of the terrible losses of World War I, France stood in need of a morale booster. In a passage truly remarkable for an unshakeable, proprietary notion of culinary destiny, Marcel Rouff, a well-known gourmet and subsequently the coauthor of a multivolume history of regional French cooking, justified his novel about an epic eater. In these traumatic times, he urged, France should adhere to its traditions. Lyrical to excess, risible for the more cynical among us, Rouff's overwrought defense and illustration of French cuisine illustrate the intimate bond so often assumed between cuisine and country.

> Great, noble cuisine is a tradition of this country. . . . a timeless and notable element of its charm, a reflection of its soul. . . . Everywhere else, people eat; in France alone people know how to eat. People have always known how to eat in France just as they have always known how to build incomparable châteaux, weave admirable tapestries, . . . create styles that the whole world steals, . . . [and we can do so] because we have taste. . . . The taste for gastronomy is innate in the race. . . . Dodin-Bouffant [the hero of the novel, loosely modeled on Brillat-Savarin] is a gourmet the way Claude Lorrain is a painter and Berlioz a musician.[14]

Controversies and Hierarchies

However much Rouff labored to place French cuisine outside of time, the very examples he calls upon, the tapestries and the châteaux that date from the later Middle Ages and the Renaissance, firmly ground cuisine and gastronomy in history. Not until the sixteenth century did distinct European cuisines begin to emerge out of the mediaeval cuisines that did not differ appreciably from one country to another. Cuisine in France, haute cuisine, arose in the seventeenth century, primarily at or around the court and the aristocracy. Much has been written about the culinary extravaganzas at the court of Louis XIV, the spectacular feasts at Versailles and their highly ritualized setting, the interest on the part of courtiers, and the prodigious appetite of the king. Few histories can resist Mme de Sévigné's breathless account of the melodramatic demise of Vatel, the prince de Condé's steward, who committed suicide when the fish did not arrive in time for a royal banquet.[15]

Still more significant for the connections of cuisine and country, a cookbook proclaimed its Frenchness for the first time. François Pierre de La Varenne's *Le Cuisinier françois* (The French chef), published in 1651, went through some eighteen editions over the century that followed, in Paris, in the French provinces, in Holland and Flanders, with additional printings in English (1653), German (1665), and Italian (1682) translation.[16] Frenchness was in the air: *Le Jardinier françois* (tied to cuisine through the kitchen garden) appeared the same year, *Le Pastissier françois* (The French pastry maker) and in 1660, *Le Confiturier françois* (The French jam maker).

Frenchness also surfaced in the express intentions of the authors of these works, who repeatedly pointed out that culinary affairs in France were not only different from but also better than elsewhere. In *Les Délices de la campagne* (The delights of the countryside [1654]), Nicolas de Bonnefons ends his instructions on making soup with the injunction to leave "depraved ragouts" to the foreigners, who in any case "never enjoy good fare except when they have cooks from France." In the polemical preface to *L'Art de bien traiter* (The art of catering [1674]), the otherwise unidentified L. S. R. justifies his severe criticisms of La Varenne on the latter's failure to distinguish between the delicate preparations suitable to the gentle climate of France and the "villainies" *(gueuseries)* that could only just be tolerated in the more impoverished climes inhabited by the Arabs. Foreign dishes had no place in "a purified climate such as ours, where propriety, delicacy and good taste are the object and the substance of our most solid enthusiasms." François Massialot, in his *Le Cuisinier roïal et bourgeois* (The royal and bourgeois chef [1691]), sets Europe against all other civilizations for its native refinement and its ability to make the most of what it takes from abroad. Within Europe, in things culinary as in so many other domains, France takes pride of place:

Only in Europe prevail the sense of what is proper, good taste and flair in the dressing of the foods found there; only there is justice done at the same time to the marvelous gifts provided by the bounty of other climates; and only there, and especially in France, can one take pride in our excelling over all other nations in these matters, as we do in manners and in a thousand other ways already familiar to us.[17]

As the excerpt makes clear, you had to be "there." Only and always, "especially in France," one finds the essence in food made more than just food.

All of these books exhibit a marked ambition to dictate practices, whether it was a question of actual recipes or general directives for running a household. To be sure, recipes must legislate, faithful to their mission to tell us what to do with food and how to do it. Even so, these seventeenth-century works stand out for their express purpose, as L. S. R. put it best, "to give rules and a method" where previously there were none. For La Varenne in *Le Cuisinier françois*, this meant separate sections for basic recipes, recipes classified by their place in the meal, a chapter for Lenten dishes, cross-references between sections, and, in the second edition of 1652, three alphabetical tables. The very next year *Les Délices de la campagne* ended a set of instructions with the injunction that everything concerning soups should apply as a "law for everything that is eaten." The very title of *Le Cuisinier méthodique* (The methodical chef [1660]) validated the importance of codified culinary techniques, and the quarrelsome L. S. R. joined the fray, promising "a method that has not at all been seen or taught, which demolishes all the works that preceded it." The observation is doubly important because it illustrates how the claim of French superiority carries inward toward a competition over the best French expression of it.

These cookbooks fit the legislative mode so characteristic of the seventeenth-century France of Louis XIV, whose fruits we see in cultural products from architecture to philosophy via literature—and not excluding table manners! French classicism tends to be identified through its reverence for form, the referral to principles that constrain cultural performance and production, and the system of formal requirements for drama, notably the "proprieties" *(bienséances)* and the three unities (time, space, and dramatic action). The Académie française, founded by Cardinal de Richelieu in 1635, declared its mission to give rules to the as-yet-unruly French language. Other national academies were established thereafter to regulate architecture, the beaux-arts, and science. The culinary writers' preoccupation with method also echoes what was long the totemic text of French culture, René Descartes's *Discourse on Method,* published in 1637. A full two centuries later, in the midst of the battles over freewheeling Romantic drama, one culinary wag came back to this very link to insist that cuisine, like comedy, should abide by the rules of Aristotle.[18] Just as writers and critics battled over the propriety of literary works—most famously, the rows over Corneille's *Le Cid* in 1636 and Molière's *L'École des femmes* (School for wives) in 1660—so, too, culinary writers and their critics engaged in furious polemics. L. S. R. attacked the "absurdities and disgusting lessons" with which the supposedly conservative La Varenne had for so long gulled "the silly and ignorant populace" and took great pains to assure his readers that his own book had nothing of the sort. For literature and cuisine, controversy worked off and incited creative ferment; for both as well, it underscored how inimitably French practices and products made the intimate connection between cuisine and country.

L. S. R. contested La Varenne, the new cuisine disputed the old, in a culinary version of the Quarrel of the Ancients and the Moderns. As was the case for literature and disputes over literary taste, almost every generation replays virtually the same quarrel in its own terms. The culinary terminology staked out ideological positions: Vincent La Chapelle made his position clear in the title of his work of 1735, *Le Cuisinier moderne* (The modern chef). In 1739 Menon published his *Nouveau Traité de cuisine* (New culinary treatise), and the third volume that he added three years later took an even stronger stand: *La Nouvelle cuisine*. In making explicit the principles that informed their cookbooks and marking their particular culinary territory, these argumentative prefaces reveal a heightened consciousness of culinary change and importance. Even though he admitted that "the old Cuisine . . . should be the basis of the new," Menon considered the chef working "in the new" preferable to one "who follows the old method." These and other programmatic prefaces make clear the will to reconfigure culinary practices and mark a further intensification in the very nature of French cuisine. Signs of a distinctive culinary sensibility, these controversies powered new initiatives and a driving desire for culinary change.

Publication made such contestation and competition possible. By pushing things culinary out of the private kitchen and individual dining room, the printed work opened cuisine up to discussion and debate. Until print culture created a reading public beyond the kitchens and the tables of the court and the aristocracy, there was not much of a public for cookery works and, hence, minimal reward for their diffusion. As was the case with literary works, publication radically changed the rules and the players of the game. The seventeenth century in France was such an important period not by the number of cookbooks but by the public arena that allowed culinary controversies to be played out in the culture at large. In fact, prior to the mid–seventeenth-century burst of culinary publications, France lagged behind its neighbors in the production of cookbooks. Culinary battles participated in the larger cultural wars that pitted the old against the new, the ancients against the moderns. We are left, however, with a vital question that *Accounting for Taste* seeks to answer: given the spread of print culture everywhere, what made France the home of haute cuisine?

Modernity was, so to speak, in the air. And modernity meant more than ever a move to lay down culinary principles that would fix constantly changing culinary practices. The very term *modern* speaks to the effort made to tie the new and the different to the state-of-the-art and to progress, an effort that inevitably entails categorical dismissal of one's predecessors. Ongoing, highly competitive culinary controversies work themselves into French culture until food and culture are inextricably united in a comprehensive sentiment of pride. The pedagogical tone is partly a function of the cookery genre—why do we read recipes if not for instruction, whether or not we put it into practice? Nevertheless, the decisive tone of many of these prefaces cannot fail to impress upon the reader the claims to "truth value" of the culinary classification that follows. Moreover, the period for replacing one text with another proves astonishingly brief. Barely twenty years had elapsed since the publication of La Varenne's *Cuisinier françois* (1651) when L. S. R. denounced his predecessor as totally antiquated.

Here the culinary sphere plays out the contradiction that Elias finds in the French conception of "civilization"—at once a superior state already attained and an ideal toward which we must work. These culinary prefaces present the works that follow as the state of perfection to which the reader can and should aspire. At the same time, the relegation of previous works to the culinary Dark Ages and the substitution of the new one assume a resolutely progressive view of cuisine as a cultural product that follows the times. Every nouvelle cuisine assumes an ancienne cuisine. By the same token, the very term promises subsequent nouvelles cuisines that will turn today's culinary perfection into yesterday's discard.

These heated debates raise the specter of cutthroat competition. Although relatively few cookbooks were published during the Ancien Régime, a number had astonishingly long careers, with many reprints as well as new editions.[19] Already the author of a number of cookery works, Menon used the preface to his *Le Manuel des Officiers de bouche* (The stewards' manual [1759]) to justify pushing his latest work on an overloaded market by touting its originality:

> What! perhaps someone will say, another work on cooking? For the
> past few years the public has been deluged with writings of this sort.
> I agree. But it is precisely all these works that give birth to this one.

Culinary differentiation followed social differentiation. Before the diffusion of cookbooks, elite cuisines remained the province of cooks and their masters. The resulting curtailment of culinary mobility—neither cooks nor recipes traveled much—all but ensured culinary and social exclusivity. Publishing cookbooks undermined this culinary exclusivity, though few explained their motives quite so baldly as the author of *Le Pastissier françois*, who made it his duty to bring to the public the art of pastry heretofore "kept secret by our most celebrated Court and Parisian pastry chefs."[20] These culinary writers played off their associations with the powerful through dedications to exalted personages (again, a strategy also followed by literary authors in quest of patronage); through the very subject of the book, as in *Les Soupers de la cour* (Court suppers [1755]); through prefaces such as Massialot's to the *Cuisinier roïal et bourgeois;* and through luxurious presentations of extravagant banquet menus and dishes, such as Menon's *Maître d'hôtel confiseur* (The confectionary steward [1750]), which includes engravings of palaces, statues, and other monuments, or La Chapelle's *Le Cuisinier moderne* (1735), with its elaborate foldouts for table settings and decorations. Such works transferred aristocratic spectacle to the printed page, where they were meant to impress or even awe. And yet, in reaching a far broader audience, the very existence of the cookbook contravened the elite associations of aristocratic cuisine, providing access to middle-class norms and values.

Even more destructive of any culinary monopoly were the works that made a point of bridging social distance by translating elite cuisine into lesser venues. The very title of *Le Cuisinier roïal et bourgeois* proclaims Massialot's firm intention to play both cards, to connect rather than separate the aristocracy and the bourgeoisie. Similarly, Audiger's *La Maison réglée* (The orderly household [1692]) presented organizational models for three householders: a great lord *(grand seigneur)*, for whose substantial Parisian establishment Audiger estimated the expenses at 9536 *livres* 16 *sous;* a lady *(dame de qualité)*, whose separate household expenses would be added to those of her spouse; and a foreign or provincial gentleman, who could set up in the capital on a smaller footing at half the cost, a mere 4879 *livres.*

The most successful appeal to a broader culinary public came in 1746 with the publication of *La Cuisinière bourgeoise* (The bourgeois [female] cook), published anonymously but by the well-known cookery author Menon. The *Cuisinière bourgeoise* wins the popularity sweepstakes hands down. It was the most reprinted French cookbook for over a century and also the only cookbook written before 1789 to be reprinted after 1800. Beyond the reprints, an even greater gauge of Menon's triumph with this work came with the string of knockoffs. From the Restoration (*La nouvelle Cuisinière bourgeoise* of 1817 and *La plus nouvelle Cuisinière bourgeoise* in 1822), to the Second Empire (*La bonne Cuisinière bourgeoise,* 1854) and into the Third Republic (yet another *Nouvelle Cuisinière bourgeoise* in 1880), Menon's *Cuisinière bourgeoise* imperturbably traversed decades and political regimes.[21]

In the culinary works that he wrote between 1739 and 1761, Menon worked diligently to cover all bases. On one side of the divide, intended for the extensively staffed kitchen of the very wealthy, he proposed *La Science du maître d'hôtel cuisinier* (The skills of the steward-chef [1749]), *La Science du maître d'hôtel confiseur* (Skills of the steward-dessert maker [1750]), *Les Soupers de la cour* (Court suppers [1755]), and *Le Manuel des Officiers de bouche* (The stewards' Manual [1759]). On the other, as with the *Cuisinière bourgeoise,* he directed works down the social ladder, or he addressed health concerns, as with *Cuisine et Office de santé* (Cooking and provisioning for health [1758]). Somewhat inconsistently, *Le Manuel des Officiers de bouche* proclaims its elite public in its title even as the same title page assures us that it is for "all Tables." The text itself, Menon says, is in response to complaints about the cost of the best cookery books and their unwieldy size, which makes them difficult to use and all but impossible to take along to country homes. The summary of his other works in this portable *Manuel,* he adds, will ensure its use as a handy reference. Further, the second edition of 1759 stresses the notable improvements upon the original, starting with a more rational order of presentation that fully integrates the material of the original into the work as a whole (the first edition had stuck some points at the end of the book). In addition, a smaller type size has allowed Menon to compress two volumes into one. Aiming at ever-greater availability and practical utility, he took evident pride in his ingenuity in making his book easier to consult and to transport.

The preface to *La Cuisinière bourgeoise* makes particular mention of Menon's previous works written for the kitchens of the nobility. Now, those credentials in hand, he wants to write a work "appropriate" to individuals of a lesser status *(condition)* "& that is what he has done here." Gender supplies the first marker of this lowered status. In proposing a cook *(cuisinière)* instead of a chef *(cuisinier),* Menon clearly sets this work in another world altogether. Apart from the invisible scullery maids, the aristocratic kitchen had no place for women. It was a military operation, as certainly was reflected in the titles that were used. The chefs *(cuisiniers)* followed the orders of Officers: the *Officier de cuisine,* later *chef de cuisine,* in charge of cooking; and his superior, the *Officier de bouche* or *maître d'hôtel* (steward), who was in charge of supplies. Proposing a cuisinière instead of a cuisinier, an Officier de bouche or a Maître d'hôtel, Menon clearly locates the *Cuisinière bourgeoise* outside the sphere of the aristocracy, its elaborate preparations, and its elite consumers. The title of the first English translation—*The French Family Cook*—captures the new audience that Menon was aiming at:

> He supplies [these households] with a Cook who, without occasioning them any expense, will help them instruct in the art of preparation those whom they provide for & who are in their employ. . . . He matches his precepts to their wealth & to the nature of the foodstuffs to which the Cook is constrained.[22]

And yet, the separation is by no means absolute. Not only does Menon derive the authority to write the *Cuisinière bourgeoise* from his many works directed to aristocratic kitchens; the very cuisine of this author-chef itself confers nobility. He is not writing for the Nobility, Menon tells the reader, he writes for the Bourgeois; "but it can be said that he ennobles plebeian foods with the seasonings by which he enhances them."

Fittingly enough, with its emphasis on economy, simplicity, and health, the *Cuisinière bourgeoise* epitomizes, as it is meant to do, *cuisine bourgeoise* and its ideological and culinary opposition to aristocratic culinary extravagance, excess, and refinement. At the same time, as Menon's presentation of self makes clear, the one draws on the other. From a culinary point of view, *cuisine bourgeoise* in the Ancien Régime simplified, or, better yet, domesticated court or grand cuisine *(la cuisine des Grands)*. It is not an "indigenous" style of cooking of the bourgeoisie in anywhere the same way that peasant culinary modes can be associated with subsistence cooking and local products. Culinary appellations deliberately confuse culinary content and its supposed producers and/or consumers. Menon clarifies the difference in the preface to *La Cuisinière bourgeoise*. This cuisine is bourgeois by its "disengagement" from "the overpowering array of sophisticated seasonings," which needs both a clever cook and a wealthy master. With these modifications, the author admits, "the Eye will be less satisfied, & taste less delighted; but, in exchange, health and the pocketbook, which certainly should be considered as much as these two senses, will come out far ahead."

Although the distinction was not, of course, Menon's alone, it characterized the dual nature of the culinary order. Even so, we do well to remember that both of these cuisines were "modern" as I understand the term, since the diffusion of each depended largely upon culinary texts. True, the patterns of circulation differed: *cuisine bourgeoise* engaged a national market (other countries had their own versions of "home cooking"), while haute cuisine attracted elites across Europe who, from the seventeenth century, increasingly called on French chefs to put those culinary precepts into practice. Having worked in London as head chef to Lord Chesterfield and later in Holland as the chef to the prince of Orange, Vincent La Chapelle wrote the first edition of *Le Cuisinier moderne* (1735) in English *(The Modern Cook,* 1733).[23]

When we actually look at the works explicitly aimed at lesser fortunes, it is evident that we have not moved far down the social scale. Even though Menon asserts that *Le Manuel des Officiers de bouche* is for "all tables," he immediately limits the range of households, which runs from "those of the great lords to those of the Bourgeois." Inappropriate the model dinners in *La Cuisinière bourgeoise* may have been for the table of a *grand seigneur,* they suited lower-level bourgeoisie even less and were totally out of the question for even the wealthiest peasants. As the *Cuisinière bourgeoise* reminds us, the bourgeoisie took its measure from the aristocracy; peasants and the urban poor were simply outside the culinary equation.[24]

With flexibility in mind, Menon grants readers the freedom to add or subtract dishes from each course according to their "fantasy" or their resources. That said, the model repast for twelve that opens *La Cuisinière bourgeoise* sets the standard at four courses, each with several dishes: first course—2 soups, 1 piece of beef for the middle of the table, 2 plates of hors d'oeuvres; second course—keep the beef and add a truffled breast of veal, mutton cutlets with basil, stewed duck, fricassee of chicken; third course—2 roasts (1 hare and 4 pigeons), 3 side dishes (a pâté of Amiens for the middle of the table, a cold cream, cauliflower); fourth course, or Dessert—a bowl of fruit for the middle of the table, apple and pear compotes, a plate of cookies *(gaufrettes)*, plates of chestnuts, dishes of red currant jelly and apricot marmalade. One wonders if the British housewife who picked up *The French Family Cook*, as the English translation was called, was as convinced of the relevance to family meals as the title implies.

However much latitude and flexibility Menon held out to his readers, he, and they, operated within a constricted social milieu—extensive if one takes the upper aristocracy and elites into account; manifestly negligible if one considers the population as a whole, especially in a period that still endured periodic famine or food shortages. Although Menon's bourgeois dishes may have been less spectacular, less fancy, and fewer per course, and the courses themselves fewer in number than those in aristocratic repasts, their simplicity was entirely relative. Like haute cuisine and because of it, *cuisine bourgeoise* supposed abundance just as it supposed the wherewithal to procure that abundance.

Geographical Diversity and the Parisian Monopoly

In the seventeenth and eighteenth centuries, *French*—as in French cuisine— made less of a geographical reference than a social statement. Ancien Régime usage did not necessarily include as "French" everything or everyone found in the domains governed by the king of France. In fact, geography restricted "French" cuisine almost as much as class. That is, geography combined with class to limit the reach of "French" cuisine—as in *Le Cuisinier françois*. In fact, "French" cuisine proclaimed the ideals and (arguably) the practices of Parisian elites wherever they might reside, but was "French" by virtue of their officially inhabiting the seat of the monarchy in the Ile de France. For example Voltaire, in exile at Ferney, kept a table every bit as sumptuous as he would (or could) have had in Paris. He lavished extraordinary care on food and dining. As befitted the great lord that he had turned himself into, conspicuous culinary consumption was ingrained in his notion of how life should be lived.[25] Authors of cookbooks may have nodded toward the bourgeoisie; they had virtually nothing to say about the diversity of actual food practices, either inside or outside Paris-Versailles. Insofar as cookbooks legislate rather than document, they necessarily construct cuisine *against* practice, which it aims to constrain and contain.

The Parisian focus of French cuisine stands out even more when we consider the whole of the country. That Parisian circles set the standard is apparent, for example, in the assumption of the availability of raw foodstuffs from all over. In the sixteenth century the Venetian ambassador noted that food came to Paris "from every country," but the list of the (now) provinces of France with which he supports this claim indicates that, for him as for others who sang the praises of French cuisine, "France" meant Paris.[26] Two centuries later the incomparable urban ethnographer Louis-Sébastien Mercier noted the same embarrassment of riches. "A hundred thousand men" scour the country to supply Parisian markets with the most succulent of fare, fish, and pheasant, even the exotic pineapple.[27] Keeping Paris supplied was a prime concern for the monarchy, which built canals and roads and strictly regulated food markets to do just that. The provinces supplied Paris first, their own needs thereafter.[28]

On the one hand, this variety of foodstuffs signals the extraordinary abundance that made Paris a gourmand's paradise. On the other, that same variety signifies the absence of location. Paris is the exemplary culinary *space* because it overrules vital connection to any particular *place*. The abstract intellectualization that makes cuisine so portable a vehicle also divests it of what the author of the *Lettre d'un pâtissier anglois au Nouveau Cuisinier François* (Letter from an English pastry maker to the new French chef) in 1739 called its "terrestriality," that is, its rootedness in the very soil, or what the nineteenth century came to term "terroir."[29] Through twin processes of intellectualization and aestheticization, cuisine works to divorce *culture* from *agriculture.*

Paris itself had more to offer the seeker of culinary excellence than would ever be surmised from works on cuisine. Cookbooks convey little of the culinary institutions and foods that make Mercier's *Tableau de Paris* (1781–88) such a treasure trove for historians of the everyday. Mercier enthusiastically roamed the city. His one volume of urban phenomena grew by popular demand to twelve volumes that seemingly cover anything and everything. "Variety, my subject belongs to you," Mercier declares at outset in the *Tableau,* and makes good on his promise. His report on the culinary worlds of Paris reveals a city with some twelve hundred cooks intently involved in satisfying gustatory desires. Thoughts of food inspire him to report on salt carriers, saltwater fish, boarding houses, cafés, pastry makers and roasters, chefs and cooks, meat during Lent, vinegar carriers, wealthy hosts, professional guests *(parasites),* taste, nouvelle cuisine, and so on for a portrait of a city teeming with culinary curiosities.

Beyond the codified, rationalized, intellectualized domain of cuisine, then, lay a remarkable assortment of foodways both urban and rural. Just how extensive the variety, and, by comparison, how narrow the construction of cuisine becomes, emerges from another remarkable work from the end of the eighteenth century, P. J. B. Le Grand d'Aussy's *Histoire de la vie privée des Français*. That he begins his work with a discussion of food is eloquent testimony not only to the salience of food in everyday life but also to the great interest to which food lays claim. In the event, Le Grand d'Aussy's projected historical investigation into all aspects of private life in France never got beyond the first three volumes on food—the foods that the French grew and ate, and the circumstances under which they did so. The first volume deals with the foods grown and cooked across France, the second discusses festive meals, and the third, drink. (The modern edition reproduces only the first two volumes.) In effect, Le Grand d'Aussy did for foods and foodways across France something of what Mercier did for Paris. He documented an astonishing array of both products and practices. Like Mercier, Le Grand d'Aussy insisted on the documentary nature of his work, though where Mercier tirelessly walked the streets of Paris, Le Grand d'Aussy took his facts and eyewitness reports from a vast array of written sources.[30]

Neither Mercier nor Le Grand d'Aussy writes as a historian, and both focus resolutely on the everyday. Mercier the journalist takes on "all classes of citizens" and vows in his preface to cover Paris from top to bottom. His success can be gauged by the criticism he received for spending—and enjoying—altogether too much of his time in the company of the dirty, the reprobate, and the ignoble. More the scholar, Le Grand d'Aussy undertakes to bring to his readers' attention everything that the historian is obliged to exclude from accounts of events of public moment—the unmemorable, the unimportant, the naturally obscure elements of private life. Thus, he will focus on

> the bourgeois in town, peasants in their huts, country gentlemen in their châteaux, in other words the French in the midst of their work and their pleasures, in the bosom of their families and with their children—that's what the historian cannot represent for us. (Avertissement préliminaire)

Such a conception of his work means that the section most like a cookbook (vol. 1, chapter 3, "Prepared Foods") has little in common with one. Nothing is farther from Le Grand d'Aussy's conception of his enterprise than legislating usage. Rather, he relates the usages that have prevailed in different places and at different times in French history insofar as they can be documented.

Whether he is dealing with spices or sugar in the thirteenth century or the kinds of soups and sauces most in evidence in earlier years, Le Grand d'Aussy ranges across time and place. He makes clear that the present trumps the past. His contemporaries, he is pleased to report, do not tolerate the obscene names earlier ages gave to certain pastries with particularly evocative forms. Yet on the whole, and again quite like Mercier, Le Grand d'Aussy earnestly and passionately evokes a multiplicity of foodways, which means for him the great variety of a people. This enthusiasm stems from the conviction that, "since the different parts of the kingdom produce different things, there necessarily resulted, following the diversity of location, a diversity in the manner of living."[31] Le Grand d'Aussy manifestly rejoices in the variety and the wealth of the French, both historical and geographical.

Thus, the end of the eighteenth century saw something of a standoff between contradictory impulses. We find culinary writings, cookbooks to the fore, working to codify and to instruct. At the same time, we confront the expansionist discourse of what the period had begun to call ethnology—the discourse that gives us the story or the analysis *(logos)* of a people *(ethnos)*. It fell to the nineteenth century to adjudicate the two drives and to reconcile the concentration of codification and the reach of geography. One early example is the *Cours gastronomique,* written in 1808 by one C. L. Cadet de Gassicourt and dedicated to the Epicurean Society of the Modern (Wine) Cellar. The fiction of the "course" is the education of a nouveau riche from the provinces, M. Manant-Ville [M. Oaf-in-Town], who very much wants to rid his son of any taint of provincial origins, the better to make a good marriage. The professor in charge of this (re)education fixes on gastronomy as the key to all knowledge and devotes chapters to history, chemistry, and geography.

The "Atlas gourmand" that accompanies chapter 28 is the first example of a kind of geographical image that we now take for granted—a map that summarizes a country not by its cities, mountains, or rivers but by its products: France by its cheeses and wines, Italy by its pastas, and so on. At the height of the Napoleonic drive for a European empire, this map looks within the borders, not without. It identifies France by regional specialties represented by symbols—a cow, a fish, and bottles—which are explained in an alphabetical index of the towns and cities of France that lists the specialties for each. The foods brought to our attention include both agricultural products such as game, mutton, chicken, and beef, and cooked preparations on the order of cider, wine, pâté, and pastry.

The dedication to a Parisian eating society indicates clearly enough that the capital runs the culinary show. Moreover, the atlas allots Paris more products than any other city (beef, peaches, melons, shrimp, eel, carp, liqueurs, pastry, chocolate, jams, bonbons, candies . . .). Clearly, the new century ratified Mercier on the subject of Parisian alimentary abundance and by extension sanctioned the hold of the capital on that abundance. Nevertheless—and this is the new element that the *Cours gastronomique* exemplifies—there is strong recognition of what is outside Paris, a new pride in the provenance of these foods and foodstuffs. The regions were making claims that they had not made before. Perhaps still more important, these claims found a hearing.[32] Yet the question remains: how would they be incorporated?

For "French cuisine" to become French cuisine, for the class-based cuisine of the Ancien Régime to turn into a truly national enterprise, these claims needed more than a hearing. Geography needed a vehicle that would translate the culinary endeavors of the periphery into terms that the metropolis would understand and accept. One man constructed just such a vehicle. Not only was Marie-Antoine Carême, by the common consent of his contemporaries, the greatest chef of his time; he was also, by common consent of his successors, the entrepreneur who did the most to bring French cuisine and cooking into modern times. To understand Carême's triumph, during his lifetime and thereafter, the next chapter takes up the extraordinary culinary instrument that he fashioned, the career that gave him star status, and, finally, the books that spread the culinary good word far and wide. It was Carême's achievement to reconcile the social and the geographical, to bring together the class cuisine of Ancien Régime elites with the geographical spread of products and produce across the whole of France.

Inventing French Cuisine

> Culture depends on cookery.
> For myself, the only immortality I desire is to invent a new sauce.
>
> —Prime minister of Russia, in Oscar Wilde, *Vera, or the Nihilists* (1883)

Is French cuisine an invention? Does it really make sense, where a practice such as cooking is concerned, to think in terms of either the originality or the singularity that invention presupposes? What could any cook possibly "invent" to earn the epithet the King of Chefs, as Carême was called? Indeed, for his contemporaries, the surname alone sufficed to identify the man and his art. Louis XVIII himself authorized the signature "Carême de Paris." To be sure, Carême forcefully defended his cooking as new, modern, and superior; still, virtually every publishing chef from the seventeenth century on made similar claims. Yet another defense and illustration of French cuisine fails to explain Carême's contemporary and continuing preeminence.

Marie-Antoine Carême (1783–1833) belongs in a class of his own, not just because he was a great chef—others could claim as much—but because he was an extraordinary cultural entrepreneur. He was the first culinary modern, a star whose celebrity extended beyond the kitchen into the culture at large. Because Carême understood that modern society favored the many, not the few, he realized that even the most celebrated individuals who ate the glorious meals that he set before them would ultimately count less than the readers of his books. By the early nineteenth century the emphasis in the culinary enterprise had shifted from the traditional marketplace of elite consumers in private settings to the visibly stratified but rapidly expanding modern market that catered, literally and figuratively, to an increasingly heterogeneous public beyond the world of Parisian elites. An urbanizing and conspicuously mobile postrevolutionary France called for cultural goods of a different order. The associations with the great that served the seventeenth and eighteenth centuries so well ill suited a market in which print media mediated more and more social as well as commercial relations. By redirecting culinary practice out of the kitchen to a general public, printed texts translated the aristocratic cuisine of the Ancien Régime for a more inclusive bourgeois public. That larger public in turn justified French cuisine as a national undertaking in place of the more manifestly class-oriented endeavor that it had been under the Ancien Régime. Only in the nineteenth century did French cuisine truly come to stand for France.

Carême's nouvelle cuisine proved compelling on many levels. It rationalized culinary practice aggressively, aestheticized culinary discourse, and "nationalized" both. In the Cartesian spirit of rational analysis, Carême formulated a discourse on culinary method. One contemporary noted the "sensation" that these works created. No one ever expected to find a cookery book with "such an analytic spirit, such a luminous method, or such varied learning." That the author announces himself a "man of letters" offers further testimony to Carême's celebrity outside the kitchen.[1] If Carême "invented" French cuisine, achieving a culinary immortality that Oscar Wilde's character only dreamed about, it was because he created not one sauce but a comprehensive system of sauces . . . and soups and pastry and meats and vegetables. Not content to refine the cuisine that he inherited, Carême rebuilt it, redefined it—in a word, reinvented it. To invoke a modern model of cultural creation, Carême's cuisine corresponded to a new culinary paradigm.[2] That this paradigm ruled French cuisine for at least a century, and made its influence felt well beyond, would have been taken by Carême as a foregone conclusion. "I repeat it without fear," he affirms in his last work, "nineteenth-century French cuisine will remain the model of the beautiful in culinary art" (*L'Art* [1833], 2:13).

I. Between the Old Regime and the New

Our French service is more elegant and more sumptuous. It is the model for culinary art.
. . . Nothing is more imposing than the sight of a great table set out in the French service.

—Carême, *Le Maître d'hôtel français*, 2:151

I destroyed old preconceptions, torturous precepts of dreadful and imbecilic routine.
. . . modern cuisine will owe me, as pastry does, elegance and a notable development.

—Carême, *Le Pâtissier royal parisien*, p. xxv

Well before he died, not yet fifty, in 1833, Marie-Antoine Carême had achieved legendary status. The author of several magisterial works on the art of cooking, Carême was fully convinced that he had indeed invented modern French cuisine: "Mine will be the honor and the merit of having been the first to treat our great cuisine in the grand manner, and to have borrowed nothing from anyone" (*Le Cuisinier parisien*, p. 20). His contemporaries agreed. Some forty years later, Alexandre Dumas, the enormously popular author of *The Three Musketeers* and *The Count of Monte Cristo*, a gastronome of renown and a cook of note, did not hesitate to call Carême "the king of cooking," one who, unlike a good many other kings who had lost their principalities over the tumultuous nineteenth century, remained firmly on his throne. "Who is to say," Dumas muses in yet another meditation on the art of cooking, "that Carême will not live longer than Horace?" Much later, even as he worked to bring the classical French cuisine of the nineteenth century in line with the mores and the mood of the twentieth, the great chef Auguste Escoffier declared flatly that "the fundamental principles of the science [of cooking], which we owe to Carême, . . . will last as long as Cooking itself."[3]

And yet, unlike his disciple Escoffier, Carême is not a household name, even in France, where he tends to be relegated to a culinary old regime, mostly of antiquarian interest. The elaborate architectural confections that made his reputation now seem overwrought, excessive, as well as fearfully expensive, a feast apparently designed as much for the eyes as for the taste buds, and as truly impracticable. The intricate pavilions and exotic landscapes fashioned from spun sugar and almond paste remind moderns of nothing so much as Emma Bovary's wedding cake with its colonnaded temple, turret, lakes of jam, and boats of slivered hazelnuts, topped with Cupid caught in midair on a chocolate swing.

To see these creations as the last gasp of Ancien Régime extravaganzas or to stress the difficulty of the preparations is to overlook the nature of Carême's contribution.[4] For it is the modernity of Carême's work that set French cuisine on the course it would follow for so long. He modernized cooking by creating a cuisine in what he saw as the "spirit of analysis of the nineteenth century" (*L'Art* [1833], 1:lxvi), a self-contained set of rules and procedures governing culinary production. Thanks to his work, albeit in ways that Carême did not anticipate and probably would not have welcomed, cooking flourished, not as the trade or craft that it always had been but as a profession. In contrast to the artisan who learns through personal example, the chef would now acquire his education through mastery of a body of systematized knowledge. Carême's culinary practice and his exceptional career provided models for the ambitious chef; his publications endowed culinary practice with the base of expert knowledge upon which all professions depend. For all these reasons, Carême counts as the first professional chef, someone who considered his work and his career in terms of an occupation with articulated rules, norms, and values that "set the example for centuries to come" (*Le Pâtissier royal parisien*, dedication).

Cascade de Rome antique

Antique Roman Waterfall

As his signature on the bottom left attests, Carême took great pride in both the execution and the depictions of his many and stunning pastry creations, and they earned him recognition as the Palladio of French cuisine. Spun sugar is the prime ingredient in this visual salute to ancient Rome. From Carême, *Le Pâtissier pittoresque* (1815). Courtesy of The University of Iowa Libraries.

Carême was unquestionably a great practitioner, but glory as an artisan was not enough. The transformation of his culinary practice into a professional norm depended on the writing that took his practice out of the kitchen. His publications put him in a singular position. Like his predecessors in the Ancien Régime, Carême cooked for the wealthy, a necessary credential for his profession at the very end of the eighteenth century, when he started out. However, unlike these predecessors, who communicated within a largely oral culture and relied on a network of personal connections, he used print to stimulate a very different kind of social interaction: more impersonal, close to anonymous, and much more comprehensive. He may have looked to the past; he wrote for the present and the future. His conception of his mission altered as he ever more self-consciously established French cuisine as a system. Carême's cuisine was modern, it was French, and it was for all French people: "My book is not written for great houses alone. On the contrary, I want it to have a general utility. . . . I would like every citizen in our beautiful France to be able to eat delicious food" (*L'Art* [1833], 1:lviii–lvix). Though Carême may have worked for the elite, he remained withal a child of the Revolution. Whatever his own preferences, his writings moved French cuisine along the path to democratization as it played to new and different publics. Brides in the provinces like Emma Bovary could have fantastic, fantasy wedding cakes because, thanks to Carême in particular, ornamental pastry making moved down the social scale and out of Parisian elite circles. The bourgeois wedding cake democratized and commercialized the *pièces montées* of the Ancien Régime and Carême's own practice. Flaubert makes a point of telling us that Emma's baker took such care with the scenic confection because he hoped to attract customers to his new business. Emma's wedding offered him a golden opportunity for publicity.

The men whom Carême revered had spent their time in the kitchen, not at the writing table. "Unfortunately for the culinary arts," these great maîtres d'hôtel, or stewards, of the seventeenth and eighteenth centuries whose names he inscribed on the frontispiece of *Le Maître d'hôtel français* never wrote "even two lines" (*Le Cuisinier parisien*, 18 n. 1). Of course, since their practice left no trace, these venerable ancestors offered no competition and could be honored with impunity. Carême even notes that he "quit the finest houses in Europe" to write up his practice along with that of "a few great contemporaries who hardly existed, when I wrote, except in my memory."[5] He judged most culinary works to be "ridiculous books that are a disgrace to our great national cuisine" (*Le Maître d'hôtel français*, p. 5), little more than "warmed up left-overs" *(du réchauffé)* (*L'Art* [1833], 1:lxv). Carême took great pains explicitly to refute their claims to culinary competence, often point by point.

Few individuals embody the old and the new quite so strikingly as Carême did. The dual allegiances that structure his work had much to do with his unprecedented culinary authority. His associations with the high and mighty and with the tradition of French cuisine counted a great deal for his contemporaries, while the innovations attracted disciples and successors resolved to institutionalize cooking as a profession. Carême's life, his career, and his work negotiated tradition and contemporaneity in a series of transactions that positioned him to establish the present of French cuisine and also, in the event, to determine its future. And however one assesses his contribution, it is indisputably true that French cuisine would have followed a different course had not so many chefs and gastronomes alike enthusiastically accepted Carême's conception of culinary excellence and the means that he devised to achieve that standard. The subsequent development of professional cooking in the latter half of the nineteenth century would not have been possible without his example and his works, the rules he laid down, the techniques he explicated, and the ideal of the creative chef that he personified.

Le Véritable Amphitryon est l'Amphitryon où l'on Dîne

Bourgogne

Champagne

WATEL.

SAUVANT.

MECELIER

RICHAUT.

LEFÉVE.

LACOUR.

DALÉGRE.

SABATIER

MECIER.

LAGUIPIÈRE

Le MAÎTRE D'HOTEL français ou Parallèle de la Cuisine Ancienne et Moderne selon les Quatre Saisons Par M. Antonin CARÊME de Paris

A PARIS
Chez l'Auteur, Rue Caumartin, N° 20.

Careme invt.

Hibon sc.

A Revolutionary Career

[A] poor young man, without education, without a protector, by my will alone and my
studies, I have recreated the art of the French pastry maker.

—Carême, *Le Pâtissier royal parisien*, p. xxv

Carême had the good fortune to make his debut on the culinary stage at an
exceptionally opportune moment. Born in 1783, with no firsthand connection to the events of the French Revolution, he was well aware of how much
and how quickly things culinary had changed from the Ancien Régime, and
how his own career was implicated in those changes. His very name changed
with the times as he moved up in the world, from Marie-Antoine to Antoine
to his apparent preference, the one he used to sign his early books, the classi-
cally inflected Antonin. He lived through several regimes, from the monarchy
of his early childhood, the various revolutionary regimes of the 1790s and
early 1800s, and the Napoleonic Empire from 1804 to the restoration of the
monarchy in 1815. Another revolution in 1830 ushered in still another
monarchy. "At the age of 48, to have lived forty years of revolution!" he wrote
in 1830 with pardonable emphasis. "What a strange concurrence of memorable events." He made no secret of his personal inclination toward the culinary opulence of the Ancien Régime and his sense of the misfortunes to
which political upheaval subjected culinary excellence. During the revolution, not least because of the widespread food shortages, cuisine went into a
decline. Gastronomy, he declared, suffered from "years of calamity and mis-
ery" because if it "marches like a sovereign at the head of civilization, . . . it
vegetates during revolutionary times" (*L'Art* [1994], pt. 4, chap. 3, p. 297;
pt. 2, p. ii). Clearly, Carême's perspective is colored by a nostalgia for a culi-

---

Title Page, *Le Maître d'hôtel français*

Carême pays public homage to the stewards who came before him in the Ancien Régime
on the title page of this menu book from 1822. The quote from Molière at the top—
"The true host is the host where one dines"—provides added cultural capital, while the
drawings at the bottom depict the extraordinary range of food elements to be applied in
the culinary text that follows. Fish caught in a net at the very bottom of the page, flanked
by vegetables to the left and the fruit to the right; the garden implements (rake, hoe and
watering can); the hunter's pouch, gun, knife, and horn; sheaves of wheat, grapevines, and
game animals and birds—all come together as ingredients for the dining table with its
splendid centerpiece. The size and form of the typeface identify Carême as the incarnation
of a glorious tradition, the French *maître d'hôtel* who simultaneously creates and celebrates
these meals. From Carême, *Le Maître d'hôtel français* (1822). Courtesy of The University of
Iowa Libraries.

nary world that he knew only through books and through working with chefs who had been part of that world, men such as Boucher, to whom he dedicated the *Pâtissier royal parisien,* or the Robert brothers, to whom he dedicated his *Maître d'hôtel.* Only the Empire (1804–14), which kept its battles outside French territory, had sustained cuisine at the level and magnificence that Carême thought appropriate to his great enterprise.

The political and social displacements as well as the economic opportunities of the turbulent 1790s opened an archetypal revolutionary path. As Dumas observed with characteristic hyperbole, "like all empire builders, like Theseus, like Romulus," Carême was something of a foundling. As the chef told his own improbable story, he was one of twenty-five children whose father, overcome by poverty, abandoned him in the street at the age of eleven. The boy never saw his family again. A providential light in a window led him to a small eating establishment, where he worked until he moved to a proper restaurant at sixteen. Soon thereafter, he apprenticed at Bailly's, a celebrated Parisian pastry maker. These years of pastry apprenticeship gave Carême his schooling. He embarked on his own education, spending whatever time he could find in the Royal Library, devouring classical and French culinary treatises along with the architectural works that defined his ambitions. A self-made man, Carême made much of his self-education, and was at once inordinately proud of his learning and obsequiously humble about his beginnings. Unlike other young men who made their mark in the world of pastry, almost all of whom, he claimed, had family behind them and several helpers in the kitchen, he would later boast that "a poor young man, without education, without any family connections, by the force of my will alone and my studies, I have recreated the art of the French pastry maker" (*Le Pâtissier royal parisien,* p. xxv).

Carême soon attracted the attention of one of Bailly's best customers, Talleyrand, the renowned connoisseur and consummate courtier-politician.[6] Again, the elements of legend are at work in the powerful man who recognizes the untutored genius striving to perfect his art. Talleyrand realized the cultural capital represented by the *pièces montées* that Carême had begun to execute (by the time he left Bailly's, he had done over 150 [*Le Pâtissier royal parisien,* p. xxv]), and he kept the chef in his employ for over a decade, "lending" him out for special banquets—*les grands extras*—one in honor of the marriage of Napoleon in 1810 and another for the birth of his son a year later, victory celebrations, and similar public displays of imperial power. Carême modeled his conception of haute cuisine on his experiences during the Napoleonic Empire, and ever after cited Talleyrand as the ideal patron.

Together, the gastronome and the chef sustain the only state of affairs where culinary genius can flourish (*L'Art* [1833], 2:vi–vii, xvii–xviii). Both through his own example and through the good offices of his head steward *(contrôleur)*, M. Boucher, who had been chef to the prince de Condé prior to the revolution, Talleyrand gave Carême a direct connection to the opulent culinary mores of the Ancien Régime, where the patron, not the customer, was an essential part of the equation. Without Boucher, Carême assures his readers in the dedication of *Le Pâtissier royal parisien* to his culinary master, Talleyrand would have sustained an immense loss. By the same token, without Talleyrand's unstinting generosity and knowledgeable support, even the "sumptuous" and "nobly disinterested" Boucher would not have attained the culinary heights that he did (*Le Pâtissier royal parisien*, 2:407).

During the occupation of Paris by the allied troops in 1814 after the defeat of Napoleon, Talleyrand loaned Carême to the tsar of Russia for his Paris sojourn. Sought after by the tsar and for a time chef to the prince regent of Great Britain, the future George IV, Carême returned to France in 1819, "his French soul" having found it impossible to live anywhere except his homeland (*Le Maître d'hôtel français*, 1:8). Back in Paris, Carême published his architectural projects, which he dedicated to the tsar, from whom he received a diamond ring—just as he had received a golden snuffbox from Metternich in appreciation for the immense pastry "trophy" that he constructed featuring the arms of all the Allies. Refusing several illustrious offers, including that of George IV (though he did "do" the coronation), in 1823 Carême entered the employ of the baron James de Rothschild, where he remained until 1829, when he retired to finish *L'Art de la cuisine française au dix-neuvième siècle*. On January 12, 1833, having dictated the second two volumes of his last work to his daughter (volumes 4 and 5 were completed by a disciple from Carême's notes, and the whole was published later that year), Carême died, apparently of intestinal tuberculosis—but "really," as Dumas advises us in the *Grand Dictionnaire de cuisine* with his usual panache, "killed by his own genius."

The most celebrated chef in Europe, Carême turned the trade he had learned into a decidedly modern occupation. He represented for chefs something of what Voltaire had earlier exemplified for men of letters: a seismic shift in the occupation itself. Like Voltaire, the bourgeois who moved from courtier to courted at his own mini-court, Carême rose from poverty to a substantial as well as an honorable estate. By his own account, he made a good deal of money from his banquets and later his books, in addition to a significant basic salary—two thousand francs a quarter from Rothschild. He could well afford his own carriage to travel to the Rothschild country estate and could afford, as most chefs could not, to assert that "the chef committed to science is more responsive to the praise given by his Patron [*l'Amphitryon*] than to the handful of gold that he might receive from him" (*L'Art* [1833], 2:xix).

This spectacular career transcended individual triumph: Carême reconfigured the occupation itself by joining to the chef's role as artisan those of the culinary performer, the scholar, the scientist, and the artist. Henceforth the chef would need to be all of these. Through his efforts, the division of the Ancien Régime elite kitchen into the domains of the Officier de cuisine (in charge of the kitchen) and the Officier de bouche (the steward responsible for supplies) was united in the early nineteenth century in the chef de cuisine or *homme de bouche,* literally "man of the mouth": everything having to do with the meal came under his supervision. No wonder military metaphors appeared so frequently in the invocation of kitchens. (They do still today: the modern restaurant kitchen is organized as a "brigade," with strictly defined lines of authority and precisely determined responsibilities.) Carême's description of the heroic commander in the kitchen is heavy with resonance of conquest in battle:

> [I]n this abyss of heat . . . the man in charge has to have a strong head, be focused on the task, and have the management skills of a great administrator. He sees everything, he acts everywhere at once; . . . And, is it to be believed? In this furnace, everyone acts promptly, not a breath is heard; the chef alone has the right to make himself heard, and everything obeys his voice. (*Le Pâtissier royal parisien,* pp. xxvi–xxvii)

Carême's distinction between the officer and the culinary foot soldier is fully justified by the sheer numbers of individuals working in his kitchens, the complex division of labor, and the exacting coordination of efforts to produce dinners ranging from the 36 to 48 guests that he served three or four times a week at Talleyrand's to the 10,000 guests at an outdoor fête for the Allies after Napoleon's defeat. This distinction is also responsible for Carême's strong sense of the honor that is due the chef and his near obsession with setting the chef apart from ordinary household servants. He complained bitterly about modern households where the chef dines with the menservants and the doormen (*L'Art* [1833], 2:viii); "wily, vain and self-important" valets come in for special opprobrium (2:xxii). The modern chef cannot tolerate this indistinction: "The chef of today's France becomes an ordinary man in the eyes of the individual who classes him among the servants" (2:xviii).

Sensitivity to status was also part of Carême's legend. When Lady Morgan, an Irish woman of letters, was invited to dine by the baron Rothschild in 1829, she was immediately regaled, the invitation barely in hand, by "anecdotes beyond number" of the "pomps and vanities" of the life of Carême: the number of aides attached to his staff, his box at the opera, and "other proofs of sumptuosity and taste," all of which only increased her desire to meet this "man who was at the head of his class." Later, having returned to Ireland, she was assured by a chef that, to the contrary, Carême had the simplest of habits: "to see him in private life, you would never suppose him to be the extraordinary and celebrated person of whom we hear so much."[7] Nevertheless, Lady Morgan, too, credited Carême with a fabulous genealogy, since she "knew" that he was descended from a famous French chef at the Vatican who invented a "lean" (meatless) soup for the pope during Lent and earned the name of Jean de Carême (*carême* as a substantive signifies Lent). That the story of his culinary antecedents was totally apocryphal testifies to the need to justify a name that would seem to bode ill for culinary distinction and to the eminence that Carême had attained. His status was so great, the social distance traversed so immense that explanation is in order. Absolutely personal artistry—"genius" in the Romantic lexicon—did not suffice, at least for a cook, however gifted and however industrious.

The Scholar

The appearance of these works created such a sensation because we were not used to finding in works of this type such an analytic spirit, such a luminous method, or such varied learning.

—M. Audiguier, "Coup d'oeil sur l'Influence de la cuisine
et sur les ouvrages de M. Carême"

Even though he worked from the cook's artisanal base, the modern chef needed much more than hands-on experience in the kitchen. He needed to know, for example, the history of cuisine, French cuisine to be sure, but also foreign cuisines and the cuisines of the ancient world. Despite the apparent loss of a complete work on the history of Roman dining—a loss that Dumas noted with great regret—there is ample testimony to Carême's knowledge of other cuisines, most notably the "Parallel between Old and Modern Cuisine" in *Le Maître d'hôtel* and the "Philosophical History of Cuisine" in *L'Art de la cuisine française*. To these formal disquisitions should be added the extensive sundry observations scattered throughout all his works detailing the differences between the old culinary regime and the new. It was the depth of his knowledge and the ability to cite the cuisine of the Ancien Régime chapter and verse that legitimated the superiority that he attributed to the new, modern French cuisine. Not that Carême expected his readers to accept this judgment on his word alone; he always took great care to prove his point. *Le Maître d'hôtel* made extensive comparisons of Ancien Régime meals and his own modern menus. Moreover, like every good scholar, Carême made a great point of citing his sources, whether Mme de Sévigné's account of Vatel's suicide or current works on cuisine, nutrition, and gastronomy. His own policy of scrupulous citation led him to denounce those who were not equally meticulous, and when the omission turned out to be one of Carême's own works, his indignation knew no bounds.

Carême also made much of the scientific basis of his culinary system, partly in the older sense that equated "science" with knowledge as such, but partly as well in the modern sense of the natural sciences. Thus, his major work on the whole of French cuisine opens with a discussion of ordinary boiled beef, the pot-au-feu. This humble dish opens the section on beef broths and stock, since that stock, in a reduced form, supplies the essential ingredient in a vast range of preparations from soups to sauces. Another reason, and one of a different order, for Carême to use the pot-au-feu to launch this work has to do with its social importance. The pot-au-feu is more than fundamental to this culinary system. As the source of the most substantial nourishment the working classes ordinarily get, it is fundamental to France itself.

Concern for health surfaces throughout Carême's work, testimony to his belief that "culinary science is more salubrious for health than all the learned precepts of those who prolong illness by their speculations" (*L'Art* [1833], 2:xxvii). What better evidence than the absence of attacks of gout when Carême had charge of the royal kitchen for the British prince regent. The brief section on the properties of herbs and spices cites no less an authority than Pliny on the virtues of salt (*L'Art* [1833], 1:lxi–lxiv). Perhaps Dumas was right to conjecture that the course in "gastronomic hygiene" given by Carême to the future George IV would have made a classic culinary work. Although gastronomy could not come into existence without an identity of its own apart from medicine, the separation always remains imperfect.

The Artist

My ambition was serious. Early on I wanted to raise my profession to the state of art.

—Carême

His apparently insatiable quest for knowledge pushed Carême to the fine arts. Architecture was his special passion, and he was immensely proud of the designs he drafted for monuments in St. Petersburg and in France, none of them much under two hundred feet! Carême's culinary work, too, associates small with pettiness and insignificance, whether in culinary creations, the work of his fellow chefs, or the shortsightedness of miserly employers who skimp on kitchen expenses. He was quite vain about having done all the drawings for his *pièces montées* (giving due credit to the engraver), and his sobriquet as the Palladio of Pastry (*Le Pâtissier royal parisien*, p. xxiv). He included a history of the orders of architecture in *Le Pâtissier pittoresque:* "The first great thing I was able to do for science was to shut myself in for almost two years to write and compose my first work; then almost three years to draw and write my *Pâtissier pittoresque* and my *Maître d'hôtel*" (*Le Pâtissier royal parisien*, p. xviii). "My ambition was serious. Early on I wanted to raise my profession to the state of art." Accordingly, Carême advises young practitioners to frequent museums in order to learn about "the nature of the rules of art . . . the eternal principle of truth and beauty" (*L'Art* [1833], 2:321).

Carême did not originate the concept of cuisine as an art. Nevertheless, his precepts gave a theoretical foundation for the distinction between the artist and the artisan. The modern chef takes cuisine beyond its artisanal grounding into the realm of the aesthetic and the intellectual. In fact, Carême's presentation of self reminds one of nothing so much as the reams written about the Romantic artist in these same years of the nineteenth century: devotion to the higher cause of art; personal sacrifices, often to the detriment of one's health; pride in one's chosen vocation; and refusal to be regarded as a hired help, that is, as an artisan.

Carême's vision of the relationship between chef and employer took as its model the ideal relationship between the artist and the unfailingly generous patron, in which the tastes of both parties coincided with and complemented one another; avarice, ignorance and vulgarity were the unforgivable sins in a patron. "The man born to wealth lives to eat, and sustains the art of the chef"; conversely, "the rich, miserly man eats to live; his life is lived out in mediocrity"; "the rich miser lives and dies in mediocrity" (*L'Art* [1833], 2:vi–vii, xii). Carême enjoyed just this kind of relationship with Talleyrand. He left Russia because he found the surveillance to which he and his personnel were subjected to be humiliating, at the very least incompatible with the status of a great artist; and he refused offers that did not carry what he judged to be sufficient support in terms of personnel and expense. At the same time, he could be positively over the top in his praise: "the wealthy man, noble in character, understands that the men who serve him ought to have some reflection of his dignity and his greatness"; or again, "the rich, beneficent man is a god on earth, his name is blessed by the unfortunate" (*L'Art* [1833], 2:ix, xii).

Such an understanding between chef and patron was rare. Even as Carême deferred to his patron, he insisted on the patron's own obligations. This curious combination of pride and humility often turns up in the same sentence. Carême complains that he had to spend his own money to further his research and that his work was better known abroad than in France: "Chefs today are not always appreciated in France; the love of knowledge *(science)* alone sustains them in their work" (*L'Art* [1833], 2:xvii). Fortunately, in Carême's case at any rate, however underappreciated the culinary artist, the chef had no lack of offers. He made a good deal of money early on; through his writings he made even more. By publishing his works himself, Carême reaped all the profit. (The usual arrangement at the time was to sell a manuscript to a publisher for a determined period [five to ten years] for a lump sum. Royalties taken as a percentage of sales did not enter publishing mores until the end of the century, and even then involved more of an ideal than a norm.) If Carême spent his own money on his culinary art, as he both complains and boasts, he had the money to spend—enough to refuse Rothschild's offer of a retirement pension (as Carême recounts the incident, the baron was all but incredulous).

Carême's discourse concerning the patron is perhaps what strikes the modern reader the most about his writings. The ephemeral nature of the cook's product requires an entirely different organization of its production to make haute cuisine commercially viable. Surprisingly enough for someone who so insisted on the modernity of his cuisine, Carême had nothing to do with restaurants. He rejected the solution offered by the restaurant because he did not countenance the overt commercialization of cooking—he closed his own pastry shop for this very reason. Haute cuisine would continue to depend upon patrons, though these would be found less and less among individuals and more and more in establishments such as restaurants, hotels, and private clubs.

The Professional

A man whose imagination greatly enlarged the variety of *entrées* and *entremêts*
previously practised, and whose clear & perspicuous details render them facile,
not only to the Artist who has already an advance in his profession, but also to those
whose knowledge of the higher code of the Kitchen has necessarily been limited.

—William Hall, *French Cookery* (1836)

Carême hardly refrained from trumpeting his accomplishments. "I have done in the science of the pastry-maker what I am now doing in the art of French cuisine" (*Le Pâtissier royal parisien*, p. xxv), ran a not-atypical boast. At the same time, he worked hard to turn his personal achievements into a general good that would serve the "estate" *(état)* or trade *(métier)* of cooking. Whatever the term, Carême conceived cooking as a profession in the modern sense of a body of socially organized expert and exclusive knowledge. French cuisine would become even more glorious, he believed, when practiced by individuals who will have learned the lessons that his works taught; works based, as he never tired of reminding his readers, on twenty-five years of experience in the most prestigious positions. Woe to French cuisine if his successors disregarded these lessons.

Carême's sharp sense of his own worth, in the kitchen and on the printed page, and his exalted sense of self were tempered by an equally strong sense of placement vis-à-vis the culinary past, present, and future. A prodigious knowledge of culinary traditions grounded his insistence on his place as the creator of modern French cuisine, and all of his works contain more or less extensive comparisons between traditional and modern culinary methods. Each book addresses his *confrères*, his practicing culinary contemporaries, of whom three receive book dedications. Carême's game was complicated because the chefs and stewards (maître d'hôtel) to whom he dedicated his works were themselves carefully situated with respect to their powerful employers: M. Mueller *(Le Pâtissier pittoresque)* was the chief steward for the Russian tsar; M. Boucher *(Le Pâtissier royal)*, the steward for Talleyrand's household; the Robert brothers *(Le Maître d'hôtel français)*, chefs who had worked in the most illustrious houses in Paris and Europe. Not until *L'Art de la cuisine française* did Carême venture to dedicate his work directly to his patron, and then the dedication was at one remove, since the dedicatee was Madame Rothschild, not Monsieur.

Carême laid great stress on his service to the profession at large, boasting that his own inventions alone more than doubled the material available to pastry chefs. "I intend to use all means to accelerate the progress of our work by making them easier to execute, all the more so as the results are the same," he declares (*L'Art* [1994], pt. 4, chap. 1, p. 288). To facilitate pastry decoration, Carême engaged master tinsmiths to make molds to his design specifications (*Le Pâtissier royal parisien*, p. xix). Not that he took all the credit. He gave effusive and, one senses, heartfelt thanks to the unknown inventor of the pastry tube. Not even the less salubrious aspects of the kitchen escape his attention. He proudly asserts that his stratagem caught 1,215 of the bugs that infest the ovens, and on the first try! (*Le Pâtissier royal parisien*, 2:410–11) Other improvements speak to Carême's perfectionism. To ensure optimal conditions for roasting, he spent his own money on skewers made to order (*L'Art* [1994], pt. 3, chap. 1, p. 162), just as he ordered a special ladle to put just the right amount of sauce on a dish. All chefs, he advises, would do well to follow his example. He also offers instructions on organizing a kitchen, enjoining the cook, for example, to label each small saucepan. Finally, for an innovation that speaks to both the accelerated pace and the restricted space of the modern restaurant kitchen, we have to look no further than his system of preparing basic sauces (stocks, or *fonds de cuisine*) in advance and then subjecting them to reduction. Easily stored, the resulting concentrates—sauce essences—could be used as wanted.

Like many other aspiring professionals, Carême based his arguments for occupational importance on the general utility of his work, and this despite the fact that he himself worked under rarified conditions for a highly select public. The very exclusivity of this practice conferred on him the cultural authority needed to impress other publics, while his written work provided the means to reach chefs who worked with a minimal kitchen staff. He admitted that chefs with their own *sauciers* would reject his new time- and space-saving manner of producing the basic sauces. His intended public, however, was "almost all cooks, who also want to expedite their work" (*L'Art* [1994], pt. 4, chap. 1, p. 288), not excluding the women who cooked for bourgeois households and had to make do with no proper staff at all. All of these cooks essentially had in common the lack of the material, time, and rigorous training necessary for the production of haute cuisine. Even so, despite their obvious limitations, these cooks could profit from Carême's works. Absent the means to make the basic sauces properly, they could not make the many lesser, or "small," sauces that grounded the whole French culinary system. Nevertheless, and even though Carême expressly omitted "bourgeois" sauces, he proposed a number of what can only be called shortcuts. And while he confesses that these sauces would not be as "rich" *(succulentes)* as the sauces properly done, they would, he assures his readers, be "agreeable" nonetheless (*L'Art* [1994], pt. 4, chap. 4, p. 303).

Most of all, Carême was preoccupied with gaining recognition for the social and artistic superiority of the estate he at once illustrated and promoted. To his way of thinking, those who benefit—the diners—should value the men responsible for the excellence of the cuisine. By the same token, public appreciation necessitates visible distinctiveness. A new product will not suffice to mark the profession as will a new persona. At the very front of *Le Maître d'hôtel* Carême placed an engraving of two chefs, one depicted old-style, the other new. As he explains it (2:279–80), the hat sets them apart. For some time, Carême tells us, he had been seeking a way to change the manner of wearing the distinctive cotton cap *(bonnet)* whose absolute whiteness is the emblematic sign of the cleanliness that is, for Carême, the hallmark of the chef ("Cleanliness is the greatest quality of the cook." [*L'Art* (1833), 2:xxi]). Reasoning that "a chef ought to look like a man in good health, but our usual cap made us look ill," Carême adopted the cap forthwith. A look at the drawing reveals the elegant curls of the young modern chef so reminiscent of the engraving we have of Carême himself. The new cap sits rakishly on the side of the head in a pose not altogether unsuitable for a Romantic poet. Although chefs did not adopt the considerably less flattering stiff high hat *(toque)* until later in the century, Carême's modifications signaled the will to raise the estate of cook in the public eye. The more entrenched haute cuisine became, the higher the hat, an unambiguous signal of the chef's claim to greatness.

The modern chef not only had to look his part, he had to play it. A lengthy discussion in *Le Pâtissier royal parisien* about orthography serves as Carême's bid to impose language itself on the profession. In a society where French still

Stéuben pinx.   *Blanchard sc.*

The Perfect Chef—Antonin Carême

This portrait carefully reduces the class distance between the working chef and his consuming elite public. Carême's stylish informal coiffure, the flowing drapery around him, his loose collar and floppy tie, and, above all, his decision to appear without the signature chef's hat—these elements take him out of the kitchen and quite possibly into a salon. Engraving by Blanchard after a portrait by Steuben in *Les Classiques de la table* (1845). Courtesy of Columbia University Libraries.

---

competed with multiple dialects and patois, where the national idiom would not become the mother tongue for the majority of inhabitants until the end of the nineteenth century, Carême's insistence on appropriate language translates the professional's desire to overcome the uneducated, even illiterate craftsman's linguistic inferiority. In reducing the discrepancy between culinary and linguistic achievement, he aimed to reduce as well the social distance between upper-class patron and lower-class artisan. He had to realize, however, that his own style was not what it should be: "it's true, I suffer about it in silence, but it's the style of a hard working man, an artisan (would that you were called artists) who for many long years has been concerned with perfecting his estate" (*Le Pâtissier royal parisien,* pp. xi–xii).

The "Vocabulary of words for writing out menus" and its list of terms from soups to desserts, which took up twenty-eight pages in *Le Pâtissier royal parisien* (1:lvii–lxxxix), was explicitly aimed at educating all cooks in the "language of our art." Incorrect spelling threw the whole estate into disfavor with the better-educated clientele and showed cooks up as "illogical or ignorant." With a handy copy of Carême's classification of all the terms relative to cooking, the chef could copy out the words in his leisure time and would soon be able to write menus in a way that is "honorable for us, and satisfactory for our masters." To learn spelling and also, primarily, the art of ordering meals, he exhorted apprentices to copy out menus (naturally recommending those in *Le Maître d'hôtel*). And while Carême thought in terms of the private patron and his circle, the restaurant relied far more heavily on correct culinary language to reach its customers. Like the seasonal menus presented in *Le Maître d'hôtel,* this "difficult and long labor" translated "the same desire of being useful to my confrères" (*Le Maître d'hôtel français,* 1:64).

Utility to the profession was Carême's byword. His great ambition "was to be useful to practitioners, by uncovering for them the fruits of the long nights I have spent studying and my voyages, by retracing the developments that we have given our science, and to leave after me a work worthy of bearing the beautiful name of *Cuisinier parisien,* and worthy as well of the great century in which I have lived" ("Observation," chapter 1, *Le Maître d'hôtel français,* 1:64). In his final illness, even as he lamented how much remained to be done, he noted with great satisfaction that, having dictated the final chapters of *L'Art de la cuisine française* to his daughter, he was certain of leaving something useful.

Carême saw himself as guardian of culinary standards and indeed, of French cuisine itself. The "critical review of the great balls" (*Le Pâtissier royal parisien,* 2:354–79), often devastating in the accusations of lack of taste, is pedagogically more useful than discussion of the successes. So seriously did he take his task that he calls for culinary organizations of various sorts: chief among them would be a culinary society formed by the most distinguished chefs of Paris that would meet every two weeks to organize regular competitions, judged by the best chefs in Paris. A member chosen to be the "censor" would be charged with judging the "great works" and promulgating his judgment. Every session would end with a magnificent supper, to show off members' new discoveries. Finally, the goal of this culinary society would be a comprehensive work on French cuisine, the outline of which Carême presents. He estimates that this work, "dictated by our great masters," would take up three big volumes, with at least fifty engravings (*Le Pâtissier royal parisien*, 1:xii–xv). Since no one else took up the challenge, Carême resolved to do it himself.

II. The Cuisine

Its character . . . was that it was in season, . . . up to its time, . . . in the spirit of the age.

—Lady Morgan, on a dinner served by Carême

What of the food Carême actually served? Culinary claims are one thing, taste another. The virtuoso architectural pastry creations that set Carême's extraordinary career in motion turn out to be, perhaps paradoxically, the least modern elements of his work. The career that began with pastry ended with a treatise on the whole of French cuisine. His first two published works concerned pastry; the two treatises that appeared in 1815, *Le Pâtissier royal parisien* and *Le Pâtissier pittoresque*, can be seen as preparation for addressing the whole of French cuisine in *Le Maître d'hôtel* (1822), *Le Cuisinier parisien* (1828), and *L'Art de la cuisine française au dix-neuvième siècle* (1833) (at the time, *pastry* covered doughs for hot and cold pâtés, rice casseroles, timbales, noodle-truffle croustades, cakes, soufflés, and fondues, as well as desserts). Whereas the gigantic *pièces montées* tied Carême's work to the great banquets of the past; his written work placed his cuisine squarely in the democratizing temper of modern society. These pages contained his bid to posterity, because they repeatedly *proved* (to use a term to which Carême had frequent recourse) the absolute and incontestable superiority of modern cuisine. Reaching beyond the elite of direct consumers who dined at the great dinners actually prepared by Carême, the written work found the far more extensive public of readers who consumed that cuisine at one remove.

Systematic Simplicity

At the same time that Carême directed his writings to the nascent profession of cooking, he addressed a larger public of gourmands, hosts, and even women in the position of instructing their (female and presumably illiterate) cooks. In other words, these culinary texts aimed both to instruct practitioners and consumers and also, more generally, to convince both groups that Carême's method was the path, and the only path, to culinary excellence. He

insisted that these *treatises* were both *elementary* and *practical,* that is, fundamental and doable. The very subtitle of *L'Art de la cuisine française* vaunted the
"culinary discussions useful to the progress of the Art." In other words, these
culinary texts aimed not only to instruct future chefs and consumers but also,
more generally, to point both groups to the way to culinary modernity and
convince them that nineteenth-century French cuisine set the standard for
times to come. Carême argued fervently that this cuisine would remain "the
very model" of what culinary art can achieve (*L'Art* [1994], pt. 4, chap. 1,
p. 291).

That Carême defined his cuisine by its simplicity startles only if we forget
that he always took the extravagant elite cuisine of the Ancien Régime as his
point of reference. He criticized the excessive decorations for which "ridiculous" was not too strong a term (*Le Pâtissier pittoresque,* pp. xxii–xxvii). Table
settings, too, benefited from simplification. Reducing the number of people
seated at table not only gave each diner more space, it set off the dishes to
greater advantage. To underscore the contrast, he appended two foldouts to *Le
Maître d'hôtel,* one from a dinner described in Vincent La Chapelle's celebrated
Le Cuisinier moderne from 1735, the other a pared-down setting for one of his
own dinners. Carême honored his predecessor, even naming a sauce for him.
Still, as he surely meant the comparison to demonstrate, nineteenth-century
France had rendered La Chapelle's eighteenth-century cuisine sorely out-
of-date.

Simplicity implies a host of other qualities—harmony, elegance, and above
all, that notoriously slippery quality, good taste. It also signals "naturalness"
in the foods used and prepared. Well before her dinner invitation, Lady Morgan knew that Carême had declared war on excessive spices, and, indeed,
Carême made much of his preference for herbs (tarragon, chervil, parsley,
etc.) over the heavily spiced cuisine of earlier years: "ordinary cooks will forever leave off their aromatic and spicy stews" (*L'Art* [1994], pt. 3, chap. 20,
p. 279). In this elimination of spices Carême continued a trend that had begun in the seventeenth century if not earlier, of setting the purified "new cuisine" of the moment against excessively heavy forerunners. He made good on
what his predecessors mostly only promised, so Lady Morgan's anticipation
was well rewarded. Carême's dinner surpassed her expectations, and her account is justifiably famous for conveying a sense of how his cooking tasted.
Many of our own culinary preferences are already present in his endeavors—
the importance of seasonal products, the dominance of natural aromas.
Carême's cuisine sounds remarkably appropriate for the twenty-first century:

> Its character . . . was that it was in season, . . . up to its time, . . . in the
> spirit of the age, . . . , no trace of the wisdom of our ancestors in a

single dish; no high-spiced sauces, no dark brown gravies, no flavour of cayenne and allspice, no tincture of catsup and walnut pickle, no visible agency of those vulgar elements of cooking, of the good old times, fire and water. . . . Every meat presented its own natural aroma, every vegetable its own shade of verdure.[8]

This simplicity defined culinary modernity. When Carême affirmed that French cuisine of the nineteenth century would remain the model for the future, this dinner must have been what he had in mind. No single element should stand out either in any given dish or in the dinner as a whole. Precise measurements where all the seasonings are "perfectly fused" were everything (*L'Art* [1994], pt. 4, chap. 4, p. 302). This ideal of fusion explains why Carême corrected the seasoning for the English turtle soup that English cooks routinely overspiced (*L'Art* [1994], pt. 1, chap. 13, p. 111, treatise on English soups). We are not surprised to find this chef, who was also a friend and great admirer of Rossini as a gastronome as well as a musician, invoking the "harmony" that he aimed for:

> [T]he art of the chef has this in common with the art of the painter and the musician; the first, through the nuances he gives to colors, . . . seduces the sense of sight and the imagination; the musician, through the combination of his notes, produces harmony; and the sense of hearing causes in us the sweetest sensations that melody can produce: the same holds for our culinary combinations: the sense of smell and the palate of the gastronome experience similar sensations, . . . when his eye contemplates the whole of a good dinner. (*L'Art* [1994], pt. 1, chap. 23, p. 157, treatise on American soups)

Even more important, this simplicity, and the harmony that results, complements the larger culinary system Carême advanced. Not the architectural creations, not the many inventions and innovations, but this system was his major contribution. Carême can be considered the inventor of modern French cuisine, because he put it all together, the old methods along with the new techniques, in a coherent structure where all the pieces, all the recipes, and all the sundry observations made sense in relationship to one another. This integration of the various culinary practices constructed a whole that no other French cookbook had attempted, much less achieved. Where there had been collections of recipes, there would now be a total culinary system.

To understand this system, culinary detail is unavoidable. We need to see how Carême constructed his cuisine from start to finish, from soups to sweets, connecting particular recipes as well as broader categories of dishes. *L'Art de la cuisine française* covers the whole of French cuisine (a first part dealing with cold entries appeared five years earlier as *Le Cuisinier parisien*).[9] Carême begins with the pot-au-feu, plain boiled beef, a preparation known to and tasted by all, and the closest France might come to a national dish. (Later in the century, almost every required domestic science textbook for girls began with a recipe for pot-au-feu.)[10] In place of a straightforward recipe, Carême analyzes exactly what happens when the housewife sets her pot on the fire, how she gets the savory beef bouillon that is the basis of the dish, and how professional chefs can obtain the same results. This basic recipe then directs the reader to a series of bouillons, from chicken to turkey, partridge, and wild rabbit, ending with a bouillon that can be used to enrich vegetable soups. The second chapter moves to consommés and fumets, the third to lean or Lenten bouillons, while the fourth examines medicinal bouillons. The fifth chapter presents court bouillons and marinades, that is, cooked and uncooked liquids used for poaching and marinating, and ends with descriptions of different doughs for deep frying and four media for frying (oil, lard, butter, beef fat). Chapter 6 then moves to the recipes for quenelles poached in the bouillons discussed in the previous sections.

In other words, there is a logical culinary progression to *L'Art de la cuisine française*. The second part of the book includes 24 chapters on soups, with, Carême specifies (*L'Art* [1994], pt. 1, chap. 23, p. 157), 196 French and 103 foreign recipes (English, Neapolitan, Sicilian, Italian, Spanish, German, Russian, Polish, Dutch, Indian, and American). Given the system he employs, which details in each chapter a basic soup from which several variations are elaborated, mastery of one preparation all but guarantees mastery of all the others connected to it. For the same reason he begins with the basics, bouillons (pt. 1) and soups (pt. 2), only then moving to whole fish (pt. 3) with more than 500 recipes (pt 3, chap. 20), sauces (pt. 4), and whole cuts of meat (beef, veal, mutton, lamb, ham and fresh pork, suckling pig), poultry, and game (pt. 5).

Perhaps the clearest sense of Carême's systematic approach to cuisine comes from part 4, which is devoted to sauces, namely the four great, or "mother," sauces (*grandes sauces,* or *sauces mères*) that provide the base for an almost infinite number of small, or lesser, sauces *(petites sauces).* (The four great sauces are l'Espagnole [Spanish], le Velouté, l'Allemande [German], and la Béchamel [basic white sauce].) Deciding (after long deliberation) against putting together all the sauces derived from a single great sauce, Carême followed another line of reasoning altogether. He grouped the small sauces by their analogous seasonings, each of which is given in both a "fat" and "lean" version to facilitate producing dinners during Lent and on the fast days decreed by the church. Far from complaining about the constraints that fasting placed on his cuisine, Carême welcomed them as the true test of the chef. The very restrictions challenged his ingenuity and allowed his cooking to shine with new brilliance (*L'Art* [1994], pt. 4, chap. 3; cf. *Le Pâtissier royal parisien*, p. xiii).

Culinary Nationalism

France is the motherland of hosts; its cuisine and its wines are the triumph of gastronomy and it is the only country for good food; foreigners are convinced of these truths.

—Carême, *Le Cuisinier parisien* (1828)

O France! My beautiful homeland. You alone unite in your breast
the delights of gastronomy.

—Carême, *L'Art de la cuisine française* (1833)

The rational presentation of culinary preparations as a system of interconnected parts arising from a singular base of fundamental principles—those principles that Escoffier claimed French cuisine owed to Carême—made it possible for this cuisine to range as far as it did, across Europe and even beyond. In the musical comparison that is so often invoked in matters culinary, the techniques of French cuisine could be learned like the rules of harmony that every musician must master. Thereafter, the meal, like the music, depends on how those techniques are put into practice. This technical basis, applicable anywhere and everywhere, supports the belief that French cuisine is "universal." In contrast with other cuisines defined not by technique but by product, Carême's French cuisine is not tied to or rooted in a particular place. Techniques and systems travel easily; foods much less so, certainly in the nineteenth century.

This universality depended heavily on language. Carême constructed his culinary model on a linguistic system, putting together a lexicon that, like every language, could be adapted by different users to their own purposes. The perfect vehicle for the diffusion of haute cuisine in restaurants, the linguistic system that carried this rationalized culinary system nonetheless remained unequivocally and intensely national. The internationalization and the nationalization of French cuisine proceeded apace. Translated editions of culinary texts mostly kept the French designations, but not just because the language of the culinary practices in question is French. The English translator of *L'Art de la cuisine française* in 1836 pointed out that Carême's terms have become technical, "like other names of science, deduced from other languages," and hence untranslatable. Anglicization would have been ridiculous and, in the event, unnecessary: given the "present universal reception amongst the profession, they may be deemed as universally understood."[11] In the *Guide to Modern Cookery* (1909), Escoffier advises that he, too, kept most of the French names in view of their untranslatability and the profusion of culinary terms, of which the French language has so many and the English language so few. Like ballet (another art formed in seventeenth-century France), cuisine would continue to speak French.

By no means did Carême invent all the dishes that he explicated. However, the names that he gave a good many of these conferred an identity, one that in this instance stamped this "universal" cuisine as nonetheless indelibly French. Rather than naming a single basic soup—turtle or fish or shrimp bisque—and specifying variations, Carême baptized each preparation, however minor the difference between it and the basic recipe. Sometimes he had the ingredients supply the names, notably for the primary soup in each category (i.e. shrimp bisque). Carême was very concerned to be clear in hopes that "young practitioners" would find them easier to remember (*L'Art* [1994], pt. 1, chap. 12, p. 110). The variants—of soups, of sauces, and of other dishes—allowed him greater scope for honorific, geographical, and historical names. Shrimp bisque, for one example, comes *à la française, à la Corneille, à l'amiral de Rigny, à la Périgord, à la princesse, au chasseur, à la Régence,* and *à la royale.* In contrast with the basic recipe, the names for the variants do not describe the dish at all. There is no connection to the main ingredients, and the names are almost entirely honorific. The point for Carême was that each variant have a distinct name, and that it be his designation. Thus, to the basic American turtle soup (chapter 23, cross-referenced to chapter 8, on French turtle soups, and chapter 13, for English turtle soup) Carême added an escalope of salmon sautéed in butter and seasoned with salt and cayenne pepper, which he served with eel quenelles made with anchovy butter for turtle soup à la Washington. A shrimp paste made from the tails of the shrimp added the finishing touch. For turtle soup à la New York, filets of spit-roasted white sturgeon and quenelles of smelts made with shrimp paste replaced the salmon and the eel quenelles.

Carême did not hesitate to "frenchify" foreign dishes to make them palatable to French tastes and practicable for French chefs. The three nominally American soups are all turtle soups, variants of the original English recipe. However, because travelers to Boston and New York reported that Americans added eel, he was obliged to alter the basic turtle soup recipe to take account of the eel's effect on the dish. Hence Carême composed "American" soups "that can be executed in Europe, and particularly in France" (*L'Art* [1994], pt. 1, chap. 23, p. 156). In other words, these soups could emigrate from American to French kitchens because of their translation by Carême into a national culinary idiom. Without this translation into the higher language of French culinary practice, these soups would remain too foreign to earn a place in a work devoted to the art of French cuisine.

Carême is steeped in the certitude of culinary predestination. For him there was no doubt that France was "the motherland of anyone who entertains; its cuisine and wines are the triumph of gastronomy and it is the only country for good food" (*Le Cuisinier parisien*, p. i; *L'Art* [1833], 2:i). He had earlier boasted that his "absolutely new Treatise . . . will give new luster to our national cuisine" (*Le Pâtissier royal parisien*, dedication). In the event, he had already refuted all the "ridiculous books that are a disgrace to our great national cuisine" (*Le Pâtissier pittoresque*, 1:5). The oxymoronic pretensions of a contemporary's cookbook entitled the *Universal English Chef* outraged Carême, so he proposed a cook-off. It was, of course, a foregone conclusion that French chefs would win any culinary contest (*Le Pâtissier royal parisien*, p. xvi).

Nowhere is this sense of national culinary destiny more in evidence than in the preliminary remarks of the *Cuisinier parisien* (1828), which Carême used to demolish one M. Martin, the "compiler" of a work he had the "presumption" to call the *Bréviaire du gastronome* (The gastronome's handbook). The "Discours préliminaire" of the *Cuisinier parisien* stands at a particularly crucial juncture, coming as it did after the publication of three major works (*Le Pâtissier royal* and *Le Pâtissier pittoresque* in 1815 and *Le Maître d'hôtel* in 1822) and at the time Carême was preparing the achievement of his career, *L'Art de la cuisine française au dix-neuvième siècle* (1833). He was able to chastise commentators for their ignorance of what he had already accomplished and to dismiss their divagations accordingly.

Carême's devastating critique of Martin as no more than a "charlatan" and "a sorry plagiarist" makes the case for the superiority of French cuisine. He can only deplore the abysmal ignorance that led Martin to bemoan the foreign presence in French cuisine: "the dishes of French cuisine on the contrary bear the most illustrious names of the French nobility: à la Reine, à la Dauphine, à la Royale," and so on, for seventeen more names. Carême then launches into a litany of other French names, mostly geographical in origin: "à la Parisienne, à la Française, à la Bordelaise . . . and many others that escape me" (*Le Cuisinier parisien*, pp. 26–27). The foreign names for the basic brown and white sauces, *espagnole* (Spanish) and *allemande* (German), had prompted the ignorant Martin to regret the absence of a single truly French sauce. Carême sets the record straight. Because the so-called Spanish sauce was brought to France to celebrate Louis XIV's bestowal of the Spanish throne on his son, it was, we might say now, functionally French. In any case, whatever the origins of the Spanish sauce, "we have perfected it so much since then" that it no longer has anything much to do with the sauce that came to France in the mid-seventeenth century. Similarly, for the so-called German sauce, it is to their credit that the French honored the presumed source of this white sauce. However, because the French "have made it as unctuous and as smooth as it is perfect," Carême concludes grandly that "these foreign sauces are so changed in their preparations, that they have long since been entirely French." In short, in French hands, with French savoir-faire, the foreign ceases to be foreign—and a good thing, too, since "no foreign sauce can be compared to those of our great modern cuisine" (*Le Cuisinier parisien,* pp. 25–28).

This Frenchness was secured and enriched by Carême's entire culinary system. At the end of the section on French soups in *L'Art de la cuisine française,* he notes that he has changed the names of several soups from his earlier work in order to confer on them the names of great Frenchmen. True to his word, of the 358 sauces in part 4, Carême gave names that I could identify to over one-third. The largest category of those honored for individual achievement come from the arts, literature, and the sciences, both contemporaries such as Victor Hugo, Rossini, and Paganini and classics such as Molière, Corneille, Pascal, and Virgil. There are also military heroes and royalty, both French and foreign, and especially important, individuals with connections to gastronomy, both chefs (4) and hosts, including, of course, his own employers—Talleyrand (*sauce Bénévent* from his title as prince de Bénévent), Rothschild, George IV, the Princesse Bagration, and Alexandre (I, of Russia)—and also the culinary writers Jean Anthelme Brillat-Savarin and A. B. L. Grimod (de la Reynière).[12] Naming dishes for famous personages seems to have begun in earnest in the late seventeenth century, a gesture that ennobled simultaneously the food and the consumer, but Carême took it further.[13]

Other sauces take us on a tour of the French provinces, from Brittany to Marseilles, from Bordeaux to Champagne. Of 112 sauces with geographical names, slightly over half carry French names. Even the sauces whose names designate a foreign person or place carry names that are linguistically French. The language frenchifies the appellations just as the cuisine frenchifies the sauces themselves. Foreign names generally appear in French dress, which makes Saint-Pierre, Ciceron, Mécène, Virgile, and Arioste fully as French as Victor Hugo or Mme de Sévigné. Whereas the names of sauces with regional or foreign variations often connect to the products associated with the region—Périgord raises visions of truffles, Provence brings in garlic and tomatoes, Normandy touts its cream and shellfish—just as often, and particularly for sauces *à la parisienne* or *à la française,* there is no relationship at all. In other words, the system confers the meaning, not the external referent. This self-referentiality and self-sufficiency identify the linguistic-culinary code that, in turn, singles out Carême's cuisine.

Given its organization around an independent system of interlocking parts, this cuisine, with its own language, could go anywhere—as, in fact, it did. And wherever it went, right along with the *batterie de cuisine,* French cuisine took French history, French culture, and French geography. For producers and consumers alike, the new world of gastronomy called for new words. Another intrepid explorer of the culinary, Carême's contemporary, Brillat-Savarin, warned his readers about the neologisms that they would find in the *Physiology of Taste* (1826). How could he not need new words when ideas and practices are changing all the time?[14] For Carême as for Brillat-Savarin, linguistic invention would shape the new worlds of French cuisine and French culture.

The international diffusion of French cuisine was originally a function of the prestige of cuisine in and around the French court. Also important factors in the diffusion of a cultural product that had its own independent elite connections were the international reach of the French language in seventeenth- and eighteenth-century Europe and its elite associations. The elaboration of a culinary vehicle that was suited to the newly expanded market of the nineteenth century took a crucial step in moving French cuisine beyond traditional elites and beyond Europe. It was Carême's great contribution to French cuisine both at home and abroad to have elaborated a rationalized eating order that could be easily transported and transposed into other settings. Yet at the same time that Carême rationalized cuisine, he nationalized it. His culinary order stands at one and the same time as a national order. The French did not wait for Carême to take pride in their cuisine, but whether they knew it or not, Carême gave them far greater reason for that pride.

Competitors?

Still and all, and as he was the first to acknowledge, Carême did not spring fully armed from the head of either Zeus or his chef. Chefs had been working at systematizing culinary practice for a good century and a half. Carême's contemporaries, chefs and authors Alexandre Viard and Antoine Beauvilliers, also made much of the rules that their works conveyed. This emphasis on order is not unexpected: after all, cookbooks legislate by definition.

Nor did it take a revolution to set culinary controversies in motion. Every generation since the mid-seventeenth century has fallen out over the same issues of old versus new. In making explicit the principles that informed their cookbooks and marking their particular culinary territories, argumentative prefaces conveyed a heightened consciousness of culinary and social change and staked out each author's place in that development.

Not even culinary nationalism originated with Carême. As in so many other domains, the French early on arrogated pride of place. Time and foreign experience had little effect on this conviction. In *Le Cuisinier étranger* (The foreign chef [1811]), published bound with a cookbook on French cuisine, the author, A. T. Raimbault, justified a work on foreign dishes largely as therapy for the "palates of our most celebrated gastronomes jaded by the excellence of

French cuisine." Though he had to admit that a work on European cuisines was "without glory"—a term presumably applicable to French cuisine alone—Raimbault could yet hope that it would not be "without utility." A page count testifies to his priorities: 53 pages of recipes from all of Europe look meager indeed up against the 280 pages allocated for French cuisine.[15]

Even the great Carême had competitors. The more than thirty editions of Alexandre Viard's *Cuisinier impérial* (The imperial chef [1806]) made it the most popular work published by a professional in the nineteenth century.[16] Viard's consequent celebrity makes his modesty all the more remarkable. He had none of Carême's overweening ambition. He advanced no claim to treat cuisine "in general," and frankly acknowledged that he did not have it in him to write the ten volumes that such an endeavor would entail, especially as a new one would be needed every year to keep up-to-date.

Antoine Beauvilliers (1754–1817) wrote with the authority of forty years of experience, primarily as a celebrated restaurateur whose establishment was frequented by Brillat-Savarin. In 1814, when he published *L'Art du cuisinier* (The art of the chef), he was still running the Grande Taverne de Londres, which he had opened over thirty years earlier. Like Carême and just about everyone else who thought about gastronomy, Beauvilliers subscribed to the superiority of French cuisine. Like Carême also, he aimed at a broad public, assuring readers that even housewives could profit by his book. In contrast with Carême's fixation on the future, and as befit an older generation that had known the Ancien Régime, Beauvilliers saw his work as an end rather than a beginning. These observations made his "final adieux."[17]

Nonetheless, in the intensely competitive culinary market of early nineteenth-century Paris, Carême stood, if not alone, then assuredly head and shoulders above his contemporaries. It was Carême whom Balzac cited repeatedly as the epitome of the creative modern chef, just as it was Carême, not Viard or Beauvilliers, whom Dumas characterized as the "apostle of gastronomes," the only chef honored with a full entry in his encyclopedic *Grand Dictionnaire de cuisine*.[18] Finally, Escoffier saw Carême, not his competitors, as the founder of modern French cuisine. As with other Romantic heroes who turn out to be very much a part of their times, Carême's genius, his "invention" of French cuisine, lay in the way he capitalized on and magnified trends well in evidence. For this we admit him as a modern. At the same time, in his tireless self-promotion we recognize the all-too-familiar hype that borders on vanity even as we respectfully acknowledge his absolute dedication to the culinary enterprise.

Gastronomical Meditation—Solitary Pleasures

Under Carême's vigilant eye in the centrally placed portrait, a gastronome dines in solitary repletion. It is appropriate that the food arrangement appears directly beneath the chef and only next to the eater. Engraving by Pauquet in *Les Classiques de la table* (1845). Courtesy of Columbia University Libraries.

And what is to be made of Carême today? What lessons do his career, his work, and his personal qualities hold for those of us who have no use for the culinary extravaganzas and who dismiss his rhetoric as naïve, pretentious, or both? Far from relegating Carême to the dustbin of nineteenth-century relics, we would do well to pay closer attention to what he did and what he had to say. Not only has his cuisine not disappeared, it turns up today in all sorts of

CONTEMPLATION.

Contemplation—Urban Delights

Although Carême severed all personal involvement in his pastry shop soon after it opened on the rue de la Paix in 1803–4, such was his fame that the shop still appeared in guidebooks as late as 1863. This 1840s engraving of the shop window shows that Carême held his place in the Parisian street scene long after his death. His confections on view remain an obligatory stop for this avid gastronomic *flâneur*. Carême's street, the rue Antoine-Carême, was inaugurated in Paris in 1894; it would disappear in the urban renewal of the central market area of les Halles in the late twentieth century. Engraving by Pauquet in *Les Classiques de la table* (1845). Courtesy of Columbia University Libraries.

ways and often in unexpected venues. The profession of cooking that Carême did so much to establish offers a mode of work that is particularly relevant to understanding certain types of occupations in modern capitalist societies. Moreover, his association of cuisine and country suggests something important about how the continuing identification of culture and country occurs, in France and also, potentially, elsewhere.

Carême has more to tell us than we might suppose on the culinary front. Even though banquets today no longer come even close to what he thought was mandatory for a proper culinary spectacle, and even if we do not classify pastry making as one of the fine arts as he did, pastry making has by no means died out. Today as in the nineteenth century, architectural fantasies spur chefs to pastry grandeur in their attempts to amaze the spectator-consumer through their challenges to the constraints of everyday cooking. Extravaganza for extravaganza, its allegories spun out of sugar and almond paste, the twenty-first-century wedding cake rivals the confection that Flaubert created for Emma Bovary.[19] If latter-day culinary competitions do not quite fit Carême's vision, they regularly feature quite wonderful pastry creations. In the fall of 2000 the Chocolate Salon in New York featured monumental chocolate sculptures of Grand Central Station, Notre Dame de Paris, an American eagle, and the Statue of Liberty, and a few years earlier one of the four compulsory models for the pastry competitors at the Salon du chocolat in Paris was an homage to Carême, a bust based on his portrait. Carême would have been pleased on all counts, though he probably would have accepted the homage as no more than his due!

Carême retains his title as a culinary modern. No one now is more aware than he was of the intimate relation between cuisine and historical context. As Lady Morgan wrote of the meal that Carême served her, cuisine must be "in the spirit of its age." For all sorts of reasons, notably the time commitment and the health regulations that rule out an open stockpot, few chefs today undertake the complex, complicated, expensive, and time-consuming Spanish "mother sauce" of which Carême was so proud. At the same time, as Carême was the first to acknowledge, any cuisine stands firmly within a tradition, no matter how innovative or "new." Contemporary chefs say much the same thing and work off the same premise. Every cuisine adapts. French cuisine today assimilates exotic foods and traditions, just as Carême told them to: remember the American turtle soup that he modified for the French palate. He also knew that every nouvelle cuisine worked off a sense of the old, of the continuing tradition constructed by the many other cuisines that were the nouvelles cuisines of their day. For all their rebellion against allegedly fustian traditions, there are signs that younger generations are discovering the basics, even as older chefs revive the traditions in which they were trained.[20]

But Carême the historical example is of more than culinary relevance. The trade that he reconfigured and transformed should interest anyone concerned with work, with occupations, and with the conditions that shape both individual acts and collective action. The theoretical aura of Carême's new cuisine, his emphasis on the principles of a culinary system defined both within and against the traditions that he inherited, fostered an exceptionally strong identity for French cuisine.[21] His romance with the modern suits the contemporary drive for innovation. Like Carême, today's chefs are ever on the lookout for new implements and appliances, methods and techniques. The food processor would have delighted the chef who made so much of his own innovations and so appreciated those of others. Do not the bouillon cubes that can be found in any supermarket today bespeak his shortcut of reducing sauces?

Shortcuts and new utensils notwithstanding, great cuisine remains a very expensive enterprise. Carême would thank his lucky stars that he did not work under the financial constraints that push chefs today to take to the media in order to market themselves, their savoir-faire, and their wares. Yet, of course, his own publications did exactly this. They publicized Carême and his cooking every bit as much as the cookbooks and television appearances, the Web sites and culinary competitions through which contemporary chefs spread the culinary good news.

The search for the innovation that will give a competitive edge puts cooking as conceived and practiced by Carême at the highest level—what I discuss as "chefing" in chapters 4 and 5—squarely within a capitalist economy. Carême kept his distance from the obvious commercialism of the restaurant or the retail shop, but his writing and his relentless promotion of himself and his profession marked him as a capitalist entrepreneur. He literally capitalized his reputation as a master pastry maker to conquer all French cuisine. His success in imposing his culinary system on contemporaries and successors offers a model of the "creative professional," and that model speaks to some vital issues in a capitalistic economy that is very different from the classic model of the nineteenth century. Like artists who emphasize the nonmonetary advantages of creative work at least partly as a function of an uncertain market and a highly unequal distribution of rewards, chefs occupy a particular niche in the contemporary workforce, and it is that niche that aligns them with artists.[22] Cooking can be regarded as an artistic occupation not because the chef is a star or because cooking is a fine art—the usual argument for the connection—but because of the affinities of the occupation and the culinary market with artistic occupations. It is not the singularity of the chef but, rather, the particularity of an occupation that places a premium on singularity. The significance of a signature dish for a chef corresponds to the identifiable style of the painter, the musician, or the writer.

Carême's culinary nationalism raises a more general issue in the study of culture. How does a particular product or practice become identified with a culture as a whole and, in the end, form a synecdoche of the largest meaning? In this case, how, why, and when was French cuisine understood as a distinctly and distinctively French eating order, and how did it come to stand for France itself? Carême's written works point us to the role that language plays in creating this cultural connection. Again and again, his culinary discourse insisted upon the intimate, indissoluble bond between cuisine and country.[23] This culinary system so forcefully identified as French gave French and foreigner alike a means of imagining their country as a community that brought together producers and consumers who were geographically dispersed, socially stratified, and politically divided. Like the gastronomic map that represented France as an assemblage of culinary particulars, Carême's cuisine assigned the particular dishes tied to people and places to the incomparably greater whole of French culture. Culinary nationalism, then, is not simply an idiosyncrasy of Carême's work. It is a fundamental element that sustains a certain conception of the collectivity that is France.

At the same time that French cuisine supplied a medium with which to imagine the nation, it provided an instrument with which to practice nationalism. French cuisine engages the nation all the more effectively because it is part of everyday life. That we practice our nationalism without having to think about it, as the cook stirs a béchamel sauce on the stove or the diner reads a menu, gives the culinary an immense advantage over cultural products that require more self-conscious ideological direction. The ordinariness of a culinary display of national sentiment, its very banality, accounts for the cohesive strength of the identification

Then, too, the range of this cuisine, from the exceptional gastronomic creation to the housewife's boiled beef, and its systematic quality meant that it could be practiced—produced and consumed—anywhere, at home and abroad, in the provinces and in Paris, among the elites, to be sure, but also reaching down the social scale. French cuisine could be (and was) put into service by republicans and socialists as well as monarchists, and probably anarchists as well. Given this association of food with France, it was only to be expected that the anti-French sentiments that surfaced in the United States during the second Gulf War should fix on rebaptizing an archetypal French dish. French fries became Freedom fries.

Like the French Revolution of 1789, French cuisine was an indelible national phenomenon that turned into an exemplar for revolutionary action. As revolutionaries across nineteenth-century Europe waved the blue, white, and red flag of the French Republic, so chefs brandished the French cuisine that Carême had taught them to consider their model and their standard. Like the French Revolution in its many, often contradictory guises, French cuisine arose in very particular circumstances and expanded in others just as it will change, and no doubt diminish, in still others. The connection is closer still. The many governments that followed 1789 worked tirelessly to create institutions and sentiments of commonality in a population divided by geography, language, politics, and culture. Carême's French cuisine became a key building block in the vast project of constructing a nation out of a divided country. A general culinary discourse created relations among consumers and between consumers and producers. How Carême's production fit with the gastronomy that opened the nineteenth century, how his culinary writing became part of an ambient gastronomic discourse—this is the province of the following chapter.

Readings in a Culinary Culture

Carême's singular success presents one story of cuisine in France; French culinary culture tells quite another one. To confront a cultural enterprise as a whole is to encounter complexities in narrative of a very different order than we deal with in individual achievement, however spectacular that success may be. What brought that venture into existence? The goal in this chapter will be to convey the energy of collective agency within a focus on emerging structure.

Looking at a culture through imagined constructs brings us to the stories that a culture tells, to itself and to others. Like all stories, these cultural tales suppose an audience. Composed of a multitude of texts and representations, the story of French culinary culture requires books, not cooks; it wants readers as well as writers. For these narratives transform the material good into something else. They convert food into cuisine, eating into dining. They transpose the culinary into the symbolic, the intellectual, and the aesthetic—the ingredients required to transform individual encounters into a collective experience. In a culture where food talk trumps food preparation as often as it seems to in France, the connection between writer and reader makes a crucial link of cook to consumer. That food so penetrates the social fabric is the work of many factors. Still, pride of place surely goes to these texts, powerful vehicles of formalization and diffusion that turn singular food events into a cultural configuration and convert physiological need into an intellectual phenomenon. The gastronomic writing that flourished in nineteenth-century France provided the mechanisms that brought the culinary arts into modern times, as these texts continually reconfigure food as both sensual object and symbolic phenomenon. In that reconfiguration, in the proliferation of culinary texts and representations, lies the secret of French culinary culture, or what the nineteenth century would likely have called its genius.

I. From Cuisine to Gastronomy

Thanks to the progress of knowledge and philosophy, gourmandise . . . has become an art.

—A. B. L. Grimod de la Reynière, *Journal des Gourmands et des Belles* (1806)

If the paradox of eating—as Georg Simmel long ago pointed out in a quirky but suggestive piece—is that this physiological activity shared by every human being should give rise to such extraordinary social differentiation, it is clear that modern gastronomy exacerbated those distinctions, enriching the social order in the process. Gastronomy—the socially prized pursuit of culinary excellence—constructed its modernity through an expansive culinary discourse and, more specifically, through texts. These texts were key agents in the socialization of individual desire and the redefinition of appetite in collective terms. The "second-order" culinary consumption of textual appreciation extended the gastronomic public, or "taste community," well beyond immediate producers and consumers. These writings converted diners into readers.

As with the performing arts, writing about food presupposes a distinct order of consumption. The cultural product in question is at one remove from the base product—the work performed, seen, or heard and, in this instance, the food prepared and consumed. These culinary texts stabilized the ephemeral culinary product and connected producers and consumers. The avid readers of nineteenth-century culinary texts were as essential to French culinary culture as the voracious eaters of nineteenth-century gastronomic practice. A set of practices and texts, cuisine codified culinary practice. *Cuisine*—from the French *cuire*, "to cook"—begat *gastronomy*—from the Greek for the laws *(nomos)* of the stomach *(gastro)*. As the etymology suggests, whereas *cuisine* emphasizes the producer, *gastronomy* engages the consumer.

The resulting culinary culture, then, is anchored in both *cuisine*—a culinary product—and in *gastronomy*—a given practice of consumption. Taken as the systematic, socially valorized pursuit of culinary creativity, gastronomy began with the nineteenth century and it began in France. It came into public view in 1801, followed by *gastronome* two years later to designate a new social status of the consumer of elaborately prepared fine food. The term is typically traced to a quite dreadful poem from 1801, "La Gastronomie, ou l'Homme des champs à table" (Gastronomy, or The man of the fields at table) by Joseph de Berchoux. But, since a word usually appears in print only well after it has been in circulation, Berchoux is surely more scribe than inventor. In any event, modern times needed new language to designate a practice perceived as new. In very short order *gastronomy* and its derivatives filled that need.[1]

Novelty itself is a password in France at the end of the eighteenth century.

Reflections on modernity cannot avoid the Revolution. What responsibility for the institution of a recognizably modern social and cultural order can be ascribed to the many and varied phenomena associated with the revolution of 1789 and its immediate consequences—the abolition of the monarchy, the elimination of traditional economic constraints on commerce, the foreign wars, and domestic political turmoil, to list only the most obvious elements? In addition, from 1789 to 1871, France had three monarchies, three republics, and two empires; three revolutions (1789, 1830, 1848), one coup d'état (1851), and one insurrection (the Socialist Commune of 1871). Napoleon I's defeat at Waterloo in 1815 ended almost a quarter century of war and put France under occupation by the allied forces of England, Prussia, Austria, and Russia; Napoleon III's rout by the Prussians in 1870 after a mere six weeks of military engagement led to a second occupation by enemy troops as well as significant loss of territory. Alsace-Lorraine was ceded to the German Empire, where it remained until Allied victory in the First World War restored it to France in 1918. How do we single out the factors that distinguish gastronomy in France—as a historical phenomenon and as a cultural practice? To what degree is French culinary culture anchored in, and therefore definable in terms of, distinctive cultural traditions and particular historical circumstances?

Like any new social practice, gastronomy drew on a nexus of social, economic, and cultural conditions. It shaped to its own ends the standard exemplar of cultural communication linking supplies, producers, and consumers in a set of common understandings. For gastronomy, this model translated first into various and readily available foodstuffs. Economic abundance and relative political stability in the first decade of the nineteenth century stimulated production, sustained a broadening social participation, and encouraged a general cultural enthusiasm for culinary excellence and extravagance. At about the same time, restaurants emerged as culturally specific sites that trained a cadre of experienced producers (chefs) whose work was supported by knowledgeable, affluent consumers (diners). Finally, a secular cultural (culinary) tradition gradually eroded religious interdictions and understandings that hampered frank enjoyment of the pleasures of the flesh. The institution of standards and models of authority ensured an acute critical consciousness that legitimated the expressions of cultural excitement. All of these elements—the food, the people and places, the attitudes and ideas—came together in early nineteenth-century France with a force hitherto unknown and, indeed, unsuspected.

The nineteenth century hardly invented the ostentatious consumption of spectacular culinary goods. Taking inspiration from models in ancient Greece and Rome, the royal banquet tables of the Ancien Régime, both in France and in the principalities and kingdoms that sedulously emulated French culinary mores, were anything but simple and never frugal. Even so, the gastronomic level of nineteenth-century Paris was unmistakably of a different order, fueled, as it was, by increasingly wealthy people as well as increasingly varied foods brought with increasing speed from increasingly farther distances. In Europe as a whole, the eighteenth century saw the end of the cyclical famines that had regularly ravaged the continent for centuries and had been such a part of everyday life for the great majority of the population. In response to demographic pressures, production increased as the expansion of the transportation system transformed agriculture from a subsistence to a commercial enterprise geared to a broadening market.

Specifically for France, with the end of the food shortages of the immediate revolutionary period and despite the British naval blockade, the early nineteenth century proved a period of alimentary abundance for the urban elites responsible for making gastronomy a distinctive social practice. Carême was especially sensitive to the deleterious effects of the "great revolutionary torment" on the "progress of our [culinary] art." He breathed an audible sigh of relief over the far more favorable conditions in the years that followed. As observers of the urban scene never tired of pointing out, every country now had its national foods produced in Paris, with the result that, as one commentator put it, the adventurous diner could take a trip around the world without leaving the table. When Brillat-Savarin observed with evident pride that a Parisian meal could easily be a "cosmopolitan whole," he meant what he said. In support of the claim that foods came from all over, a foreign visitor to Paris in the sixteenth century had given a list of the French provinces as the provenance of foods to be found in Pairs. Making much the same claim, witnesses describing dining in nineteenth-century Paris talked about Europe, Africa, America, and Asia.[2]

The haute cuisine of the Ancien Régime served the court and the Parisian aristocracy; modern culinary creativity centered in the restaurant. Although restaurants preceded 1789—the first urban establishment by that name dates from 1765 and Antoine Beauvilliers opened the Grande Taverne de Londres in 1782—the revolution set the restaurant on its modern course of development. By doing away with all restrictions concerning which establishments could serve what foods in what form, the abolition of the guilds in 1791 spurred culinary competition and prompted a number of chefs who had served the now-exiled aristocracy to put their culinary talents in the service of a more general though still elite public. The restaurants they opened became a notable feature of the urban landscape. Finally, the demise of the monarchy and the court ended the partition of political, commercial, and cultural life between Versailles and Paris; henceforth it was concentrated entirely in the capital.

Giving strong support to gastronomy by enlarging the pool of potential diners (and readers) was the dramatic increase in population between 1800 and 1850 that caused Paris to double in size. Politicians and businessmen, journalists, writers, and artists flocked to the city and to its restaurants. This fluid transient population stimulated the development of eating establishments of many sorts: the hundred or so restaurants found in Paris in the late eighteenth century increased by a factor of six during the first decade and a half of the new century. By the 1820s the city counted over three thousand restaurants of various types that ranged across the social as well as the culinary spectrum. As Brillat-Savarin recognized at the time, competition became intense once it became clear that "a single well prepared stew could make its inventor's fortune." As a result, self-interest "fired every imagination and set every cook to work."[3] Competition made everyone better, if just by process of elimination. Against the lone observer who regarded gastronomy as the one social force left untouched by "successive upheavals of civilization," several others were equally convinced that it was part of a new regime, political, social, and economic. Gourmandise, like elections, had moved from the "summits" of society to its "lowest classes," with the result that the social division that really counted in contemporary France was the one drawn between cooks and diners. If Brillat-Savarin did not rank the restaurateurs among the "artists" and the "heroes of gastronomy," he recognized the significance of their contribution to the social order.[4]

The connection between gastronomy and suffrage became something of a cliché. Both phenomena were taken as signs of modern times and of the (very relative) democratization of French society. At the time much of this culinary commentary was written, during the Bourbon Restoration (1815–30), the right to vote was determined by the amount and kind of taxes paid and enfranchised approximately 1 percent of the adult male population. The July Monarchy (1830–48) expanded the voting base to some 8 percent of the population without altering the basic system of taxation. But, just as political life actively involved many nonvoters, notably impecunious scholars and intellectuals, so, too, gastronomy might touch a public that did not dine in the great restaurants. The striking development of publishing and journalism was a prime mover in this general cultural diffusion. There were, of course, other populations, untouched by either restaurants or the texts that talked about them and about whom few culinary journalists had anything to say. Briffault's *Paris à table* stands out with even his minimal attention to hunger and to "People Who Do Not Dine," from unemployed workers to prisoners.

The diners who rushed to the Parisian temples of gastronomy were assuredly as affluent as the aristocrats who had sustained the haute cuisine of the Ancien Régime. Socially far more mixed than their predecessors, this new elite was markedly more insecure. Some carried over their *savoir-vivre* from the old to the new regime; others, no doubt the majority, had the wealth but

Nineteenth-Century Takeout

Early restaurants sent fine food out
as well as took diners in, as this delivery
boy attests, with his bag and platter
containing a special creation. Illustration
by Bertall in Briffault, *Paris à table*
(1846). Courtesy of Columbia
University Libraries.

sorely lacked the savoir-faire. These were the opulent *arrivistes* addressed by
the journalist A. B. L. Grimod de la Reynière. In his *Manuel des Amphitryons*
(Manual for hosts) of 1808, Grimod gives detailed instructions for hosts and
their guests, in effect translating the aristocratic culinary culture of the Ancien
Régime for the consumers in the new world of gastronomy.

This new regime pursued gastronomic pleasures in public, not private, a re-
location that was not inconsequential. It designated the restaurant, not the
private gathering, as the primary vehicle institutionalizing gastronomy as a
social and cultural practice. Even the eating societies that served as essential

points of culinary encounter met in restaurants that not only put gastronomy on view but opened it to every comer who could afford the fare. By relocating culinary creativity and fine dining from private homes into public space, the restaurant offered an ideal, semipublic venue for the display and affirmation of status in a bounded space that simultaneously defined nondiners as nonelite and marked all diners as members of the elite. As Edmond Goblot argued for other practices that circumscribed the bourgeoisie such as the acquisition of Latin and the baccalaureate degree, the restaurant both erected a barrier against outsiders and made all insiders equal. The resulting competition among diners drove the competition among restaurants that so impressed Brillat-Savarin.[5]

The participatory disposition of the restaurant contrasted sharply with the imposing banquet spectacles of the Ancien Régime where the king often dined in solitary splendor in full view of the court. The differences between these two culinary modes are by no means trivial. Whereas the banquet makes use of elaborate, often multitiered culinary creations to manipulate space in the service of a communal spectacle, the restaurant regulates time to create intimacy. The public setting legitimated a new conception of the meal. Courses were no longer served French style, à la française, which lays out the several different dishes for a single course on the table at the same time—but in the simpler, modern style, à la russe (the Russian ambassador imported the order of service usual in his homeland), which serves a single dish for each course to all diners. Against the dramatic display of the traditional French service so appropriate to the hierarchical arrangement of the Ancien Régime banquet, where one's place at table largely determined the food one actually consumed, its adaptability to variable numbers of individual diners made Russian service a perfect system for the restaurant and, not so incidentally, made it possible for diners to eat their food hot. Despite their persistence for ceremonial occasions, elaborate banquets gradually receded before the gatherings at select restaurants.

A secular culinary tradition laid the final building block of modern gastronomy. Conceptual autonomy presupposed the consideration of food for its own sake and the subordination of religious, symbolic, or medical concerns to the gustatory, however imperfect the separation of the culinary from the symbolic and the medicinal might actually have been. Even though religious interdictions and directives center a great many cuisines, they do not themselves constitute a cuisine. There is no Jewish or Christian or Muslim cuisine; there are, rather, a multitude of culinary traditions that negotiate dietary restrictions, ambient cultures and agricultures to construct a localized set of culinary practices. For largely Catholic France, liberation from religious prohibitions diverted attention from negative to positive associations of gustatory pleasure. First to fall among the negatives was gluttony (gourmandise), classified by the church as one of the seven deadly sins.[6] Parallel criticism from secular quarters invoked sobriety as well as the physical and moral health of both individuals and the social order but left the ultimate test to individual reason rather than institutional censure. In eighteenth-century France the *Encyclopédie* (1751–80) joined gluttony to a second deadly sin in its definition of *cuisine* as "the lust for good food" and *gourmandise* as the "refined and disordered love of good food." "Experiments in sensuality" denatured foods by transforming them into "flattering poisons" that "destroy one's constitution and shorten life." Following a tradition found in writings as divergent as the Old Testament, Plato, and Herodotus, the authors of the *Encyclopédie* articles conjured up lurid descriptions of the excesses of the late Greeks and the flagrantly decadent Romans to make the point that any thing or practice that reached beyond nature and reason was not only useless but noxious, as destructive of political character as of personal integrity. Gourmandise, the *Encyclopédie* ruled, is considered a merit in countries "where luxury and vanity reign [and] . . . vices are elevated as virtues." From an individual sin, gourmandise became a social vice, its diffusion a conspicuous sign of the flagrant corruption of the body politic. Jean-Jacques Rousseau was perhaps the best-known advocate of basic foods prepared simply in order to keep as close to nature as possible. It is fitting that, as readers of Rousseau's novel of education, *Emile*, will recall, milk should figure prominently among his culinary preferences.[7]

Fortunately for the development of French cuisine, strong countervailing pressures from the monarchy and the court offset these negative judgments of delectable pleasures; it was these pressures, not the prohibitions, that set the course of fine French cooking. In France, as at many other European courts, public dining rituals elaborated spectacular displays of status and power that reinforced attachment to ruler and court through the manipulation of social distance and spatial proximity. Voltaire's affirmation of the necessity of the unnecessary in his poem "Le Mondain" (The man of the world [1736])—"le superflu, chose très nécessaire" [anything superfluous is a real necessity]—offered a basic definition of gastronomy that spoke to and for the elite around the court—the very milieus against which the *Encyclopédie* inveighed so vehemently.

Given that indulgence and restraint are the two poles in any sensory experience, we should not expect resolution of the tensions between the two. But the terms of the debate over culinary excess shifted noticeably from the eighteenth to the nineteenth century, and they did so because gastronomy changed the rules of the game. For a privileged witness, we may take Pierre Larousse's monumental dictionary-encyclopedia (1866–79), a work that was taken as a reference point at the time and a window on the nineteenth century ever since. Larousse accords *gourmand* and *gourmandise* two columns of discussion; he allots more than four to *gastronomie*. More significant still is the way he makes gastronomy a moral force. In a turnaround from the eighteenth-century culinary discourse of the *Encyclopédie*, Larousse assumed the heightened social significance of this practice. He felt no call to argue a case; in any case, a dictionary is not an appropriate forum for argument. Instead, Larousse constructed a modern culinary hierarchy. Next to *gastrolâtrie* ("the passion for good food pushed to a sort of cult . . . incompatible with generosity") and *gastromanie* ("love of good food pushed to excess"), *gastronomie* appears the very model of discipline, control, and moderation. In contrast with the pejorative associations that cling to the *gourmand* ("eats eagerly and to excess"), no negative connotations besmirch the connoisseur who entertains a more intellectual relation to food. The *gastronome* "loves, [and] . . . knows how to appreciate good food." The gourmand has only a belly, whereas the gastronome has a brain, which explains why the gourmand only knows how to "wolf food down," whereas the gastronome "moves from effects to causes, analyses, discusses, seeks, pursues the useful and the agreeable, the beautiful and the good. He lives a worthy life, and must be endowed with sure senses, with judgment and tact." To be sure, "no one blushes to be a gastronome any more," Larousse declares with his habitual assurance, "but at no price would one want to pass for a gourmand or a drunk."

These and other works reconstrued pleasure—properly controlled—as both morally admirable and socially beneficent. Insofar as gastronomy was both a science and an art, the gastronome could even be a philosopher-diner, the antithesis, in any case, of the unreflective eater whose lack of self-control led to the gluttony reproved by the church and castigated by the *Encyclopédie*. Larousse's modern construction of culinary fervor sloughed off negative connotations onto the gourmand, the glutton (*glouton* or *goinfre*), or the *gastrolâtre* (who "makes a god of his stomach"). Once again, the careful articulation of distinctions helps to explain the emergence of a largely autonomous culinary practice.

This characteristic disciplining of appetite and restraint of sensuality also made the gastronome the epitome of the modern self-made man, the individual whose consumption practices defined his place in society. Those practices themselves turned out to be as worthy of our approval as the practitioners. In a recasting that recalls Mandeville's *Fable of the Bees; or, Private Vices, Publick Benefits* (1714) as well as a good many similar claims about the general economic utility of luxury, gastronomy became a force for prosperity and union. Far from the oxymoron that it might appear to be, the disciplined extravagance of gastronomy now appeared to sustain social harmony and economic prosperity. What was good for gastronomy could only be good for France.

Of the many texts that recast the vice of gourmandise as a virtue and the sin as socially useful, one work stands out. *Gourmandise* was one novel in the series devoted to *The Seven Deadly Sins*, written by the wildly popular novelist Eugène Sue. In it, the demonstration of the social value of all the deadly sins accords gluttony *(gourmandise)* the pivotal role. The eight nephews and nieces of the hero engage in food production as pastry maker, fishmonger, grocer, bread maker, game supplier, butcher, wine merchant, and captain of a merchant vessel with the emblematic name of *Gastronome* who imports foodstuffs from the colonies. The reformist socialist author sets up a profit-sharing scheme not unlike those proposed in others of his novels, and assembles all the "sinful" and "sinning" protagonists of the first six novels for a final joyous repast. At the end of *Gourmandise*, conviviality reinforces the practical functions of this one-time sin. Sue's novel, like the *Encyclopédie*, Voltaire's poem, and Larousse's dictionary, offers us glimpses into the changing ways French culinary culture thought about and imagined food.

II. Food Talk

To the extent that cuisine depends on oral transmission, its general cultural status remains precarious. Writing stabilizes experience by giving it a form amenable to commentary and criticism. Language allows sharing what is at once the most assertively individual and yet, arguably, the most dramatically social of our acts: eating. Further, texts translate the material into the cultural. The ephemeral, private nature of the material culinary product severely limits the cultural currency of the culinary arts. To consume food, we have to destroy it, and, in purely alimentary terms, that consumption is strictly individual. The original material product itself cannot be diffused. As both cooks and diners know full well, they cannot duplicate a meal, they can only replicate it. This inherent instability requires an intellectual form for food to enter into more general cultural circulation.

The nineteenth century built upon the legacy of the Ancien Régime, the better to herald a new era. Culinary writings moved into the rapidly expanding publishing and journalistic market. It was this expansive culinary discourse, not the dishes and meals of a confined culinary practice, that is responsible for the iconic status of the culinary in French culture. The genres of gastronomic writing range from the most instrumental cookbook to the loftiest of philosophical treatises; from pedestrian journalism to the great novels and essays of nineteenth-century France. These authors bore witness to the society modernizing all around them. Each aimed to systematize culinary knowledge and to establish what that knowledge meant for French cuisine.

The greater the association of nonspecialists in the gastronomic enterprise, the more numerous the social connections and the greater the social impact. Five exemplary genres—cookery books, journalism, social commentary, the philosophical treatise, and the novel—give us a key to understanding the place of gastronomy within French society. Defining gastronomy as a practice and establishing the modes of culinary writing, these texts offer us a precious textual archive of the beginnings of gastronomy in modern France.

It is not by chance that men wrote virtually all of the texts I examine. Despite the "natural," "logical," and traditionally dominant associations of women with food and feeding, gastronomy owes its existence to founding fathers, not mothers. It represented the public pursuit of sensory pleasures, not the private satisfaction of physiological needs. Female associations concerned the domestic order; gastronomy occupied a public domain, which explains that, like the chef, the gastronome was invariably male. Beyond the realities of men holding the purse strings and haute cuisine incurring vast expense, the public culinary sphere was inhospitable to women. The host whose duties Grimod de la Reynière spelled out with such care could only be male. At the most extreme, the gastronome dined alone, and it is telling that all but one of the six frontispieces for Grimod's *Almanach des Gourmands* (1803–12) show a man by himself—in his library, receiving purveyors, writing, dreaming about gustatory delights. Moreover, as with other urban spaces (shops, parks, public transport, and, above all, the street), its inherent promiscuity gave the restaurant an uncertain moral status that effectively excluded upper- and middle-class women. Even a superficial run-through of the *Almanach* turns up misanthropic and outspokenly misogynistic gems such as the "Discourse of a True Gourmand: Advantages of Good Food over Women."

The most instrumental and for that reason the most feminized of the culinary genres was the cookbook. Both its utility and its association with women placed it low on the scale of prestige, despite the exceptions of writers such as Carême early in the century and Auguste Escoffier at the end. But professional cooking did not dominate the culinary book market in nineteenth-century France. It was overshadowed by the great expansion of the domestic market, and from the evidence of titles of cookery books published over the century, that market dominated culinary publishing.

This increasingly strong public presence of domestic culinary concerns reshaped culinary culture accordingly; most strikingly, it drew women into the culinary public sphere. A sample of fourteen years of the *Bibliographie de la France,* the official record of modern French publishing from its inception in 1811 to 1898, points to the changing shape of this culinary book market. The very rubrics under which the *Bibliographie de la France* classified cookbooks confirm the growing importance of the domestic market. The two cookbooks published in 1811 came under the heading "Physics, Chemistry, Pharmacy." By 1821 and through 1847 the expanded *Bibliographie* placed them with "Agriculture, Rural, Veterinary and Domestic Economy." In 1848 the listing becomes "Sciences and Arts, Section on the Useful Arts, Subsection, Foods *[Aliments]*." The next year separated "Food Arts" *(Arts alimentaires)* from "Domestic Economy." The last half of the century reverted to placing cookbooks under "Domestic Economy," which was itself to be found under the larger heading of "Industrial Arts." The most interesting aspect of these titles is neither their number nor their presumed readership. About the latter we know little beyond the evident popularity of republished works. On the basis of titles alone, the skewed gendering of culinary publication is as striking as it is unremarkable—striking given the gender markers of so many of the works published, yet unremarkable given the culinary bifurcation that continues to allot domestic cooking to women and reserves professional "chefing" for men.[8]

Journalism, too, was a male preserve. Successors to the *flâneurs* (strollers/idlers) who wandered about the city reporting on its flora and fauna, journalists took it upon themselves to explore the new France that was taking shape in the early nineteenth century. In that society gastronomy loomed large, and the gastronome offered prime material for observing a society in the throes of change. The practice, in its current guise, was certainly perceived as new, like the restaurants that catered to this emerging public. Like cookery books, though in a very different mode, journalistic works put forward information and techniques, standards and values, to guide the consumer. Rather than informing chefs, the gastronomic journalists aimed at enlightening and amusing diners. The most striking expansion of journalism did not occur until the 1830s, when advertising reduced subscription rates and the introduction of the serial novel increased subscribers, but the first decade of the century saw the journalistic model solidly in place. (The term *journalism* dates from the late seventeenth century.) Following in the footsteps of L-S Mercier in the late eighteenth century, urban explorers such as Étienne de Jouy ventured forth into the city to bring back news of the indigenous populations.[9]

Correspondingly, the gastronomic journalist pounded the pavement with a shiver of anticipation for the unexpected gastronomic pleasure. Because it moved the Ancien Régime legacy down the social scale and into the public domain, gastronomy could claim more than gustatory significance: it was another frontier. Like other urban adventurers, then, the gastronomic journalist guided the reader through unknown territory. Unlike them, authors of the more obviously instrumental gastronomic guides offered advice and counsel along with information. Like most gastronomic reviewers since then, these authors saw themselves as pedagogues with a duty to educate the reader's palate.

Grimod de la Reynière's Gastronomic Journalism

The greatest of these educators, and certainly the most insistent on his duties as such, Alexandre Balthazar Laurent Grimod de la Reynière (1758–1838) stands as the first gastronomic journalist. Beginning with the *Almanach des Gourmands* (1803–12), Grimod put the culinary conscience and wisdom of the Ancien Régime at the service of the new. Known before the Revolution for outrageous culinary extravagances, this one-time literary critic made use of his extensive knowledge to bring nineteenth-century elites up to gastronomic speed in an era of accelerated culinary and social change. For, unlike Grimod himself, who was steeped in Ancien Régime culinary practices, the new-age gastronome was not to the manners born. A self-made man, and in Grimod's estimation devoid of the most elementary knowledge of what dining is all about, this apprentice gastronome stood in great need of instruction. The subtitle of the *Almanach*—a "guide to the ways of eating very well"—linked his goal to his status as "an old amateur." Grimod presents himself as a disinterested party, untainted by professional or commercial interests of any sort, firmly credentialed by his familiarity with traditional, elite culinary practices. Grimod's Ancien Régime pedigree provided him with a vital marketing tool, a constant reminder of his intimate connection to the glorious past now, of course, gone forever.

As Carême worked to form the exemplary chef of the future, Grimod labored mightily to fashion the model consumer in the present. Again like Carême, Grimod lamented the instability and incertitudes of the revolutionary era. His assessments of culinary establishments (restaurants, food suppliers, stores, and products) and practices ordered a culinary world turned topsy-turvy. If, for example, the fine art of carving had been lost, Grimod would rectify the situation. After all, the ignominy of a host who did not know how to carve was every bit as great as that of an owner of a magnificent library who did not know how to read. (One senses that, for Grimod, *infamy* would not be too strong a term.) He worked from the assumption that gastronomic science had advanced by quantum leaps. As he declares categorically in the coauthored *Journal des Gourmands et des Belles* of 1806, undoubtedly thinking of his own contributions, "Thanks to the progress of knowledge and philosophy gourmandise . . . has become an art." [10] To further this progress and to control the unregulated market, Grimod proposed establishing still more culinary institutions, including professorships in the lycées, gastronomic societies, and an elaborate system of what he called "legitimations," whereby product samples were sent for evaluation to "tasting juries" composed of "professors in the art of Gourmandise." In contrast with Carême, who intended culinary competitions for the instruction of chefs, Grimod proposed his "legitimations" to train the consumer.

Grimod's success was immediate. By his own estimation, twenty-two thousand copies of the *Almanach* sold in several editions over the four years following publication, and although he may well have fabricated some sales, there is no doubt about his celebrity.[11] His influence lies above all in the model that the *Almanach* proposed for, and for that matter imposed on, gastronomic journalism. Like every restaurant reviewer since, Grimod navigated between description and prescription. Like every other culinary commentator, he continually confronted the real with the ideal, the meal actually prepared and consumed with the imagined repast of unimaginable delights. The delicate balancing of criticism and commentary places the gastronomic reviewer in the position occupied by other commentators in an open market. For food as for literature and even for politics, writers need to attract readers, assert their authority, and justify their tastes. Some works, such as the 1816 *Gastronomiana, ou Recueil d'anecdotes, Réflexions, Maximes et folies gourmandes* (Gastronomiana, or collection of anecdotes, reflections, maxims and gourmandizing follies) stressed the genial tale. Others, such as the aptly named *Code Gourmand, Manuel complet de Gastronomie contenant les lois, règles, applications et exemples de l'art de bien vivre* (The gourmand code, being a complete manual of gastronomy containing the laws, rules, applications and examples of the art of living well) of 1827 championed a code.[12] Nowhere were the rules of culinary conduct more highly and more authoritatively codified than in nineteenth-century France, inspired at least in part by dismay over evident but uncertain social change. Still other works, like Eugène Briffault's *Paris à table* of 1846, which summed up three decades of dedicated dining in the metropolis since Grimod, called attention to the social landscape beyond the anecdotes and the reportage.

Brillat-Savarin's Sociability

From Carême and Grimod de la Reynière to Brillat-Savarin, gastronomy progressed from a practice and a technique to a topic of general interest in polite society. For although Jean Anthelme Brillat-Savarin (1755–1826) wrote about food and physiology and history and geography, it was all the talk about food by a wonderful, witty conversationalist that turned his *Physiology of Taste* (1826) into the totemic gastronomic text that it is today.[13] To the culinary paradigm of chef-diner Brillat-Savarin added the reader, the consumer for whom the cultural rather than the material product is the primary concern. Unlike the journalist, who addresses actual and potential customers, clients, and diners, or the chef, who targets practitioners of the culinary arts, the commentator-analyst speaks to indirect consumers—the readers, whose culinary consumption is indirect because it is noninstrumental. The culinary commentary practiced by Brillat-Savarin and generations of his disciples places gastronomy within the larger intellectual and social universe. Whereas Carême and Grimod de la Reynière took the culinary text as chiefly instrumental, a means to the primary end of producing or consuming what anthropologists term the "food event," that is, the dish or the meal, Brillat-Savarin made the text its own end. The few recipes included in the work hardly alter this status. The often noted stylistic qualities of the *Physiology of Taste*—the anecdotal mode, the witty tone, and the language play—give this work an almost palpable literary aura.

More decidedly than Grimod or even Carême, Brillat conceived of gastronomy as a distinctly modern social practice. His admission that a fear of falling behind the times had prompted him to undertake the study illustrates the degree to which he equated gastronomy with modernity, an intellectual enterprise representative of a contemporary body of knowledge and a nontraditional, analytical attitude toward food. The many anecdotes and the bons mots should not obscure the claims this work made to theoretical, historical, and even scientific understanding. The subtitle, *Meditations on Transcendent Gastronomy—An up-to-date theoretical and historical work,* confirms that these bonds are not incidental and singular but structural and generic. Gastronomy is both comprehensive and foundational, since it draws on the natural sciences—physics, chemistry, physiology—and on learning of every sort, including cuisine, commerce, political economy, and medicine. The youngest science was born, Brillat tells us, when the chemist, the scholar, and the political economist took cuisine out of the kitchen and into the laboratory and the library.

Never again could food be confused with either a sin or a mere bodily function. Like Grimod de la Reynière and Carême, Brillat made much of the distinction between gourmandise and gluttony. To him, reason made the difference. Gourmandise was "the passionate, reasoned and habitual preference for objects that flatter taste" (meditation 11), just as gastronomy was "the reasoned knowledge of everything that concerns man and nourishment" (meditation 11). Conceived as an intellectual activity dealing with the senses, gastronomy relied on refined sensuality but even more on intelligence: "Animals fill themselves; people eat; the intelligent person alone knows how to eat" (aphorism 2). Four decades later, Pierre Larousse followed the same line of reasoning when he defined the gastronome as master of a body of knowledge.

The second component of Brillat-Savarin's analysis is more obviously sociological. In effect the *Physiology of Taste* suggested a model for a sociology of taste and taste communities. This eighteenth-century Enlightenment philosopher and nineteenth-century sociologist before the fact always considered the "pleasure of the table" with respect to its varied and shifting social contexts and justified what he called "social gourmandise" by its exceptional social utility. Although the *Physiology of Taste* offers some menus, describes a number of dishes, and gives a few recipes, the variety of French cuisine interested Brillat less than the correlations that he posited between the social and culinary attributes of taste. The science that explores those relations, gastronomy is also a social science by virtue of its discourse on class and class distinctions in which taste becomes yet another powerful marker of social status.

As a new science, gastronomy faced a formidable task because the social diffusion of gourmandise complicated the gastronomic hierarchy. If there are individuals whom nature has "predestined" to be gourmands and whose very physiognomy betrays their predilection, more interesting to Brillat-Savarin were those professions which he assessed in terms of their penchant for gourmandise: financiers, doctors, men of letters, and the pious *(les dévots)* head the list. Brillat-Savarin devised a series of "gastronomic tests" calibrated to income. His menus range from 5 courses for a 5,000-franc income and 6 courses (including truffled turkey) for the 15,000-franc income bracket to the 9 courses of extravagant, complex dishes appropriate for those with an income of 30,000 francs and over. Nonetheless, money supplies a necessary but not sufficient factor in the hierarchy of taste preferences: an indicator of "gastronomic class," it intersects with social class. Consequently, Brillat prudently avoided ranking the financier's fare above the less extravagant fare. In keeping with the neutralizing language of science, the evaluations of the *Physiology of Taste* call on the "dynamometer" to register increasing force as one ascends the social ladder. The dishes capable of testing the gastronomic faculties of the stolid bourgeois *rentier* are not worthy of examination by the "select few" who are likely to be invited to the opulent table of a banker or governmental minister (meditation 13).

Brillat-Savarin's approach was inclusive, neither overtly elitist nor misogynistic; he concerned gastronomy with every social condition. Cultural event more than culinary construct, the meal offers a privileged, and managed, setting for the performance of human relations. It then follows, as Brillat-Savarin both assumes and verifies by example in his text, that cuisine varies according to the social setting, the participants, the occasion, the time of day, the historical period. It is this variance that allows and requires correlation of cuisines and taste communities. The dining table also turns out to be society in miniature, minus conflict. The fellowship of the table offers an ideal that the larger society would do well to emulate. Bringing together the different social groups, dining "bonds them into a single goal, animates conversation" (meditation 11), and, in a great gesture of political reconciliation, "smoothes out the sharp angles of social inequality" (meditation 11). With its own hierarchy and its variable standards, eliding social class even as it builds upon class division, the world of gastronomy delineated by Brillat-Savarin reproduces the contradictions and the ambiguities of postrevolutionary France.

However, the *Physiology of Taste* does not take full account of that society. Brillat-Savarin's "philosophical history" places the restaurant among the "latest refinements," an institution so new in the 1820s that no one had thought about it enough. He devoted only one "Méditation" (28) to restaurateurs, for their establishments disconcerted as much as they intrigued him. On the one hand, the restaurant put into circulation an element of democratization; on the other, those catering to solitary diners fostered an individualism that was potentially destructive of the social fabric. In any event, and however significant a social phenomenon the restaurant might be, Brillat took the private gathering as his model of sociability. This concern for social relations, and the consequent emphasis on sociability, led him to look upon the gastronomic competence of women with more favor than the frankly misanthropic and overtly misogynistic Grimod de la Reynière. Whereas Grimod regarded dining as a gastronomic event, Brillat reveled in the meal as an eminently social activity. With no possibility of conversation, then, the solitary diner offers a sorry spectacle. (A quip that Pierre Larousse cites in his entry for *Gourmand* captures the egotism ascribed to the individual who dines alone. The abbé Morellet, an eighteenth-century gourmand in the mold of Grimod, agreed that two are needed to consume a truffled turkey, and there were in fact two at his dinner: "the turkey and me.")

Grimod de la Reynière had already made it clear that this world, too, had been greatly altered by the increased circulation of individuals and their culinary habits, the availability of goods and services, and the culinary pluralism of the restaurant. By virtue of its interpretation of cuisine as a collective enterprise defined by the consumers rather than the producers, the *Physiology of Taste* places cuisine squarely in the public domain. In it, Brillat turns the science of human nourishment, gastronomy, into something more: a science of society and, at the same time, a model for society. In the face-off between Brillat-Savarin and Grimod de la Reynière in French culinary history, the laurels for originality of conception undoubtedly go to Grimod. But in the larger landscape of French culinary culture, Brillat's amiability wins easily over Grimod's misanthropic pedagogy. The value placed on sociability has a lot to do with explaining why the *Physiology of Taste* has never been out of print since it first appeared in 1826 and why so many English translations exist, just as Grimod de la Reynière's very different sensibility explains why his celebrity faded, why there are no significant English translations of his works to date, and why his works are hard to come by even in French. Whereas Grimod de la Reynière established a model for gastronomic journalism, Brillat-Savarin exemplified a recognizably French model of social relations, one in which conversation plays a prime role. Grimod *lectures* his audience; Brillat *talks with* them.

Fourier's Gastrosophic Utopia

Beyond the texts directly concerned with culinary production and consumption, those of Carême, Grimod de la Reynière, and Brillat-Savarin, are others that dramatize food as a total social phenomenon. More emphatically than any other text at the time, and by its very utopianism, the social order imagined by the philosopher Charles Fourier (1772–1837) demonstrates how food works in France to mold institutions as well as individual behavior.[14] Fourier based his philosophical system on the social utility of pleasure, specifically the principle of attraction, the two most powerful aspects of which are sex and food, or, in his terms, love and gourmandise. No more than sex is gourmandise an individual matter, so Fourier constructed an entire social system to turn these individual pleasures to social account. The vast majority of gastronomic writing finds the parallels of its topic with sexual activity irresistible. It is not by chance that collectivities so assiduously regulate the one and the other to keep individual appetites from disrupting the social order. Second-order consumption also looms large for both activities. In this as in other domains, Fourier's writing conspicuously mixes tones and genres, all of which add up to what can be fairly characterized as controlled delirium. He wrote to convey the fundamental attraction of a new social order predicated on neither justice nor equality but, quite simply, happiness: "The events resulting from this Order will give you, not the objects of your desires, but a happiness infinitely superior to all your desires."[15]

Although Fourier sets his work apart from the ambient gastronomic discourse, he invokes many of the same themes and principles: the scientific nature of gastronomy, the importance of culinary judges and juries, the crucial distinction between gastronomy and gluttony, the social utility of gastronomy in a time of rising economic prosperity. He takes these precepts outside the contemporary social order, which he derisively refers to as Civilization, in contradistinction to the projected social order that he calls Harmony. Gastronomes, writers as well as practitioners, produced nothing better than "gastro-asininities" *(gastro-âneries)*. Fourier's distant cousin by marriage, Brillat-Savarin, fares no better than any other so-called gastronome ignorant of the higher or combined gastronomy, which Fourier baptizes "gastrosophy." Gastrosophy alone allowed "a profound and sublime theory of social equilibrium," and it did so through "the principal mechanism of the equilibrium of the passions" governing one of the two primary bases, sex and food, of the new social order. Gastronomy occupies such a central place in Harmony because it develops rather than suppresses the senses. Fourier premises his entire system on material abundance as the sole guarantee of spiritual abundance, for example happiness. Contemporary society is based on differential scarcity, whereas the increased production of Harmony will spread abundance throughout society. Indeed, Fourier broke fractiously with his mentor and fellow utopian, Henri, comte de Saint-Simon, on just this issue. The emphasis on plenty sets this new culinary order against gastronomy as Civilization understood the practice. The moderation preached in nineteenth-century gastronomic circles is anathema to this philosopher of the appetites: "A hundred thousand philosophers eat only to keep their passions under control." Because he considered moderation a "travesty of nature," he placed all activities in Harmony under the twin signs of profusion and the absence of moderation: Harmonians' prodigious appetites will necessitate five meals plus two snacks a day, men will be seven feet tall, easy digestion will make children strong, and life expectancy will reach 144 years.

Few works tie the culinary and the social order so visibly or so tightly. Like Grimod de la Reynière, Brillat-Savarin, and Carême, Fourier transcended the materiality of food. Also like them, he was maniacally concerned with detail. Where they saw gastronomy in terms of art and science, he made it the stuff of economics, philosophy, and politics. His gastronomical political economy endowed the proverbial land of milk and honey with an elaborate, complex social organization grounded in a visionary social science. More than any other culinary text, Fourier's writings intellectualize gastronomy. They make connections to established intellectual enterprises of unimpeachable legitimacy—philosophy and political science, or what nineteenth-century France called the moral and political sciences.

Balzac's Tragedy of Gastrolatry

As Fourier carved out a place for philosophy and the social sciences in French culinary culture, Honoré de Balzac (1799–1850) set forth the literary relations. A generation younger than the other founding gastronomic fathers, he knew their work well. With gastronomic credentials that include a *Gastronomic Physiology* (1830), the entry on Brillat-Savarin in the *Biographie Michaud* (1835), and the *New Theory of Lunch* (1830), Balzac built on a long tradition of literary culinary commentary that, in French literature alone, dated from at least Rabelais and Montaigne in the sixteenth century. His perspective differs from that of his predecessors because it is so resolutely modern. To the contemporary literary enterprise of tracking the society emerging in post-1789 France, he joined the traditional prestige of literature. One of the striking contributions of Balzac's novels—one greatly appreciated by Marx and lavishly praised by Engels—is the dramatic ethnography of the nascent industrial capitalism of postrevolutionary France. As self-appointed secretary to that society, he could not pass over a social practice so patently modernizing as gastronomy.

Balzac put food and dining to many purposes. First, the consumption of food offers the realist novelist a precious social and psychological indicator. What budget-conscious visitor to Paris does not identify with Lucien de Rubempré in *Illusions perdues* (1837–43), when he decides to initiate himself in the pleasures of Paris at a restaurant where a single dinner eats up the fifty francs that would have lasted him a month at home in the provinces. Small wonder that the impecunious young man soon finds his way to the Latin Quarter and a menu at eighteen sous. Balzac understood what Grimod, Carême, and Brillat only intuited, namely the significance of the restaurant as a privileged location of gastronomic and other innovation—a semipublic, semiprivate urban space of dubious moral and variable culinary quality. As Lucien's saga tells us, dining in modern Paris obliges us to interpret gastronomic opportunities as markers of distinction in the urban social order. For Balzac as for Brillat, dining is a distinctly social experience defined by the company that one keeps. It is, nonetheless, a sociability rooted in the material. Note how Balzac fixes on the intersection of the physiological and the social, on the material basis of intellectual satisfaction:

> When a dinner starts to wind down, some guests start playing with the seeds of a pear; others roll breadcrumbs between their fingers; . . . misers count the pits. . . . Such are the little gastronomic pleasures that Brillat-Savarin did not take into account in his otherwise complete book. . . . No one is bored. . . . We like to stay in a kind of calm, between the reverie of the thinker and the satisfaction of ruminating animals, a state that we might designate as the material melancholy of gastronomy.[16]

But Balzac also understood the deeper forces at work when we eat, the primal forces that appetite puts into action, the material sensuality of a pleasure that vies for control of the individual. He takes Brillat-Savarin to task for not placing enough importance on the "real pleasure" derived from the physiological struggle: "Digestion, by using human forces, constitutes an inner battle which, for gastrolaters, is the equivalent of the greatest climaxes [*jouissances*] of love." The danger, as with sexuality, is that appetite so easily overwhelms reason: "one feels such a great displacement of one's vital capacity that the brain gives way to the second brain, located in the diaphragm."

Balzac's last, and darkest, novel, *Cousin Pons* (1846), takes gastronomy still higher in the literary pantheon. It becomes the stuff of tragedy, a "bourgeois tragedy," as Balzac calls the genre in *Eugénie Grandet*, "with neither poison nor dagger nor blood but . . . crueler than all the calamities in the house of Atreus." *Cousin Pons* makes gastronomy a social actor, an agent of the dramas that construct Balzac's world. In giving gourmandise tragic dimensions, he broke with a philosophical and aesthetic tradition that restricted expression of the baser senses—touch, smell, and especially taste—to baseborn characters and to the baser genre of comedy. Gastrolatry is the good-hearted Pons's tragic flaw; his sin, gourmandise. In the narrative, Balzac brings the sin and the punishment up-to-date. The hapless Pons is beset by identifiable social forces, which take the form of avaricious relatives who defraud him of an incomparable collection of antiques. Like the exceptional collection that he has amassed with such loving care, his worship of fine food compensates for personal disappointments:

> For him celibacy was less a preference than a necessity. Gourmandise, the sin of virtuous monks, opened her arms to him, and he threw himself into them as he had thrown himself into the adoration of art. . . . For him good food and Bric-à-Brac were substitutes for a woman.

Others, less inhibited than Pons, turn to exquisite food as they would turn to a courtesan, yielding to their appetites. With so many restaurants competing for customers, all too often, ruin awaits. "You have no idea," Balzac warns us, "how many people Dining [*la Table*] has ruined. In this respect, in Paris, Dining follows the courtesan." Gastronomy joins all the other seductions of the city: "How can one resist the clever seductions in this city? Paris has its addicts, whose opium is gambling, gastrolatry or sex [*la courtisane*]." The writer in particular must guard against such seduction. The *flânerie*, the art of exploring the city that Balzac assimilates to a science, he also defines as "the gastronomy of the eye," a knowing gaze that reveals the innermost secrets of the city and its inhabitants. Unfortunately, just as most people do not know how to walk in Paris to discover its riches, most do not know how to eat. We have now come full circle to the gastronome as the superior consumer, for whom consumption depends upon both knowledge and reason.

III. The Gastronomic Field

We call culture the ethnographic whole, which, from the point of view of the study,
presents significant differences from other such entities. . . . The term of culture is used
to group an ensemble of significant differences whose boundaries,
experience tells us, approximately coincide.[17]

—Claude Lévi-Strauss, "Social Structure" (1952)

The strong links between the gastronomic and literary enterprises go far to explain the singular place that gastronomy occupies in France. A characteristic feature of French culinary culture, this connectedness reveals the presence of a cultural field in which an intense awareness of other actors leads in turn to struggles for position in the network of ties. Although French culinary culture reaches beyond the gastronomic field, this field marks that culture in myriad and unexpected ways. However much French culinary culture shares with other culinary cultures, the structure of gastronomy as a field is distinctively French.

Many strands come together to form a cuisine. But even with these strands in place—the economic factor of alimentary abundance, the rise of the restaurant, the unapologetic celebration of pleasure in an increasingly secular society, the heroic figures who created cuisine, and the emergence of genres that textualized food in all of its aspects—we are still left with the fundamental question with which this chapter began: How do we tell the story of French culinary culture? More particularly, we might add, what story does the sociologist tell?

The concept of *field* has been applied to make sense of complex economic, intellectual, and cultural interaction. Elaborated in its specifically sociological usage by Pierre Bourdieu, *field* designates the state of a cultural enterprise when the relevant production and consumption activities achieve a certain degree of independence from direct external constraints. As a "particular social universe endowed with particular institutions and obeying specific laws," a field translates external economic or political phenomena into its own terms for its own use or, more correctly, for the use of its occupants.[18] To the extent that the norms governing conduct, the values inducing behavior, and the rewards determining production operate according to field-specific standards, a field is self-regulating, self-validating, and self-perpetuating. The example of gastronomy fits this model particularly well. From the middle of the eighteenth century to the middle of the nineteenth, the articulation of gastronomy in all of its independent importance as a cultural system supplies us with an important answer to the evolution of French cuisine.

Against the functional divisions that tend to be drawn for cultural activity, a field constructs a social universe in which all participants are at once producers and consumers caught in a complex web of social, political, economic, and cultural relations that they have woven and continue to weave. Against unilinear, univocal approaches that focus on discrete structures, historical incident, or extraordinary individuals, the dynamic configuration of social and cultural relations proposed by a cultural field does greater justice to diverse modes of cultural participation. Neither the singular cultural product nor the producer lays the foundations of the cultural field, but rather a spectrum of products and practices that displays the workings of the field in all of its synergy.

Cultural fields offer the added advantage of focusing our attention on tangible products and identifiable pursuits. A sustained concentration on particular cultural fields—their internal disposition as well as their external relations—stocks the sociological arsenal with the kind of controlled studies that integrate empirical, historical evidence into a conceptual framework. The most successful studies work within a given sphere of cultural production. The "literary field" proposes a delimited space for investigation; a vast construct such as the "field of power" invites speculation. A more limited focus usefully situates the field as a historical entity as well as a sociological concept.

In any case, a sharper use of the concept of *cultural field* helps to explain the specifically sociological import of gastronomy in nineteenth-century France. As a relatively circumscribed cultural enterprise, the pursuit of culinary excellence that we call gastronomy speaks to the vexed issue of antecedents. Any search for causes or origins in such a multifaceted configuration is doomed to fail. At what point do structures and sensibilities, institutions and ideologies, practices and practitioners cohere to "make" a cultural field? To this question gastronomy proposes some interesting answers.[19]

The gastronomic field works off the split between the material product— the foodstuff, the dish, or the meal—and the critical, intellectual, and aesthetic by-products that discuss, review, and debate that original product. The relentless intellectuality so characteristic of culinary discourse in France is as necessary to the gastronomic field as the insistent materiality. In a paradigm of what cooking is all about, culinary discourse transforms the material into the intellectual, the imaginative, the symbolic, and the aesthetic. The cultural construct that we know today as French cuisine is largely the accomplishment of this discourse. Secured in texts, this discourse consolidated the gastronomic field in a period of great political and economic flux. The resulting interlocking networks of individuals and institutions forged a multitude of links within French society. These linkages, and their careful articulation, solidified the prestige of gastronomy both at home and abroad.

The associations between the gastronomic and literary fields situate cuisine favorably among French cultural products and position the gastronomic field in the hierarchy of cultural fields. Although the second-order consumption of this "literary gastronomy" places it on the outer reaches of the gastronomic field, intense textual consumption supplies a crucial element for the diffusion of the values and the traditions that govern the field. The literary work is particularly valuable in this instance because it encourages transcendence of the material and transformation of the sensual in the manner that cuisine demands. In fact, this work of transformation points to the decisive distinction between cuisine and gastronomy and their respective functions in the gastronomic field. Cuisine, or culinary codes, concerns production; its injunctions are largely instrumental, its practice more or less site specific. Grounded in primarily gratuitous, that is, noninstrumental, discourse, gastronomy pertains to consumption. Each of these cultural products operates within the gastronomic field; each is a necessary component of the cultural consciousness characteristic of that field. For the gastronomic field to come into existence, cuisine had to connect with gastronomy. Moreover, culinary production had to link to culinary diffusion, and did so through texts that also made connections to other cultural fields, literature especially prominent among them, but also, as we have seen, journalism, philosophy, and social commentary. The end result is a whole that is markedly greater than the sum of its parts.

The concept of the *gastronomic field* encourages as well cross-national comparisons. It allows us, for example, to make better sense of the affinities so often posited between French and Chinese cuisine. A highly codified Chinese cuisine, too, built on prestigious culinary traditions tied to a central government and an urban elite and disseminated by texts. Aside from very different techniques of cooking, Chinese cuisine differs most from the French in its philosophical overlay. In more recent times, in contrast with the strong support of the French government for culinary initiatives, the Communist regime that did so much to destroy elite institutions in China interrupted the course of culinary tradition and thwarted the practice of gastronomy. Although there are signs of change, such close, direct political control makes it unlikely that a gastronomic field in the full sense of the term could be identified in present-day China.[20]

If China is often compared to France for the refinement and complexity of its cuisine, the United States is more likely to be invoked as a polar opposite. Although culinary America is a substantially more sophisticated place than it was only a few decades ago, it does not offer the unity, the articulation, or the authority that a field requires. There is no cultural product on which to base a cultural field because there is no American cuisine, that is, no culinary configuration identified with the country as a whole. Regions yield more or less local, product-based cuisines. Identified by dishes, these cuisines are subject to great variation. As we saw in chapter 1, chowders alone take us on a tour around the country. More recently, this distinctive American pluralism has come to include the foodways of newer immigrant groups, a number of which, through fast-food chains, have become an integral part of the American diet and patterns of food recognition. In Pizza Hut and Taco Bell, McDonald's, Burger King, and Kentucky Fried Chicken, foreigners as well as Americans find the most salient common element of American foodways. (In the absence of an American cuisine, there is an identifiable American diet—predominance of fast food eaten outside the home and prepackaged foods eaten at home; high levels of animal protein, salt, fat, and processed sugars and correspondingly low levels of fresh fruit and vegetables; preference for soda over water.)[21]

Whatever other culinary unity Americans may have comes not from food but a food event: Thanksgiving, which may make the United States the only nation that has made a meal its foundational event. As a national food event, Thanksgiving is the product of texts, relayed by a panoply of representations that range from the journal of Edward Winslow recounting the meal of 1621 to the proclamation of 1863 by which Abraham Lincoln first declared Thanksgiving a national holiday and the annual presidential declarations since. The dinner itself is one of the perduring myths of a singular American destiny. Yet here as well the legendary meal of turkey, pumpkin, and cranberry gives rise to innumerable variations fixed in regional or ethnic custom or simply idiosyncratic preference. In other words, pluralism wins out even for a food event that is relentlessly constructed as a defining national occasion.

This cultural pluralism means a relative lack of cultural authority at the national level. None of the various American tourist guides begins to approach the authority of the Michelin Guide, whose annual restaurant ratings in France arouse such expectation and anxiety on the part of diners and restaurateurs alike. Moreover, the American guides—Mobil, AAA—are regional, not national. Surely it is emblematic of pluralistic American foodways that the well-received Zagat restaurant guides for a number of cities and regions in the United States (and now Paris as well) rely on self-selected informants rather than experts. In culinary as in so many other matters, the American federal system places little stock in regulations and rules promulgated by a national system.

Given that every society has a culinary culture, it falls to the ethnographer to chart that culture and track down indigenous foodways. A culinary culture is more comprehensive, less concentrated, less competitive than a gastronomic field. Hence French culinary culture includes but reaches well beyond French (haute) cuisine and the gastronomic field. Similarly, American culinary culture comprehends much more than the ubiquitous fast-food eateries. Texts are essential to the intellectualization of food and therefore the constitution of the gastronomic field, whereas a culinary culture incorporates a wide range of representations, most of which will not be intellectualized or even written. Visual images lend major support to the gastronomic field; they are absolutely central to a culinary culture. By the same token, the texts that play the major role for a gastronomic field are less salient in the more loosely construed culinary culture.

If the gastronomic field makes no sense for an adamantly pluralistic American culinary culture, what account can be made of the America that dines out, not at McDonald's but in restaurants situated at the antipodes of industrialized fast food? How do we interpret the America that reminds one suspiciously of France, with its adulation of avant-garde chefs and taste for culinary adventure both close to home and in far-flung places? How do we discuss the urban America in which restaurants have been so significant in the reconfiguration of the cityscape and the practices it generates? We are in the presence of what may be termed a *restaurant world,* to adapt the technical variant of *art world* as "the network of people whose cooperative activity . . . produces the kind of [culinary] works that [restaurant] world is noted for."[22] Such cooperative networks can exist only in fairly circumscribed social and/or geographical settings endowed with mechanisms that promote connection. The sheer size of the United States, the ambient cultural pluralism, the conflicting occupational identifications of chefs and cooks dictate that restaurant worlds in the technical, sociological sense are the exception rather than the rule.[23] A network of high-end restaurants run by self-consciously innovative chef-entrepreneurs structures the American restaurant world. Broad professional support comes from a number of organizations and periodicals, but foremost for these elite chefs are the elite media that diffuse critiques and praise of given restaurants as well as anecdotes about star chefs. Centrifugal economic factors (each restaurant produces a singular cultural product and competes with others in the same market niche) are countered by centripetal social forces generated by close personal and professional connections. While the density of these elite restaurants is highest in New York City (and Paris), the network of chefs is nationwide in the United States as well as France, and, not infrequently, international as well.

Each of these models fits within a larger paradigm of relations undergirding the relationship of food and society. A *restaurant world* focuses on production of a more or less well-defined culinary product and coheres through networks of individuals. By contrast, a *culinary culture* is fixed in consumption practices and values. Finally, the *gastronomic field* is structured by a textual discourse that continually renegotiates the systemic tensions between production and consumption. Culinary culture and the restaurant world take us to food; the gastronomic field points us toward other cultural fields and particularly toward literature and the arts.

Considering gastronomy as a field refines our understanding of cultural fields generally, how they operate and evolve, the respects in which they are similar and those where they differ, their connections to the larger field of cultural production. The simultaneous susceptibility and resistance to change, the drive toward innovation against the force of tradition, aligns gastronomy with other modern arts, which also occupy fields that similarly negotiate invention and convention. Every field will have its distinctive networks and strategies, its bastions of traditionalism along with outposts of innovation. By simultaneously containing and promoting competition, the field generates the inevitable struggles that are the signs of cultural ferment and creativity. The gastronomic field serves as a particularly telling example of such activity, because it enables us to talk more concretely about cultural experiences that are easily lost from sight when language and practice are not aligned in theoretical understanding.

But, for my purposes in this book, the great value of the gastronomic field lies in what it tells us about cuisine in France. This conceptual frame allows us to see exactly what is French about food in France. A structuring feature of the "ethnographic whole" that Lévi-Strauss put on the agenda for cultural analysis, the gastronomic field uncovers an "ensemble of significant differences" that sets French culinary culture apart and accounts for its power. Beyond foodways, beyond food, we have reached the culinary imagination that has impelled the French to tell stories about their cuisine for two centuries and more. As the next chapter will argue, those stories are central to this culture that has made food so much more than just food.

CHAPTER FOUR

Food Nostalgia

I. In Search of Cuisine Lost

The cook and the poet are just alike: the art of each lies in his brain.

—Athenaeus, *The Deipnosophists*

Marcel Proust's novel of artistic redemption, *À la recherche du temps perdu* (1913–27), counts as one of the great works of the twentieth century, and a monument to Western literature. Often paired with James Joyce's contemporaneous *Ulysses* (1922), the *Recherche* reflects a modernist sensibility and aesthetic.[1] But, while the modernist reading raises Proust to an international pantheon of literary greats, it obscures the deeper roots of his novel in a specific time, place, and culture. A fundamental text of twentieth-century literature, the *Recherche* is also an emblematic text of French culture as Proust found it; and it is this "Frenchness" that makes the novel both a monument to country in Proust's France and a keystone in the construction of nationhood out of the nineteenth century.

Culinary affairs play a major part of Proust's sense of this development. Just as this culinary culture gives us access to the dynamics of nation building, so, too, it opens up the *Recherche*. A cultural icon in its own right, the *Recherche* resonates beyond the pages of the book, and it does so through its resurrection of a bygone France—a France accessible through gustatory communion. As Proust makes clear in the later volumes, war and changing times have destroyed the society that he is writing about. Even so, the novel tells us, we can reclaim that past through the foods we prepare, eat, and appreciate. One can go further. The modernist novel can express the moment in a French understanding only by an act of nostalgic recovery that continues to construct a na-

111

tional tradition. The *Recherche* produces a national culinary landscape that reconciles province and capital, periphery and center, a landscape in which the French recognize an idea of country. That they are able to make that connection is in good part because of the many texts, particularly literary works, that insist upon it.

I asked the steward about his job, and he replied with a discourse on the science
of the maw delivered with magisterial gravity and demeanor as if he had
been expounding some great point of theology.

—Montaigne, "On the Vanity of Words"

As long as writers have been writing, they have written about food and cooking in both mundane and extraordinary terms. The sacrificial meals of the *Iliad*, like the welcoming repasts of the *Odyssey*, give us entry into an everyday life beyond armed conflict and harrowing adventure. The greatest culinary text of the ancient world, the multivolume *Deipnosophists* by Athenaeus, a Greek living in Rome about 200 B.C.E., discusses Homeric diners and draws on a vast number of poetic, philosophical, and medical works relating to food and feeding with seemingly endless lists of foods, dishes, ingredients, and tidbits of every sort thrown in for good measure. This compendium of the mores of an ancient culture draws from a great many works of which Athenaeus gives us the sole remaining record. Given the significance of texts in the constitution of French culinary culture, it is fitting that the *Deipnosophists* was first translated into a modern language in France. Along with the cookbooks that began to appear with increasing frequency in the mid-seventeenth century and even a poem that sings the praises of Pont l'Eveque cheese, the translation of Athenaeus, *Les Quinze livres d'Athénée* (1680), takes an important step in the "textualization" of French cuisine. Here, in the seventeenth century, Montaigne's derisive "science of the maw" *(la science de gueule)* had already become a touchstone of French culture, bridging elite and popular culture.

The realist novel and the industrializing, urbanizing society of the nineteenth century combined many forces to bring conspicuous culinary consumption into general view. People eat a great deal in nineteenth-century French novels, and it is easy to understand why. To the novelist intent on analyzing the relationship between group dynamics and individual psychology, commensality offers a wonderfully exploitable situation. Meals put groups on display, set the scene for dramatic interactions, and foster unexpected relationships across class, gender, and generations. In a society increasingly perceived as fluid, where constantly shifting borders dictate ever more complex strategies of distinction, dining allows a dynamic group to interact in a fixed setting—a setting that in France comes close to a stage.

Balzac zeroed in on the new culinary force field of the restaurant. He fixed on dining as shorthand to chart his characters' relations as they sometimes diligently, often desperately, try to make their way in the world. As his saga of the gastrolater demonstrates in agonizing detail in *Cousin Pons*, the evident pleasures of eating are never pure, unalloyed, or uncontaminated; social and economic constraints impinge at every moment. Pons's failure to take these dimensions into consideration leads to his being plundered by those who are cannier than he, and who make dastardly use of the tool that his love of fine food places at their disposal.

Considerably further down the social scale, gourmandise also does in Gervaise, Zola's laundry woman in *L'Assommoir* (1877). With its outsized goose, endless courses, and rivers of wine, a gargantuan feast centers the novel. Here we find both the high point of Gervaise's success and the beginning of her fall—a fall that will soon have her piteously begging for scraps of food. The prestige traditionally accorded literature in French culture redounds to the benefit of cuisine, while the pervasiveness of the culinary grounds literature in the everyday. This symbiosis is the surest sign of a gastronomic field at work: the culture stresses cuisine, and France's greatest writers augment that emphasis in a higher discourse of the human condition.[2]

Whether or not they have actually read the *Recherche*, a good many readers are familiar with Proust's use of taste to reconnect with the past as an iconic experience. Reinvoked everywhere by cultural commentary from literary criticism to cookie advertisements, the madeleine is surely the most celebrated literary cookie ever baked. Unquestionably delicious, these buttery little cakes will, however, do nothing for us on their own. Proust's narrator learns that tasting something means nothing unless it is a "re-taste." The madeleine works its magic only in conjunction with the narrator. Far from the passive ingestion of foodstuffs, consumption in the *Recherche* repeatedly creates a conversation between consumer and consumed that reaches well beyond everyday eating. Years before the taste of the madeleine on a dreary afternoon in Paris transforms the narrator's life, a picnic in Normandy renders the evocative power of food through just such a dialogue. The foods brought along by his new friends do not tempt the young man away from home. To him the foodstuffs are devoid of a history, lacking a vital connection to the past. The cakes and the tarts, on the other hand, are eloquent:

> [W]ith the chester cheese sandwiches and the salad, foods that were
> ignorant and new, I had nothing to talk about. But the cakes were ed-

ucated, the tarts chatty. The first had the blandness of cream and the second the freshness of fruit that knew everything about Combray.(2:257/1:965)

In this picnic moment and more dramatically in the episode of the madeleine, the memory in question belongs to the collectivity no less than to the individual. The taste that transforms the narrator's life by giving him the subject of his book resurrects a communal history through a personal incident. The little cake that the despondent adult dips in what turns out to be a magic potion does not resuscitate only his past; it restores the irretrievable past of a now irreversibly contemporary France. As the title of the novel proclaims, that time is indeed lost. The community of the narrator's childhood has disintegrated, altered beyond recognition. Henceforth it exists only in the narrator's memory and the novelist's work. A singular incident opens the novel—the child's anguished bedtime remembered by the sleepless adult and the one incident that, contrary to all expectation, realizes his every desire. The title tells us what the rest of *Combray* (part 1 of *Swann's Way*) confirms, namely that the cup of tea that bleak afternoon in Paris calls up not a particular event in the life of a small boy but a span of time in the life of a small French town.

> And, as soon as I recognized the taste of the madeleine . . . immediately the old gray house on the street . . . and along with the house came the town, from morning to night and in all kinds of weather, the Square, . . . the streets . . . , the country paths . . . the people of the village and their little houses and the church and all Combray and its surroundings, . . . rose out of my cup of tea. (1:47/1:51)

Through food, Proust recreates town and country. For, in fact, "these short fat cakes" (1:44/1:50) have no particular connection to the Beauce near Chartres where the Proust family regularly spent vacations. As a regional specialty, the humpbacked Proustian madeleine (other kinds are flat) comes from Commercy, located in the Lorraine, and in the last volume of the novel Proust shifts Combray to the eastern front. By setting his paradigmatic provincial town in the middle of the war zone, Proust records the ravages of war sustained by all of France. The bombing of St Hilaire, the church that centered life in the Combray of the opening volume, destroys more than a building; it obliterates a way of life. The extraordinary happiness that overwhelms the older narrator when he retrieves his past via the madeleine extends to the hopeful readers who, through Proust's text, possess what the narrator recovered through the madeleine—the coherent, self-contained life of a village with deep roots in both nature and history, a social setting where food, its preparation and consumption, centers the existence of its inhabitants. The

PROUST ORDERS FROM THE CART

"I'm out of madeleines, Jack. How about a prune Danish?"

The Celebrated Literary Cookie

The magic madeleine is a talismanic cookie everywhere after Proust. We laugh at the cartoon because the proposed substitution evokes a very different setting and vernacular. The prune Danish cannot possibly revive the ailing writer, because the memory that the madeleine evokes is indelibly French—and clearly beyond the scope of the very American pastry hawker. Cartoon by Lee Lorenz, *The New Yorker,* July 24, 1989. © The New Yorker Collection 1989 Lee Lorenz from cartoonbank.com. All Rights Reserved.

France of the early twentieth century, the France in which Proust was writing the *Recherche,* looked back nostalgically to what seems a simpler era. Part of that assumed simplicity came from belief in an intimate bond between foods and the land, one that bound consumers and producers together in an organic whole. That belief anchors the entire novel. Proust raises the discourse of *terroir* to the realm of faith in the permanence of place.[3]

Proust's recreation of the nineteenth-century world exerts such a strong pull on the narrator, especially from the distance of his adulthood in a palpably and disconcertingly more complex society, because life in this village of his childhood is so profoundly motivated. In Combray no one is a stranger; every person and every thing is accounted for. Every event and every food has its raison d'être in the social contacts that circumscribe the purchase, preparation, and consumption of food. Françoise, the incomparable cook who epitomizes the locus of this lost culture in the land, unconsciously creates a legion of associations through the lowliest item of everyday life. The menus that she puts together illustrate how the personal—what she serves the family—depends upon the communal—the extensive network of her socio-culinary relations:

> To the staples of eggs, cutlets, potatoes, jams, biscuits, . . . Françoise added—according to what came in from the fields and the orchards, from the catch of the day, the good luck of the market, the kindnesses of neighbors and her own genius, . . . so that our menu . . . reflected . . . the rhythm of the seasons and the events of everyday life: a brill because the fish seller had guaranteed its freshness, a turkey because she had seen a beauty at the Roussainville-le-Pin market, cardoons in marrow because she hadn't yet fixed any for us that way, roast lamb because fresh air sparks the appetite and there was plenty of time to digest before supper at seven, spinach for a change, apricots because they were still scarce, red currants because in two weeks there wouldn't be any more, raspberries that M. Swann had brought just for us, . . . a cake because she had ordered it the evening before, a brioche because it was our turn to offer it at church. (1:70/1:76–77)

Everything is accounted for. The mantra-like repetition of *because* puts everything (each foodstuff and dish) and everyone ("just for us") in place and in perspective. Justified and explained by ties to the land and to social life in town, Françoise's menus attach the Parisian family to a specific provincial place and through that place to the whole country. The dishes that appear on these menus do not derive from a readily identifiable location—no quiche lorraine, no provençal tomato or garlic. They belong instead to the culinary repertory of *cuisine bourgeoise* that could be found across France: roast chicken, steak, roast lamb, brioche, chocolate pudding, glazed cream puffs, white cheese with strawberry cream, and not forgetting the asparagus that turns up so often one year. The fishmonger works with what comes in every day, although nothing indicates any local provenance for fish.

A cornucopia, the table at Tante Léonie's, which overflows with the plenitude of nature (the bounty of the land) and the talent of culture (the cooking of Françoise), affirms a generalized ideal of life in *la France profonde,* the heartland of France. The narrator recalls his aunt's sitting room, where he used to be given a taste of the madeleine, as typically, that is, generically, provincial. From the many smells avidly "tasted" by the child as he entered the room to greet his great-aunt, the heat of the fire bakes an invisible provincial cake whose warmth and succulence surrounds him like a sort of gastronomic womb. Like so many other French novels before it, the *Recherche* lets us have our cake and eat it, too:

> It was one of those country rooms that . . . enchant us with the in-
> numerable smells given off by virtues, wisdom, habits, a whole se-
> cret life . . . the fire baking the appetizing smells like a dough . . .
> made an invisible and palpable country cake, an immense turnover.
> (1:48–49/*1:54*)

The want of culinary specificity in Combray stands out against the evocation of Normandy in the specific terms of its produce and its dishes. Reminders
of the particulars of place range from the litany of pears that begins with the
local variety, louise-bonne d'avranches (3:398–99/*2:1043*), to the spooner-
ism of the local elevator boy who is so much a part of Normandy that he metamorphoses the marquise of Cambremer into the marquise of Camembert
(3:251/*2:833*). More to the point, the very Parisian Mme Verdurin, summer-
ing in Normandy, makes much of featuring the Normandy countryside at the
dinners she gives her Parisian friends at her country home, firmly convinced
that "the great affair was not to look at it [Normandy] like tourists, but to have
good meals there" (3:290/*2:927*). She takes great pride in offering more-
authentic fare than the nearby hotel. Parisian that she is, she serves "real"
galettes ("I'll give you a Normandy galette to eat, a real one, and cookies too"
[3:360/*2:1002*]), Norman puff pastries (3:389/*2:1033*), and the local lan-
gouste known as the young ladies of Caën (3:293/*2:931*). Mme Verdurin's
dinners realize her conquest of Normandy. So, too, the craving of Albertine,
the narrator's girlfriend, for the local calvados and cider translates her desire
to possess the countryside (3:403/*2:1047–48*).

Cooking and art weave their way together through the *Recherche* to reach
well beyond the classic notion that sees cooking as an art in its own right.
When the narrator's father invites his supervisor to dinner, Françoise sets to
work with "the burning certitude of great creators" (1:437/*1:481*).

> Knowing that she would have to compose a beef in aspic, according to
> methods known to her alone, [she] had been living in the efferves-
> cence of creation; since she attached an extreme importance to the in-
> trinsic quality of the materials that went into the production of her
> work, Françoise went herself to the central market to get the best cuts

of rump steak, beef shin, calves' feet, like Michelangelo spending eight
months in the mountains of Carrara choosing the most perfect blocks
of marble for his monument to Julius II. (1:437/*1:480*)

We are surely meant to smile at the ironic disparity between marble and aspic, between one of the great achievements of Western art and the eminently
fragile and very ordinary cold beef, between the sculptor acclaimed by thousands over several centuries and the cook known only to the narrator and his
family. Proust does not let us off so easily. Smile though we may, he keeps the
comparison in play, and he does so to make us realize that this dish is not ordinary at all. Françoise expends so much time and energy on the preparations
that the narrator's mother is afraid that she, too, will fall ill from overwork
"like the author of the Tomb of the Medici in the quarries of Pietrasanta"
(1:437/*1:480*). When it comes time to serve, the *boeuf mode* comes forth, "laid
by the Michelangelo of our kitchen on enormous transparent aspic crystals
like blocks of quartz" (1:449/*1:493–94*). In this novel so profoundly about
artistic creation, the insistent comparison elevates Françoise the sculptor to
the company of the other great artists of the *Recherche*—Elstir the painter, Vin-
teuil the composer, Bergotte the writer. It is eminently fitting, then, that the
narrator returns to this monumental dish for the work that he is about to undertake. "Why wouldn't I make my book the way Françoise made the boeuf
mode that M. de Norpois liked so much, where so many pieces of choice meat
enriched the aspic?" (4:612/*3:1091*)

The model for Proust's novel becomes even more compelling when we consider in detail just how *boeuf mode* is made. Proust makes clear what cookbooks
confirm: once the ingredients have been assembled—no small task—this dish
calls for a great deal of time and concentrated effort. Enriched by the many
different pieces of carefully selected meat, the stock from which the aspic is
prepared must simmer for hours. To attain the transparency that so enchanted
M de Norpois, the stock must be purified—the culinary term is clarification—
which entails filtering the liquid through egg white or eggshells. The set aspic
then has to be cut to provide a base for the roast—the "enormous transparent crystals." Michelangelo does indeed work in that kitchen. It is not hard to
see why Proust would find this such a convincing exemplar for the painstak-
ing work required to convert the raw material of his life into his novel. Transformed by the artistry of Françoise, the materials of everyday life become art
recognizable to all. In the flurry of creation, an artist in the fullest sense of the
term, "Françoise accepted M. de Norpois' compliments with the proud simplicity, the joyful and—if momentarily—intelligent expression of an artist to
whom someone speaks of his art" (1:475/*1:522*). Proust himself had made the
connection earlier on his own account, writing to Céline Cottin in 1909 after
a meal that must have provided the basis for the comparison in the *Recherche:*

"I should like to succeed as well as you what I am going to do this evening, may my style be as brilliant, as clear, as solid as your aspic, my ideas as savory as your carrots and as nourishing and fresh as your meat" (4:1311).

In contrast with the bid for permanence that Françoise makes with the sculptural *boeuf mode,* her musical chocolate cream captures the fragility and the impermanence of the culinary, "fleeting and light like an occasional piece of music into which she had put all of her talent" (1:70–71/*1:77*). The apparent solidity of the one counters the elusiveness of the other. The literary, like the culinary, works in both modes.

Cooking is not the only art of the everyday promoted to full aesthetic status by association with arts of unassailable legitimacy. The artist in the presentation of self is also a woman. Odette Swann's dress supplies the narrator with another model for his novel: "I would build my book," he muses, "I don't dare say ambitiously like a cathedral, but, quite simply, like a dress" (4:610/*3:1090*).[4] Unlike the other great creators of the *Recherche,* Odette and Françoise are artists of everyday life. Their works accomplish what every other artist of the *Recherche* accomplishes (or hopes to) and what Proust effectively achieves. They give material expression to the sensations of a moment, which they endow with the permanence of form ordinarily denied to the sensual. The links to the *Recherche* are plain; they had to have been for the Proust who, when criticized for his "microscopic" attention to detail, pointed to his "telescope" and his attention to structure (4:618/*3:1098*). The two perspectives, the microscope and the telescope, join in every aesthetic creation in the *Recherche,* from Elstir's paintings to Françoise's cuisine. In all of these arts, the fleeting, even secretive detail conveys the immediate apprehension of the sensual. The overarching structure—of the *boeuf mode,* of the cathedral, of the dress, of the book—depends on the materialization of the immediate, sensual detail. Materialization gives it permanence through the writer's, and then the reader's, recognition.

Like every artist, the cook struggles against time; the cook, too, dreams of a permanence that can resist the aggressive orality of the Proustian "alimentary object."[5] In a parody of the narrator's style (and of Proust's own), Albertine, the young woman whom the narrator has sequestered, makes the paradoxical connection between the aspiration for permanence and the urgency of destructive consumption. Inspired by the calls of the food vendors in the streets, she launches into flights of overblown prose that turn the most ephemeral of foods, ice cream, into architectural constructions worthy of Carême's celebrated *pièces montées:* "temples, churches, obelisks, rocks—were like a picturesque geography that I look at first and then convert the raspberry or vanilla monuments into freshness in my throat" (3:636/*3:125*). *Conversion* supplies the operative term. Albertine's transmutation of the momentary into the monumental provides Proust with a model for turning the transitory into the permanence of prose. The ruthlessness of consumption produces a narrative parallel in the destructive fantasies of Albertine:

> [A]fter all these lemon ices are miniature mountains . . . at the bottom of my yellowish lemon ice, I can clearly see coach drivers, travelers, and coaches onto which my tongue rolls glacial avalanches that will devour them . . . just so I take it upon myself to destroy with my lips, pillar by pillar, these Venetian churches made of marble that is strawberry and crush the faithful with whatever I have not eaten. (3:636–37/3:125–26)

Albertine produces a sensual landscape and a narrative, a mini adventure novel in which, as the omnipotent author, she holds the power of life and death. She undertakes the kind of melodramatic overkill that Proust definitely does not write. Unlike the excessive Albertine, but like Odette and more particularly Françoise, Proust works his art in the ordinariness of the quotidian. Still, the parallels are there in Proust's insistence on just how much can be made of food. Its preparation is an art; its consumption, the proof of worlds known.

Things culinary lay the foundation of the Proustian enterprise. In the *Recherche* food is also a literary phenomenon: without the culinary context we miss a good deal of what Proust is about. He serves French culture so well not because the *Recherche* stands alone in its attention to culinary matters, but because his culinary landscapes fit within the project of creating, sustaining, and inspiring a national community. The architectures of his food are at once imaginative flights and technical recognitions for a French reader to conflate in a more general appreciation: yes, that is the way it tastes because yes, that is the way it was.

To the extent that the *Recherche* endows French literature with a truly national work, one that identifies the nation in culturally significant terms, the Proustian culinary landscape deserves no small share of the credit. Proust comes the closest to a truly national writer that France has, and he does so in part by completing the nationalization of French cuisine.[6] Of the many works that contributed to an emerging national consciousness in late nineteenth- to early twentieth-century France, none occupies a more privileged place in French culture generally than the *Recherche*, and no other writer matches the gastronomic imagination that Proust brings to his art. The Proustian culinary order ties cuisine to country.

An earlier text, very different from Proust's work, exemplified such a balance in the making. (Mme) G. Bruno's *Tour de France par deux enfants* first appeared in 1878 and went through new editions regularly over the next thirty years. This work, used and venerated by generations of students, accorded the parts of France with the whole and harmonized the claims of the regions with those of the nation. On their "tour" of France, the orphans from the Lorraine that had fallen into German hands after 1870 recognize that the evident diversity of the country not only does not compromise, it actually strengthens the fundamental unity of the nation.[7] The *Recherche*, too, gave France a text that balanced the part and the whole, the provinces and Paris, and it did so importantly through food. Like the national education system that made Bruno's exemplary text both possible and necessary, the expanding culinary system gave Proust's novel an exceptional resonance, making its work of harmonization all the more striking. For the *Recherche* tells us that the multiplicity of culinary practices neither undermines nor contradicts the unicity of French cuisine as a product of the whole country but, instead, celebrates that country.

II. Country Cooking

A quiche lorraine . . . or a Marseillaise bouillabaisse . . . or a potato
gratin from Savoy has all the refined richness of France, all its spirit and wit, its
gaiety . . . , the seriousness hidden beneath its charm, . . . its malice and its gravity, . . .
the full soul of its fertile, cultivated rich earth.

—Marcel Rouff, *La Vie et la Passion de Dodin-Bouffant-Gourmet* (1924)

When it appeared soon after the end of World War I, Marcel Rouff's perfervid declaration of culinary faith was timely. A well-known culinary commentator, coauthor of a twenty-seven-volume inventory of the gastronomic treasures of France, Rouff announces at outset that he intends this tale of the quintessential gourmet to recall its glory to a country demoralized after four years of destructive combat. Is he wrong to give us the saga of a man who "devoted his life to one of the oldest and most essential traditions of his country"? To talk "with conviction and love about a work where [France] has always surpassed other nations"? To reaffirm the place of cooking among the fine arts? After all, "Dodin-Bouffant is a gourmet the way Claude Lorraine is a painter, Berlioz a musician." The very essence of Frenchness, cuisine bespeaks as no other subject the superior claim of its culture. "Grand, noble cuisine is a tradition of this country," Rouff writes. "It is a time-honored and noteworthy element of its charm, a reflection of its soul." Rouff turns Brillat-Savarin's general dictum— "Animals fill themselves, people eat, intelligent people alone know how to eat"—to specifically French account: "Everywhere else, people eat; in France alone, people know how to eat."

He insists upon the "natural" bond between cuisine and country—"The taste for gastronomy is innate in the race"—between the abstract entity that is France and the material phenomena of everyday life. The culinary landscape that Proust evokes so subtly, Rouff paints in the broad strokes that come close to caricature. Whereas Proust's memories retrieve cuisine from a particular time and place, Rouff's overwrought gastro-lyricism tries to fix cuisine outside history. The French, Rouff proclaims, have always been the French that they are today, endowed with the same (good) taste:

> We have always known how to eat in France just as we have known
> how to build incomparable châteaux, weave admirable tapestries, . . .
> create styles that are stolen by the whole world, invent fashions that
> set women dreaming in all four corners of the earth.[8]

This more than typically chauvinistic passage and the larger discourse of culinary nationalism from which it derives show how cuisine could serve the country. Rouff insists that France *is* its cuisine, that cuisine *is* France. The bond is indissoluble, and, as the recurrence of *always* tells us, even eternal. France in the nineteenth century had to form a nation, that is, a political entity that configured politics into a whole. Beyond the obedience secured by the state, a nation requires loyalty. It requires hearts and minds as well as bodies. And though *nation* inevitably proves as slippery in the real world as it is to conceptualize, we can usefully understand a nation as a state plus culture, power plus persuasion. In France, cuisine became part of that cultural work of persuasion and identification. Like other nation-states-in-the-making, it set about mobilizing past glories in support of the present. Cuisine along with other cultural phenomena helped by translating people, places, and practices into traditions impelling belief.[9]

The France envisioned by the republican government of the late nineteenth century and imagined by Rouff is a country beyond political strife, beyond the humiliating defeat and occupation by the Prussians in 1870, and especially beyond the bloody civil war of the Paris Commune in 1871. Like Rouff's celebration of cuisine and country, the "law of the stomach" ingested the parts into the whole. Gastronomy belonged to an evolving sense of nation. That cuisine could become such a privileged vehicle of Frenchness lay in its ability to reconcile center and periphery, to harmonize the exigencies of the countryside with the demands of the city, and to do so without manifest conflict. To the degree that the unity of French cuisine triumphed over the multiplicity of culinary practices, the culinary offered nineteenth-century France a model for national unity—a model all the more powerful in that cuisine somehow seemed to exist outside the political in a realm of Frenchness all its own, a Frenchness that the rest of the world accepted and continues to embrace, if at times with misgiving.

> The most significant characteristic of the metropolis is [the] functional extension beyond its physical boundaries.
>
> —Georg Simmel, "The Metropolis and Mental Life" (1904)

The very existence of Paris challenges all readings of France. Does the city concentrate the country in the same way that it focuses social, economic, political, and cultural life? Or is it the cosmopolitan Other, an alien site, the great escape for the women and men whose fortunes we follow in so many novels both French and foreign? To this problematic relationship between city and country, culinary Frenchness offers no exception. In things culinary, Paris is both enduringly French and undeniably cosmopolitan, not just a city, but, as Emperor Charles V declared in the sixteenth century, a world—"non urbs sed orbis." The rapidly changing metropolis of the early nineteenth century set the stage for and trained the actors in the institutionalization of modern French cuisine. Paris supplied goods and services, ideas and innovations. It provided patrons and practitioners for the evolving profession of chef and publishers for the gastronomic texts that circulated throughout France and Europe. Its chefs, too, circulated, Carême and Escoffier only the most celebrated among them. As the prestige of the French monarchy had radiated outwards from Versailles, so, with its many vehicles of diffusion, nineteenth-century Paris reached beyond the still-extant city walls. At the same time, like any other culinary code, French cuisine remained tied to place, tributary to the land, its foodstuffs, and the dishes that went with them.

Simmel's contention concerning the spread of the metropolis certainly obtained for nineteenth-century culinary Paris. Yet diffusion was never a one-way street. National identity emerged from a complex interaction of center and periphery, a negotiation between Paris as the center of a culture and the provinces as repository of that culture. The relentless centralization of political and economic activities over the nineteenth century, and the consequent concentration of cultural and artistic life, reinforced the dominance of the capital. The specificity and the rootedness of regional culinary place were particularly useful in this regard in their negotiation of urban cultural space. With its supplies of foodstuffs, the countryside literally fed a natural hierarchy that placed Paris as the "head" of the country. At the same time, the concentration of elite cultural organizations and governmental institutions, by making use of the country's products, conferred honor on all. Hence all of France could join in exporting Frenchness Parisian style, and this was particularly the case with the developing gastronomic field, where local product fueled urban production.

The associations of Paris with intellectuality and with intellectual and artistic achievements made cuisine a central cultural enterprise there. As the very term *chef* would lead us to imagine, Parisian chefs had a natural affinity with the "head" of the country. Carême's career, to take only the most obvious example, was not simply impossible but unthinkable anywhere but Paris. Later in the century the establishment of a number of culinary institutions reinforced this culinary supremacy. Between 1860 and 1900 more than ten associations were founded in Paris alone, along with twelve journals in France between 1870 and 1900, and another ten in England and the United States. On the domestic front, a very different category of magazines came to the fore. The evocative subtitle of *Le Pot-au-feu—Journal de la cuisine pratique et d'économie domestique* (Boiled beef—The magazine of practical cuisine and household economy [1893]) pointed to middle-class housewives and their cooks. Culinary competitions and exhibits sponsored by the professional associations gave the culinary arts institutional publicity, while the World's Fairs held in Paris in 1857, 1867, 1889, and 1900 showcased French culinary achievements, particularly the great advances in the preservation and transportation of foodstuffs.[10]

How did the union of Paris and the provinces become quintessentially French despite the domination of the capital? All cuisines turn on questions of identity. Just so, the French provinces and regions assert theirs against the metropolis, often seen as not only pervasive but frankly invasive. Most obviously, the countryside supplies Parisian haute cuisine with products. Eugène Briffault, the author of a droll exploration of the dining customs of the capital at midcentury, puts it succinctly: "when Paris sits down to dine, the whole world gets going." Whereupon he proceeds to detail exactly how much the city consumes—from the number of animals slaughtered and the amount of wine, beer, and alcohol consumed to the quantities of oil and vinegar used in salads. The provinces exist to feed Paris. "Dinner in Paris," Briffault asserts, "concerns the whole country in a big way."[11] City joined countryside around a table and the communal act of dining.

Paris became the hub of a gigantic wheel. The development of the railroad system in midcentury speeded up the circulation of goods. The train routes primarily connected the provinces to the capital rather than to one another. More than ever, in the second half of the nineteenth century, Paris turned into a redistribution center. That tomatoes from Provence or Camembert from

Normandy had to be procured via the capital placed chefs in the provinces at a clear disadvantage for all except local produce, while it gave the master chef in Paris the first choice of everything. Small wonder that ambitious chefs made their way to Paris sooner rather than later.

The often conflictual interaction of principle and practice mirrored the oppositions between city and country but with a larger consensus always in view. Regional products, too, passed through Paris—through the official standards imposed by the government, through the scarcely less stringent standards of the market, and, above all, of the elite Parisian gastronomic public. On the one hand, there was Les Frères Provençaux (The Provençal brothers), a restaurant that opened in Paris in 1786 and remained a temple of gastronomic excellence until the middle of the nineteenth century. As the name implies and as contemporaries corroborate, the three brothers (in-law) introduced provençal dishes to the capital. On the other hand, those exotic elements had to be enhanced for the Parisian public. Convinced as he was of the absolute superiority of French creations, Carême made a great point of frenchifying foreign sauces.

The real thing could elicit fiercely negative reactions, which probably explains why the chef Alexandre Viard claimed that only people from the south of France used garlic on a regular basis. Another commentator in 1825 railed against the depredations that foods from far and wide visited on the French "national taste." Anglomania notwithstanding, unless French diners were endowed with "iron clad palates," they had better stay away from the plum pudding, mutton soup, and salted beef favored by the English (roast beef and boiled potatoes passed muster) along with the garlic-laden dishes from the south of France. Whether from the deep south or the far north, these were alien cuisines "unsuitable to either our health or our climate."[12] "National taste" could only mean Parisian. Any borrowing occurred in terms of an already defined national idiom—much as the French typically give foreign words a decided French pronunciation, rendering the word incomprehensible to a native speaker of the foreign language. Neither phonetically nor culinarily is "un hot-dog" identical to the American version, although each is a recognizable variant of the basic German wiener. In both cases, the dominant linguistic norm and culinary code adapted the foreign element to meet the expectations of the indigenous public.

In the nineteenth century as today, it was virtually impossible to say what, exactly, was authentic or, for that matter, what exactly authenticity might entail, and who had the authority to make that determination. How far back did one have to reach for the essence of authenticity, and what difference did it make? Given the mobility of people and foodstuffs, which precludes culinary isolation, the promotion of indigenous products as authentic has to be seen as a move in a collective strategy of distinction designed to publicize and certify a particular identity against others. Authenticity, then, is not a given but a construction.[13] In turn, it is logical that organizations to celebrate various regional cuisines were established and, moreover, established in Paris. Gastronomy was a Parisian eating order, its practices of consumption as well as production codified in a range of texts. Lacking such codification, the very notion of a provincial gastronomy could only be a contradiction in terms. The nostalgia for the traditions ascribed to the country is a function of the distance from, and consciousness induced by, the city.

The network of culinary connections long resembled the map of train (and subsequently automobile and air) routes that connected Paris and the provinces but not, or with difficulty, one region with another, another reason all became "French" under Parisian hegemony. Even so-called regional cuisines owed their existence to Paris. Not until the nineteenth century, and especially toward the middle and end of the century, did gastronomic interest seriously consider the provinces, and this despite the traditional dishes that in some cases can be traced to the Middle Ages.[14]

In the broadest sense, culinary nationalism operated within a general movement of culinary modernization. These changes, in turn, were associated with both increasing governmental control of production and distribution and also the developing national (and international) markets for foods and services. The 1855 classification of the wines of Bordeaux originated in a move to regulate the production of wine and to assure a stable market. A product marketed beyond its point of origin requires some measure of standardization, and the larger the market, the greater the need for identifiable goods. As long as Camembert remained a local product sold in Normandy, producers had little incentive to standardize or even label their cheeses. As soon as they aimed at a Parisian (and therefore national) market, standardization and distinctiveness became essential in identifying the authentic product, along with a new level of visual appeal to stimulate demand. Here is the explanation of the evolution of Camembert's distinctive appearance. A pristine white crust replaced the original unappetizing motley blue, and the characteristic, easily recognizable packaging that made travel possible (the round box and waxed paper wrapping) came into usage along with the colorful labels that publicized the cheese, its provenance, and its producer.[15]

It is important to see exactly how these mechanisms of the periphery under the auspices of the center worked in nineteenth-century France before proceeding further with the role of cuisine in that process. In short, the complexity of the relationship undercuts the oppositional model of city against province. The center does not simply impose its values and norms (even if we make the highly dubious assumption that these are constituted in isolation). To the extent that communication from one part of the periphery to another passes through the center, that center—Paris—makes connections that would otherwise not be made. Support for the whole comes from the constituent parts and through the creation of bonds between those parts.

Thus, the essence of Frenchness rests on the codified distinction, and distinctiveness, of the many different territories within its borders. They, in turn, are controlled by the central value accorded education, particularly primary education. The Third Republic zealously pursued a pedagogy of national distinctiveness through complementary difference. The high degree of centralization of the educational system offered a critical means of shaping that identity and integrating the often disparate cultural and linguistic entities into the whole that was France.

We are not as far from culinary matters as it might seem. Traveling spread knowledge of the culinary patrimony of France and made contacts between regions, but so did the books and journals that acquainted middle-class women throughout the country with a range of culinary traditions. Schools did their part with domestic economy courses intended to shape the republican woman as the army was taken to mold the republican man. Culinary republicanism also worked off the "educational cookbooks" aimed at the domestic market. A work such as Edmond Richardin's *La Cuisine française du XIVe au XXe siècle—L'Art du bien manger* (French cuisine from the 14th to the 20th century—The art of good eating [1913]) shows culinary republicanism at work. Richardin takes his readers on a tour of the provinces, stressing the diversity of French products and recipes. He calls on celebrated writers for recipes and includes numerous engravings of kitchen-related scenes over several centuries. In a patently patriotic tone, a note in the 1913 edition of this work gives especial emphasis to the bond between the regional part and the national whole and points us to the politics that can lurk behind the culinary. At a time when Germany held Alsace and part of Lorraine, ceded by the French after the defeat of 1870, it is understandable that Richardin included over thirty pages of foods from Lorraine. The province may have been lost to the French, but Richardin assures that its cooking will live in France.

The note that he added—all the more remarkable given its lack of culinary significance—reveals the depth of the tie between the country and the province that this book sought to convey. At his summer home in the Pyrenees, Richardin tells us, wishing to recreate "a bit of" the country of Joan of Arc (about whom he also wrote a book), he has transplanted wild rose bushes from his native Lorraine for "the enchantment of my eyes and the joy of my heart, always faithful to the fatherland [*patrie*] of Lorraine." The sentiment is not in itself noteworthy—the "lost" provinces were a common topic from 1871 until their "return" after World War I. But the place in which these feelings find expression—a cookbook—is definitely worth notice. The national and the regional are as inextricable on the culinary as on every other level. Should we be surprised at the adoption of this book by both the Ministry of

Public Education and the City of Paris for use in schools? Schoolchildren all across the country could leaf through Richardin's cookbook and see for themselves the bounty that their country had to offer, the better to understand the crucial link between provincial part and national whole.[16]

As written products, these recipes were already at one remove from local, primarily rural culinary practices, which were likely to be uncodified because they still belonged to an oral tradition. Because the dominant code was Parisian, culinary sophistication meant modernization, which in turn implied the refinement, luxury, and complexity of preparation characteristic of at least the bourgeois versions of French cuisine. Culinary refinement moved outward from the city as urban gastronomes took to touring the country in the latter part of the century. Locals might accept the pits in the cherries in the clafoutis dessert typical of the Limousin in mid-southern France, but not travelers accustomed to greater sophistication and more concerned about their teeth. Peasant recipes required every bit as much modification as the foreign preparations so conscientiously reworked by Carême. Accordingly, Curnonsky and Marcel Rouff, in their gastronomic tour of the French provinces, advised tourists to stay clear of locals unless they had impeccable gourmet credentials. The regional cuisines that we know today, with their special dishes tied to local produce, evolved out of an extended confrontation of those products with the codes and practices imposed by Paris, the norms diffused by the culinary journals that flourished at the end of the century.[17]

This promotion of the regional points to a shift in culinary as well as political priorities. The great Parisian restaurants only became more important centers of culinary creativity as the century advanced. The culinary pantheon becomes a national monument—in Paris. Proust rightly places the emblematic meal of the *Recherche* in Paris, even though he conceives of Françoise as the spirit of Combray and specifies that for this special dinner she once again found "her incomparable Combray manner" (1:450/*1:494*). Françoise does not reproduce Combray for that Parisian dinner: the capital requires a more conscious craft and more evident luxury. For the distinguished guest, she adds truffles to the pineapple salad and transforms the simple pot roast (*boeuf à la casserole* or *boeuf mode*) that figured regularly on the menu in the country into the extravagantly elaborate *boeuf à la gelée*. High cuisine belonged in high culture, bourgeois cuisine to bourgeois culture, one more pursuit secured by the educated, monied leisure that connected elites.

Cuisine or, more particularly, culinary practice, embraced a distinctly new political, social, and economic order. Exclusionary by virtue of the community it sanctions and thereby perpetuates; a meal signals allegiances and affinities to insiders and outsiders alike. Particularly in a society as seized by political controversy as nineteenth-century France, politics can never be far away. For example, the July Monarchy eventually banned banquets as hotbeds of republicanism, and the Third Republic celebrated its success with ceremonial banquets for its elected officials, the most spectacular of which, in 1900, brought close to twenty-one thousand French mayors to Paris! The culinary pantheon may have been represented as a national good, but the Panthéon itself was anything but a politically neutral monument. Even the great men buried there were moved in and out as the many different regimes of nineteenth-century France adapted the space for their own purposes. By the end of the century, like the Panthéon, cuisine had become a rallying point for a republican tradition in the making.[18]

Culinary Geographies

Not that the provinces were absent from the national scene, culinary and otherwise. Collections of regional recipes began to appear in the nineteenth century, although to the extent that they addressed primarily a local public, they exerted little influence on what we might see as the national culinary consciousness. To exist within that consciousness, to stake out territory in the national culinary patrimony, regional cuisines required a term of comparison, a cultural configuration against which they could be both defined and judged. Paris long supplied the terms for that comparison. To the extent that French cuisine is Parisian, it is not because of particular products or dishes but because Paris supplied the template of French culinary civilization. Put another way, the culinary capital associated every identifiable periphery in France with the center. A national discourse not only accepted but actively promoted regional difference but on the assumption that all were subsumed in the greater whole. As with Le Grand d'Aussy at the end of the eighteenth century, that discourse came from Paris, even when, again like Le Grand d'Aussy, it catalogued the foodways of the provinces. The continual negotiation of the part and the whole fueled the cultural construction of "Frenchness," the character of each dependent upon the shifting characteristics of the other.

The interest of the gastronomic register of French culinary treasures published by Rouff and Curnonsky (Maurice-Edmond Sailland) between 1921 and 1928 lies in just that interdependence. The title of *La France gastronomique: Guide des merveilles culinaires et des bonnes auberges françaises* (Gastronomic France: Guide to the culinary marvels and the good inns of France) proclaims its culinary-geographic ambitions. The adjective puts the very definition of France at stake: *gastronomique* stands less as a modifier of France than as a component of the substantive. France is to be apprehended not just through gastronomy but as itself a gastronomic entity, thus recalling the culinary-geographical maps that began to appear in the early nineteenth century. Rouff's *Dodin-Bouffant* characterizes France by its dishes—"a quiche lorraine . . . or a Marseillaise bouillabaisse. . . . or a potato gratin from Savoy has all the refined richness of France, all its spirit and wit"—and by the bounty of the land—"the full soul of its fertile, cultivated, rich earth . . . of which its perfumed creams, snowy poultry, delicate vegetables, juicy fruit, savory beef and frank, supple and ardent wines are the blessed manifestations." A particular locale fixes each dish, and yet every dish exhibits the essential, ineffable quality of the whole. This assertively national cuisine incorporates all others in a perfect synecdoche of France. Individual products and preparations commend the incomparably greater whole. However inconceivable Dodin-Bouffant appears outside his small town, the cuisine that he champions belongs to a recognizable, national tradition.

This culinary symbiosis of provincial part and national whole emerges with especial clarity from a deceptively unpretentious cookbook by Marthe Daudet, who wrote under the name of Pampille.[19] Straight off, the title, *Les Bons Plats de France—Cuisine régionale* (The good dishes of France—Regional cuisine [1913]), announces the author's ambitions. Even in a cookbook, *bon* means more than simply "good" to the taste. Beyond the senses, *bon* carries overtones of authenticity, of tradition, of distinction. Pampille herself tells us right away that she has absolutely no interest in the "complicated" menus of fancy dinners. Her goals are simpler: to bring together a few of the "good traditions of French cuisine," and to give recipes for the most characteristic dishes of each province. Pampille and her readers would not find the two incompatible, because each actually implies and depends upon the other. Before launching her culinary tour of the provinces, she offers a section on National Dishes—four "great soups," four culinary "poems" that come from the four corners of France—pot-au-feu, onion soup, cabbage soup, leek and potato soup.

Throughout, Pampille scatters observations about the superiority of these simple dishes over the excessively ornate cuisine that all too often flaunts the name of French. She ends *Les Bons Plats* with a mordant sketch of just the kind of meal to avoid at all costs. Her version of "The Dreadful Dinner" takes us from one awful, pretentious dish to another, from lukewarm soup and viscous sauces to old fish and overcooked beef. The dissatisfied and thoroughly disgruntled guest must wait for good food until she gets home. "You have no idea," she tells us in a withering comment, "how good an apple tastes at midnight." Like Rouff, like Richardin and others committed to culinary regionalism, Pampille defined her culinary ideals against a bastardized French cuisine. She proposes recipes to counter the extravagant preparations associated with the frightfully expensive luxuries of the big hotels *(les palaces)* that catered to an international clientele.

Even so, and admirer as she was of this traditional France rooted in time-honored traditions, Pampille wrote from Paris and for a public that took

Parisian standards for granted. Readers of *Les Bons Plats de France* could appreciate the setting of the dreadful dinner for having themselves on occasion been subjected to similar disasters. Also, they would have expected culinary sophistication—a refinement that nonetheless recognizes the superiority of simplicity and the imperative of pleasing the palate first, the eyes a distant second. Indeed, part of that sophistication would have been apparent to the gastronome through the originality of a dish such as *crêpes Léon Daudet* (which Pampille named for her husband).

Even as Pampille, Richardin, Rouff, and others brought the provinces to Paris, their work connected the provinces with one another. These writers and many more besides in effect extended to the public at large the home economics classes that taught girls about ways of cooking across the country. In the process they mounted a larger celebration of the riches and the diversity of the country. Culinary works turned readers into practitioners, natives into cosmopolitans, and most important, provincials into French. The culinary geography constructed by these works, novels and cookbooks alike, translates country traditions for a city audience. When Mme Verdurin receives guests at her summer home in Normandy, Proust notes that this most Parisian of hostesses has the local lobster grilled according to Pampille's "incomparable recipes" (*3:293/2:931*). These cookbooks and guides transmit dishes and foods as emanations of the very soil. Fixed in an eternal present, they take cuisine out of history, doing their share of nation building by defining the nation in an implied conflation of nature and culture.

III. Cooking and Chefing

Women Cooking

Slave to routine, the impassive cook never leaves the beaten path, her crude and uninspired character is below the nobility of her functions . . . if a man hadn't grabbed a hold of the frying pan, [culinary] art would have stayed where it was, and we would still be eating Esau's lentils and Homer's roastbeef.

—A. B. de Périgord, *Nouvel Almanach des Gourmands* (1825)

To the degree that it remains in the kitchen, confined to a culinary place and to the affective relations and informal communication that govern domestic culinary production, cooking will remain local: "home cooking" for Americans, *cuisine bourgeoise, cuisine de femmes* for the French. Surely it is significant that English does not have the same equivalence. Anglophones do not routinely talk about "women's cooking" or, for that matter, about "middle-class cooking." Just as the counterpart of *cuisine bourgeoise* is not, as logic would require, *cuisine aristocratique* but haute cuisine, so the counterpart of *cuisine de femmes* is not *cuisine d'hommes*. Gender and class distinctions alike blur in the conflation. *Cuisine d'homme*? Man's cuisine? Certainly not, when there exist so many apparently neutral, ostensibly ungendered terms. *Grande, haute, savante, nouvelle, professionnelle, avant-garde, créatrice* fill the bill quite nicely, masking the very real—that is, socially grounded—foundation of culinary vocabulary. The hierarchy implicated in gender, like the gender implied in hierarchy, structures French cuisine and the culinary discourse that accompanies, reinforces, and disseminates this cuisine. The oppositional pairs of French cuisine— *grande-populaire, haute-bourgeoise, traditional-nouvelle, domestic-professional*—implicitly and often, as in the epigraph above, explicitly construct such a gendered hierarchy.

The broader distinction between written and oral culture reinforces the polarity of masculine and feminine culinary domains. The more prestigious of each culinary pair shares a reliance on texts that transport the relevant culinary practices beyond a specific culinary place into a broader cultural space. French cuisine—the formalized code of culinary practices—partakes of a culinary discourse that intellectualizes the material and rationalizes the sensual. Confined to the home kitchen, excluded from the public culinary life of the professional kitchen, and, for that reason, excluded from the cultural space occupied by culinary texts, women's cooking/*cuisine de femmes* was long absent from the prestigious culinary-cultural space of professionalized haute cuisine. The distinction between *chef* and *cook* in English obscures (without obliterating) the gender divide that the French language makes obvious with *cuisinier* and *cuisinière*. At the same time, the English use of *chef* sets everyday food preparation against and apart from the "fancy" foreign, or frankly French, food preparation for public consumption. In the cross-Channel selective adoption and redefinitions of terms, English differentiates between *cooking* and *cuisine* (sometimes rendered as *cookery*), which French conflates, since *cuisine* refers at once to material food preparation, the place where that process occurs, and a culinary style.

Yet *cuisine de femmes* is not necessarily, primarily, or, for that matter, even usually a negative ascription, despite the many misogynistic comments we can dredge up to impugn the lesser culinary abilities of women. Its affective associations—the childhood memories of comfort food, of food that comforts—ensure a ready audience for simpler foods reminiscent of simpler, presumably better times. To become more than individual memories tied to individual culinary experience, to become a cultural creation, as chapter 3 argued, a culinary product needs texts, recipes, journalism, literary works. Without Proust's novel neither the cookie nor the cook would have made it out of

Combray. Similarly, regionalists such as Pampille and Richardin often invoked the minimalist rootedness of *cuisine de femmes, cuisine bourgeoise, cuisine du terroir* (local cuisine), or *paysanne* (peasant cuisine), which they set against the perceived excesses of the "fancy" fare of haute cuisine.

Denigration of haute cuisine continued a long-standing discourse that condemned the artifice of elaborate culinary preparation, which was also criticized on health grounds. Rousseau opposed Voltaire on this very issue, and Menon conceived his *Cuisinière bourgeoise* in just these terms. In a reversal of the aristocratic priority accorded spectacle, *cuisine bourgeoise* gave pleasing the palate precedence over charming the eye. Setting simple food against complicated preparations long antedated these debates and continued well after. Indeed, the quarrel undoubtedly intensified with the institutionalization of haute cuisine over the nineteenth century. Against the undeniable prestige of haute cuisine are strong reactions against its sophisticated preparation and exotic products. Excluded from the realm of haute cuisine, women earned praise for their very limitations. Cooking is not, nor is it intended to be, "chefing."

Cooking as such is both more and less—more because of the affective ties of the cook, less because of the domestic venue. The praise heaped on the cook of Dr Véron, the cultural entrepreneur who entertained many artists and writers in mid-nineteenth-century Paris, offers a case in point. "Sophie is a cook of the right school, disdainful of the charlatanism of all the artificial procedures currently used by those who are ambitiously known as 'chefs.'" The home cook presses her own claim to culinary consideration. Where chefs complicate, she simplifies. Where chefs add on, she pares down, trading ornament for essence. She "disguises as little as possible, . . . and by both simple and sophisticated means achieves culinary results of which women alone are capable."[20] The home cook does not lead, she follows.

A half century later, Pampille followed in Sophie's footsteps. She does not talk to us about system or method, as Carême, Escoffier, and others do, and still less about decorating desserts. She stresses instead ingredients that no recipe can convey—the "special touch" *(tour de main)* and the love without which no dish will succeed. Cuisine, she concludes, is neither a trade nor a profession, but a vocation, a "calling" that requires "the sense of joy in reality."[21] While Proust's Françoise is by no means a joyful character, she, too, makes a gift of her meals to the narrator's family. She finishes the dinner with a special flourish:

> [C]omposed expressly for us but dedicated especially to my father, who was a connoisseur, a chocolate cream was offered to us, fugitive and light as an occasional piece into which she had placed all her talent. (1:70/*1*:77)

A Sixteenth-Century Chef   An Eighteenth-Century Chef

The rather slovenly sixteenth-century cook equipped with only the most basic utensils
becomes a rotund and more carefully dressed purveyor and displayer of elaborate dishes
two centuries later. From Alfred Franklin, *La Vie privée d'autrefois—La Cuisine* (1888).
Courtesy of Columbia University Libraries.

The division of culinary labor inherited from the aristocratic kitchen and
the food guilds took on new dimensions in the public culinary market of the
nineteenth century. Men—*cuisiniers*—wrote the cookbooks published during
the Ancien Régime, and most of them leaned heavily on their elite associations to recommend themselves to the public. By the time the upscale restaurant (and the gentleman's club in England) came into existence in the late
eighteenth and early nineteenth centuries, women cooks disappeared even in
private homes as one moved up the social scale. Larger establishments tended
to collapse the functions of chef and steward into the Chef de cuisine, or what
contemporary restaurants in the United States call the executive chef (as opposed to the line cooks, or, in French, *cuisiniers*). The exclusion of women
from the most public, upper reaches of the French culinary world brought by
professionalization over the nineteenth century is by no means entirely out-
dated, though France can claim no monopoly on the gendered divisions of
culinary labor. The "haute-r" the restaurant, the closer to the French model,
the fewer women are likely to be found running either the kitchen or the

restaurant.[22] The French ascendancy among the world's cuisines extended its model well beyond the borders of the country. The explanation lies in the combined effects of the aristocratic culinary norms inherited from the Ancien Régime and the professional ideal that dominated in the nineteenth century: food in public spaces was the province of men, as defined by the Ancien Régime; moreover, before they were abolished in 1791, guilds not only closely regulated the purveyance and preparation of food, they required both masters and apprentices to be male.[23]

Men defined the parallel hierarchy for the aristocratic and the royal household even more emphatically. The aristocratic esquire trenchent *(écuyer tranchant)*, or carver, served at court in full regalia; the steward *(maître d'hôtel)*, often noble himself, served with his sword at his side. As late as 1822, in an engraving in *Le Maître d'hôtel français* depicting the old and the new chef, Carême shows the steward with a sword at his side. However mightily scullery maids labored to get extravagant dinners on the table, women had only the most ancillary role in the aristocratic kitchen run on the military model, where cooks (male) worked under the orders of Officers. The Officer of the kitchen *(Officier de cuisine)*, later Head of the kitchen *(Chef de cuisine)*, was in charge of all the actual cooking, while the Officer of the mouth *(Officier de bouche)* or steward *(maître d'hôtel)* supervised supplies and cold preparations, including desserts. Vatel's suicide when the fish failed to arrive in time for a banquet honoring Louis XIV illustrates just how much at least one steward took the aristocratic military model to heart.

Another legacy from the eighteenth century was a generalized imitation of aristocratic mores and a promotion of the chef. As the great gossipy urban ethnographer Louis-Sébastien Mercier observed, chefs at the time had almost gotten to the point of calling themselves culinary artists. Everyone, Mercier opined, took great care not to upset them, and as a result they lorded it over all the other servants.[24] For the first time a sharp distinction appears between cook's cuisine and chef's cuisine *(la cuisine de cuisinière/la cuisine de cuisinier)*. Mercier claimed that the two operated according to very different principles and created contrary expectations. Separate is not equal, and in this world of conspicuous consumption the new urban elites looked to chefs for something to set themselves apart from, and above, their neighbors. Anyone with pretensions to elevated social standing had to have a man in the kitchen, which, as contemporaries remarked, represented a notable change from early in the eighteenth century, when the bourgeoisie largely contented themselves with cooks.

The gender discrimination in the world of French cuisine stands out even more dramatically when we look across the Channel. Where the French maintained a strict separation of the domestic and professional culinary spheres, English practice undertook far fewer strategies of distinction. Although the

The Old and the Modern Chef

The nineteenth-century chef on the right, contrasted sharply with his eighteenth-century counterpart, takes a stance that is more self-conscious of his own more dramatic persona. Carême's modern rendition gives us a figure at once young and stylish, while his hand on the shoulder of his predecessor reveals continuing reliance on the old. His fine boots show his legs to good effect, and his elegant curls display Carême's newly designed chef's cap in a pose not dissimilar from ones assumed by the Romantic poet. From Carême, *Le Maître d'hôtel français* (1822). Courtesy of The University of Iowa Libraries.

The Paris Chef

The title page of this journalistic tour of the Parisian restaurant and culinary scene claims
that even the River Seine is filled with broth from a pot-au-feu while other provisions
seem to fall from the sky. To complete the absolute symbiosis of the city and cuisine, the
fork stuck into the Left Bank carries the seal of the City of Paris, and the wine bottle set
somewhat precariously on the Right Bank stands in for the Vendôme Column. Illustration
by Bertall in Briffault, *Paris à table* (1846). Courtesy of Columbia University Libraries.

The Writing Chef

Chefs cook, but they also must write with care to complete their acts of creation. Here a chef contemplates the text of his menu, taken quite possibly from one of Carême's own cookbooks. Illustration by Bertall in Briffault, *Paris à table* (1846). Courtesy of Columbia University Libraries.

English aristocracy adopted the French model, based in the court and later the urban elites, English cooking professionals, including considerable numbers of women, evolved out of the largely domestic culinary practices associated with more modest households and the countryside.[25] Where the French bourgeoisie cooked within the shadow of the aristocratic standards, the English gentry and prosperous farmers, which had no real French equivalent, evolved their own cooking norms, quite separate from those of urban elites.

The most strikingly new elements in early nineteenth-century France, the restaurant and the professionalization of cooking, reinforced the restriction of upper-class women to the home and lower-class women to the lesser ranks of the occupation. Carême's many culinary treatises addressed future professional cooks as the *hommes de métier* (men of the trade). Today's apprentices would be tomorrow's chefs, who would carry on the cuisine that he had perfected. His works would show the way and start them down the right path, the one, of course, that he marked out. But because the consummate professional was anxious to capture as wide a public as possible, he proposed shortcuts for professional chefs, including women, who had to make do without proper staff. *L'Art de la cuisine française* (1833) detailed ways in which women could profit by this book, which was directed largely to (male) professionals. Not that Carême expected the working-class, presumably illiterate cooks to use his work themselves. He aimed, rather, at their mistresses, who could rely on his analyses to instruct the cooks on proper preparation.

On a more symbolic plane, an age-old and apparently universal discourse associating food and sexuality kept women in their place as the objects, instead of the producers, of consumption goods. In the dichotomous perspective that sustained this discourse, consumption excluded production, since insofar as women are "consumed," they cannot produce. If premodern societies generally tied women to home and hearth, a capitalist society founded on the promotion of production placed women at a particular disadvantage symbolically, materially, and legally—disadvantages that professionals set out to uphold. The strategies of distinction that professionalizing chefs pursued so energetically situated professional practice fully in the public sphere, where women's cooking had no place. The domestic associations of cooking with women led chefs to insist upon their corporate status all the more fervently. In his memoirs of various apprenticeships in the 1890s, including a stint with Escoffier, the son of one chef (or "culinary worker," as he puts it) noted the lack of respect for men doing a woman's job. When the other students laughed at another boy who declared his father a *chef de cuisine*, the youngster said nothing about his own father's occupation, proffering instead the far more dignified "property owner."[26]

These strategies relegated women to the culinary sidelines of domesticity. Nonetheless, Châtaillon-Plessis, author of *La Vie de table à la fin du XIXe siècle*

(Life at table at the end of the 19th century [1894]), had to acknowledge that "good cooks" could be found. No cook, however, could ever give the "attractions of form and content" that a chef alone could bring to an important occasion. Paternalism reinforced the condescension. Women needed protection from the "strenuous tasks that only a man can confront" (among which he included restaurant work); and in any case, professional cooking also required "elements of ingenuity that a woman would not know how to put into effect." About the same time, the chef Philéas Gilbert firmly drew the line between chef and cook. Writing for the professional journal *L'Art culinaire,* of which he was also the editor, Gilbert justified adding courses in "culinary theory" to the household management curriculum in girls' schools, and he set up other such courses for young women who had quit school. Even as he acknowledged women's instinct for cooking, Gilbert demurred on the grounds that "this instinct does not always go with the real knowledge which, in the last analysis, is the result of experience and practice." Like Carême, he focused his efforts not on the cooks themselves but on their mistresses: "The study of this science [of cooking] . . . is indispensable for those whose . . . modest means will require them at a given moment to take the household management in hand." For the nineteenth century and for many decades thereafter, women cooking meant women either cooking in home kitchens or directing those who did. Just as its respect for the gendered kitchen surely played an important role in the success of the École du Cordon-bleu, founded in 1890 to teach young women, failure most likely awaited those who sought to cross culinary lines. In 1891, promoters dropped the project of a professional cooking school for women because the subsidy promised professional organizations by the City of Paris concerned men only.[27]

Women's Cooking

Yet the all too familiar tale of obstacles and barriers does not tell the whole story. Things are not—and were not—so neatly disposed. Undeniably useful as a heuristic devise, with the triple sanction of tradition, convention, and the law behind it, a strictly gendered modern society neatly divided between a female private sphere and a male public sphere cannot account for the discrepancies between principles and practices that allowed women access to public space. The dominant exclusionary discourses have made it all too easy to take representations for unvarnished reality. Critics have not always appreciated the range of appropriative modes used by women to make their presence felt in the public social world; whatever the formidable barriers to meaningful female participation, agency has never been a male prerogative. Contemporary feminist critics focus on the ways that women made their presence felt in the

The Cook

In striking contrast with the chef's association with the city and his clear professional context, this female cook appears informally and in a rustic domestic setting, complete with vine-covered, slightly decrepit cottage and the distractions of a small child and caged bird. Without the title to the engraving, "Le cordon bleu," the term applied somewhat ironically to a good (female) cook, we might be hard pressed to identify the sweet young thing as a cook, and this despite the pile of game in the foreground and the vegetables at her side. Her primary function is further undercut by dreamy abstraction from her work as she listens to the song of the bird. This illustration surely nods to a growing domestic market for cookbooks and cooks. From *Les Classiques de la table* (2d ed., 2d printing, 1844). Courtesy Boston Public Library.

public arena. If women were not *flâneurs* who freely wandered about the city taking its measure, neither were all the women in public space prostitutes or easy marks despite a discourse that persistently made the equation. To be sure, (proper) women made few forceful claims to public space in French society, particularly political space. George Sand, for one, raised scandals, not the red flag of revolution. Still, very much like George Sand, under the best of circumstances, they infiltrated that space, working their way around the official absence of women from political life, the legal barriers to independent participation in professional activity, and the unilateral conjugal power structure made official by the Civil Code.

It may well be that our conception of *public sphere* is too narrowly political, tied as it tends to be to the claims of Jürgen Habermas and other theorists of modernity concerned with the development of an autonomous realm of political action. For a more commonsensical, simpler understanding of the public sphere as the social world outside the home, we do well to look to Michel de Certeau, for whom everyday life is the province of opportunistic tactics, of "making do," of "poaching" on otherwise forbidden territory. Resistance to hegemonic discourses and practices can never be publicly acknowledged. Unobtrusively, insidiously, resisters infiltrate what from the outside seems like a closed system. The very real limits of "making do"—absent effective political action, all the barriers remain in place—should not mask an equally real involvement in public life.

This understanding enables us to perceive the mobility hidden by a dichotomous discourse of "either/or." The modernizing city of a nascent industrial capitalism thrived on change. Not for nothing is frenetic movement a characteristic topos of urban life. Continually shifting urban life allowed women to move about in public, though differently than men. Working-class and lower-middle-class women went outside the home to work; elite women did so in pursuit of their domestic duties or personal pleasures. In addition, lower-middle-class women might very well be shopkeepers. Hence domestic duties secured niches for women in the larger social arena. If cooking kept them in the kitchen, it got them out as well. In one of the ironies of women's work, this archetypical domestic activity connected women vitally to the larger society. Françoise's kitchen in Combray overflowed with the "offerings" of the dairyman and the fruit and vegetable sellers, who often came from far away to supply this incomparable, and exigent, culinary deity (1:71/1:77). Her forays to the market near Combray and in Paris to get the best cuts of meat for her *boeuf mode* illustrate the ways in which food shopping brought working-class cooks in bourgeois households in contact with the foods and practices of different social groups.[28] The migration of both people and produce from the provinces to cities in the mid–nineteenth century increased the range of culinary contacts. Although the upper-middle-class Parisienne might not herself go to the central food market, still, like the mother of Proust's narrator with Françoise, she most likely supervised her cook, who did—precisely Carême's rationale for directing his work to women as well as to professional chefs. The contact was nonetheless real for being indirect or episodic.

In this as in many other domains, the larger social sense of domestic attachments that kept women out of the professional arena also supplied the vehicle through which they entered that arena—as nurses (if not doctors), as teachers (if not professors), and as cooks (if not chefs). Here, too, domesticity provided the ticket to public life in the literal publication of an indisputably female private space, the cookbook, which offered a vehicle of cultural appropriation. With the advent of the cookbook, like their English sisters if considerably later, French female cooks "went public." Pushing things a bit, one could even say that this development took a revolution, since the first French cookbook by a woman came out of the French Revolution and proclaimed its political allegiances—no longer to high and mighty patrons, as with cookbooks published over the seventeenth and eighteenth centuries, but to the new Republic. Mme Mérigot's *La Cuisinière républicaine, qui enseigne la manière simple d'accomoder les pommes de terre* (The republican cook, who teaches the simple way of fixing potatoes [1795]) staked out a female claim to cookery that became increasingly important as the nineteenth century progressed. Titles show the dominance of women as cooks and as authors. That Mlle Marguerite, author of *Le Cordon bleu* in 1834, should turn out to be the Horace Raisson who expressed such misogynistic comments only a few years earlier as A. B. de Périgord testifies to the place women were coming to occupy. Rather like romance novels today, which "must" have a female author, these works so tied to domestic economy needed the imprimatur of someone who knew what running a household was all about—a woman.[29]

Economy necessarily brings women into the picture. Although it was written by a man (Menon) and published anonymously, the *Cuisinière bourgeoise* (1746) was aimed at women's cooking, if not necessarily female cooks. In perhaps the most striking gender connection, Menon presents the text as itself a *cuisinière*. With this book he seems to be saying that the reader will not even need a(nother) cook, although the dishes certainly seem elaborate enough to require one. With the substitution of lowly potatoes for scarce and rationed bread, *La Cuisinière républicaine* gave a sure sign that frugality took precedence over gustatory pleasure. Over the nineteenth century, increasing numbers of similar cookbooks along with household management works targeted the domestic market, still more symptoms of the separation of spheres that marked so many other domains.

Take the cookbooks published over the century. In a sample of 14 years from the *Bibliographie de la France* beginning in 1811, when it began publication, to 1898, I found 70 cookbooks (see appendix B). Of these, only 11 books specify women as authors, and one of these, as we saw, turned out to be written by a man using a female pen name. But authorship gives little idea of the feminization of cookbook publication, primarily because many works were published anonymously while others carried only the initial and surname. The most revelatory gender sign surfaces in the titles that actively invoke women's cooking. Of the 70 titles, 41 are tied specifically to women and less than half that number, 18, to men. And the most popular cookbook of all, in reprints and knockoffs, was *La Cuisinière bourgeoise* (The bourgeois [female] cook).[30]

Here we can track another shift from the Old Regime to the new. As under the Ancien Régime, many of the male authors stressed their public status—*chef de cuisine* or *homme de bouche*, imperial or royal chef. Many other works insisted on economy and utility, as coded by "housekeeper" *(ménagère)*, "bourgeois cuisine," or "bourgeois cook" in their titles, thereby blurring the dividing line between male and female. Obviously female works such as *La Petite Cuisinière habile* (The clever little cook [1821]) were not the only ones to stress the practical and the economical. Finally, despite the bid for elite recognition made by his title, *Le Cuisinier impérial* (The imperial chef), Alexandre Viard's subtitle specified that this work offered recipes "for every purse"—and this as early as 1806. Economy sold. Insofar as ambitious chefs looked to a broad diffusion of their work, they could not afford to ignore a public whose scope compensated for its limited resources and proficiency. To make inroads into the domestic market, cuisine reverted to cooking, plain, simple, economical. Chefs also went back to being cooks. Consequently, readers got a taste of both worlds.

As the titles of these cookbooks make clear, women's cooking fits with de Certeau's arts of making do. The cook incarnates the *bricoleur* (tinkerer) as she sets her *savoir-faire*, her know-how, against the prescriptive knowledge, the *savoir*, of the recipe and the professionalism of the chef. Escoffier cites just this "making do" as a primary distinction between women and men in the kitchen: although *bricoleurs* may be admirable people, they don't make good cooks. The disposition that makes women such admirable domestic cooks, he explains, disqualifies them as professionals.

> A man is more particular over the various little details which are necessary to make up a really perfect dish. A woman, on the other hand, will manage with what she has handy. This is very nice and obliging of her, no doubt, but it eventually spoils her cooking. . . . One of the chief faults in a woman is her want of accuracy over the smaller items—the exact amount of flavoring, the right condiments to each dish; and that is one of the chief reasons why her cooking pales before that of a man, who makes his dishes preferable on all occasions to hers.

Still, Escoffier is no essentialist. Attention to detail is not inborn, it is learned—in places like his own kitchen, where he trained so many chefs. While he never went so far as to propose instructing women chefs (perhaps mindful of the failed attempt to do so only a few years previously), Escoffier nonetheless held out a glimmer of hope.

> When women have learned that no trifle is too small for their consideration, then we may find them at the head of the kitchens of the chief clubs and hotels; but until then there will certainly be at least one place where man can reign supreme.[31]

The professional adheres to standards that transcend the individual (*accuracy*, the *exact* amount of flavoring, the *right* condiments). Yet Escoffier himself knew full well that "making do" plays an important part in any good chef's culinary practices. A chef, he decrees, must never be caught unawares. The suicidal Vatel offered a pernicious example, absolutely off the mark for the true professional, whose honor consists in getting a meal on the table. If he had been in Vatel's place with no fish in sight, Escoffier comments in his memoirs, he would have done up chicken fillets as fillets of sole. The dinner would have been saved, with no one the wiser.[32] Although he most certainly would have rejected de Certeau's term, with all its implications of makeshift work, Escoffier, too, recognized that in the end, good chefing demands a practical sensitivity.

What, then, of women's cooking? How does the culinary division of labor figure in French cuisine? That there is a strong sense of gender relations is evident. Beyond what it says explicitly about cooks and chefs, the culinary division of labor assumed by French culinary discourse also feeds into the construction of a national sense of self. To the extent that culinary discourse in France is vitally concerned with the intimate relationship between cooking and country, the gendered division of cuisine operates on several planes at once.

Most visibly, the gendered discourse of French cuisine extols the home as a site of female culinary competence, a site that exists to counter male, elite, originally aristocratic foodways. Take the following assessment of the reciprocal relationship between elite consumption and domestic production. For Escoffier—the most influential French chef after Carême—the connection between elite consumption and domestic production reaches well beyond the court and the kitchen to lay the very foundations of Frenchness.

> For a country to have a good cuisine, it needs a long past of courtly life that leads people to appreciate the pleasure of a good meal among friends; it needs as well solid domestic traditions that transmit the secrets of good food from mother to daughter.[33]

In contrast with a French cuisine that exists above and beyond particular practitioners, women's cooking is prized for the attachment to the particular. As with regional practices, distinction derives from place. Despite the fact that dependence on place sorely circumscribed women's culinary achievements, late nineteenth- and early twentieth-century republican France actively promoted just this attachment to local venues and to the land. Curnonsky and Marcel Rouff's gastronomic tour of the French provinces emphasized the homey virtues, the farmer's wives who, like Proust's Françoise, were "artists" in the kitchen. As men of a certain age, they set themselves resolutely against the fast-changing, palpably modernizing world of the postwar years. They will not, they tell us in the introductory volume, say a word about the "cosmopolitan hotels," where one goes for "the Fox-Trott, the Two-Step and the Shimmy." For "Gastronomy is a Great School of Regionalism and Traditionalism," which, like the great artists, writers, and thinkers of France, "makes us feel, understand, and love the prodigious variety, all the fertile diversity, of French earth."[34] No shimmy here!

What might be called culinary republicanism also brought women into the national fold through domestic economy courses and culinary journals that aimed at the domestic economy market. The journals proposed a national culinary consciousness, and they did so through the publication of the regional. With an array of recipes at hand, the Breton woman could prepare a quiche lorraine as knowledgeably as her counterpart in eastern France, the Marseillaise housewife could serve up a savoyard potato casserole no less readily than a fish soup, from Provence garlic recipes could travel the length and breadth of France.[35] To what degree this integration actually occurred in everyday kitchens must remain a matter for speculation. But, increasingly, the models were there. Proust ties his cuisine to place, to family, and to the feminine. As I shall detail in the next chapter, the French restaurant chefs I interviewed a few years ago stressed the vital importance of the social relationships created by food, of generosity and conviviality—a lesson they all ascribed without fail to time well spent in the family kitchen. This is what Escoffier meant by "solid domestic traditions."

The printed word identifies the connections between these traditions of a lesser and greater cuisines, haute cuisine and *cuisine bourgeoise;* between a national construct and regional practices; between the traditional and the innovative. To return to my earlier Proustian example, Françoise and her cuisine need the *Recherche* to be known beyond the tables of Tante Léonie or the narrator's parents. Yet it is not far-fetched to submit that, in his turn, Proust needs the "incomparable recipes" (2:293/2:931), the "dishes discoverable in Pampille's delicious books" (2:792/2:521). He needs "this true poet" (3:546/3:29) to find the truth of his past. The recipes of regional cuisine, along with the chatty narratives that accompany them, emphatically reconnect a national, largely urban culinary space to local customs and practices. They establish culinary place, and in so doing they establish cultural space. The disadvantage under which women and their cooking labored pays off in unexpected ways.

French culinary discourse, then, fluctuates between cooking and chefing, the domestic and the public, the feminine and the masculine, the *bricoleur* and the *homme de métier*, the professional and the domestic. While this bifurcated discourse is by no means unique to France, this society, which has so strongly invested in culinary matters, gives it an especially clear and focused expression.

And what of culinary France? Is it best conceived as a hierarchy of culinary practices or a clearly defined rank order? Or, with its emphasis on the distribution and diffusion of people and practices, is geography or landscape the more apposite model? Is the ideal "chefing," steeped in the spectacular feast and dependent upon its quasi-military kitchen brigades? Or should we look to "cooking," to the comforting family kitchen and its female practitioner? Is it more useful to think of cooking as a craft or as a profession? Do the traditions rooted in local cultures, where recipes are passed down over many generations from mother to daughter, take precedence over the legacy of Carême and Escoffier, the modernity that prizes innovation and creativity? Should we see this culture in a set of culinary precepts or in the *tour de main*, the special touch of the individual, that owes little to principles and everything to practice? How does culinary France resolve the Pascalian opposition of the *esprit de géométrie* and the *esprit de finesse*?

We cannot resolve these tensions, but we are in a position to appreciate their underlying implications. The act of posing these alternatives gets us closer to the distinctive nature of a culture that lives its relationships to food so intensely. No one of these qualities, not even a pair, does justice to culinary France. We must take all of them into account. For together, whether in concert or in conflict, these predispositions sustain the heightened culinary consciousness that long set France apart from its neighbors. Not that France has a monopoly on choices between plain foods and fancy cuisine, cooking and chefing, the everyday and the festive, the recipe and experience, the professional and the amateur, the expert and the dilettante. They are the very stuff of everyday life. Like all modern myths, French cuisine draws power from its intimate connection to and careful articulation of the everyday. We make one choice or another as our tastes dictate or our moods vary, as the venue or the company shifts or the occasion demands. What sets France apart is that, more insistently, more ardently than elsewhere, its people express, weigh, and debate these choices not just as individuals shaping their private lives, but as public instances of representation, information, evaluation for the culture as a whole. Anyone who has spent much time in France knows just how easy it is to become a culinary convert. You do not need to be French to find yourself "acting French," criticizing or disputing judgments about food and defending others. Like the gastronomic field but on a broader, more diffuse scale, culinary France offers a site for the performance of things culinary. In that performance of those values and expectations, of those practices and precepts that this art entails, we all, French or foreign, make our contribution to a certain idea of France and Frenchness.

Consuming Passions

What of French cuisine today? Carême and his contemporaries would surely wonder at what has become of the culinary world that they did so much to define. Phenomena of every sort have transformed not only what we eat and how we eat it, but also how we think about the whole enterprise of cooking and eating. We can no longer eat—and, for the most part, we no longer *want* to eat—the way our parents did. In our turn, we wonder at the unfamiliar, alien culinary world of just two or three generations ago. Can we imagine working in a kitchen dependent upon the coal-burning stove that so damaged the health of the nineteenth-century chef? Then again, we know tastes that earlier chefs never dreamed of, so like Brillat-Savarin we might consider ourselves fortunate. By the same token, however much we might prefer a world without McDonald's, the twenty-first century does not give us the option. Losses counter the additions. We do not really know what Camembert tasted like forty years ago, much less this cheese as it first appeared in the Paris market at the end of the nineteenth century; and in the unlikely event that we resurrected a nineteenth-century Camembert, we would be tasting with twenty-first-century palates formed by a modern range of sensory experiences, which, willy-nilly, includes Big Macs and cheese made with pasteurized milk. The tradition-in-the-making over the nineteenth century, the integrity and the individuality that it both assumed and promoted, turns out to be exceedingly vulnerable. To appreciate what has happened to French cuisine in the past century; to understand our evident passion for consuming; in brief, to read the contemporary culinary landscape, we need to look at the factors that have reconfigured that landscape over the past one hundred years.

It is surprising, all things considered, not that the culinary landscape has altered so much but that it is recognizable at all. Consider the turbulence of the past century for France: two world wars followed by colonial wars in Indochina and Algeria that sealed the loss of empire; the exhilarating yet patently disruptive postwar economic boom that edged French society into modern times; the globalization of trade and the much-feared "Americanization" of French culture; the constraints imposed by both European Community regulations and U.S. trade policy; the increasing salience of foreign foodways; frozen and prepackaged food; and, more recently, genetically engineered food, not to mention mad-cow disease. Just listing these phenomena—many more could be added—suggests the fragility of the connections to time, place, and the practices of everyday life that shaped French cuisine from the nineteenth to the early twentieth century. The more France opened itself to the outside world, the more vulnerable French society became to exogenous practices and beliefs. Just as the integration of the provinces into the nation over the nineteenth century attenuated the uniqueness of local foodways, the increasing and increasingly complex links to European and international markets work to obliterate the distinctive features of any particular culinary landscape. Current debate in France unquestionably plays on the fears of losing a unique French culinary identity.

More than ever, practitioners of French cuisine must recognize its many contraries and balance them. They must confront national understandings with both international pressures and newly resurgent local traditions; they must weigh the claims of time-honored practices and products against those of new foods and innovative preparations; they must reconcile the very public spectacle of the restaurant with the understatement of the home kitchen, plain cooking with fancy chefing, the routine of the everyday with the extraordinary event, continuity with change. And while cuisine is by no means the only cultural product buffeted about by such crosswinds, the ephemeral nature of the culinary product leaves it exceptionally vulnerable to the effects of change.

Of these effects on the culinary world, the most far-reaching and certainly the ones that have most marked the culinary landscape are the spectacle of production and the internationalization of the exchange of foodstuffs and culinary traditions. Our postmodern society puts world cuisines on display on an unprecedented scale, media of every sort publicize them worldwide, and small-time entrepreneurs as well as multinational corporations market all things culinary. Billboards and advertisements, magazine spreads and television impresarios all spread culinary good news and, as it unfortunately happens, much bad news as well. Contrary to what one might expect given the frequently overwrought and downright tendentious rhetoric of globalization and its critics, this maximal display of the culinary has not destroyed indigenous traditions. What it has done is to modify profoundly the means by which those traditions survive in today's hectic, often confused world. Through it all, the tenacity of French culinary culture is one of its major attributes.

I. Conspicuous Cuisines

Dining on Display

A restaurant is an absolutely admirable center for sociological studies.
—Gilbert Le Coze, New York chef-restaurateur, 1991

The most striking feature of our contemporary culinary landscape is surely the ubiquity of what can only be called the culinary spectacle. More and more of us beam out images of food over an increasingly global food culture. If food has lent itself to culinary extravaganzas as far back as history gives us records, and probably well before, only in the last quarter century or so has spectacle come to dominate our eating order. For most of history and the vast majority of individuals, subsistence has dictated culinary horizons, and tt continues to do so today for most of the world's populations. Extravagance is, however, an entirely relative notion. Given the opportunity, the most impoverished will indulge in foods that take them beyond the rations of their daily fare, often in a spirit of celebration, occasionally with a mind set on transgression. In short, display precedes consumption. Extravagance for the wealthy proves equally relative. From antiquity to the present day, as any number of records can attest, culinary opulence can attain uncommon proportions. Kings, emperors, or simply the very, very rich have flaunted fabulous displays of rare foodstuffs, intricately presented, the better to astound and amaze. Every bite taken, every "oooh" and "aaaah" uttered, pays homage to the power behind the proverbial groaning board. Sumptuous banquets put the social stratification system on parade.

There is a hitch. The ephemerality and the individuality of food consumption restrict the numbers directly involved in the culinary enterprise and severely limit the exercise of its power. The problem of governance then becomes one of determining how such consumption can have an effect beyond the immediate confines of the dining table. How can a good as transitory as food be turned to greater social account? The most obvious strategy has been to expand the dining arena and multiply the diners. In 1814, Carême superintended an open-air banquet for some 10,000 French soldiers. Some three-quarters of a century later, in 1900, more than 22,000 French mayors dined together in Paris as guests of the Republic that they served. Every era and every society can adduce its own examples of this expansive commensality.

Adding spectators to the diners further mitigates the transience of the material good. The politics of display dictates that for some, dining becomes primarily, perhaps entirely, a spectacle. At times, "gastro-voyeurism" has become a matter of state policy. Roman hosts invited nondiners to convivial spectacles, which Plutarch likened to "a procession and a show." Spectators in Naples packed the theater to watch Nero dine in solitary splendor in the orchestra section while lesser Romans similarly used the banquet as a strategy of distinction to reinforce their control over their households and to set themselves apart from the rest of society. A millennium and a half later, Louis XIV, alone or with his family, regularly dined in full view of nondining courtiers. One banquet at Versailles records 134 spectators standing behind the guards: only when the royal party finished were the bystanders allowed to enter and eat up the leftovers. This custom of dining before nondining spectators continued well into the nineteenth century; as late as 1867 onlookers joined diners in the upper galleries at a banquet given by Emperor Napoleon III in the theater of the Tuileries Palace.[1]

A more effective means of extending the spectacle and the only way we know about these meals comes from textual account and visual representation. Words and images extend the dining experience in time and space. The symbolic record sends the repast well beyond the particular dining table. By breaking through the confines of time and space, that is, by moving the meal off the dining table and into the culture at large, these media turn the singular occurrence into a cultural phenomenon. The voluminous writings of the early third-century Greek writer Athenaeus take modern readers to lavish Greek feasts in many venues. Other writers, from Suetonius to Tacitus and Petronius, along with anonymous painters and artisans, make us privy to the Roman banquets that for centuries served as the archetype of luxurious food consumption. The advent of the printing press in the fifteenth century broadened the potential culinary audience immeasurably. The greater the numbers reached by these representations, the more extensive the social networks involved and the greater the implications for the eating order.

In the twentieth century the diffusion of prosperity stimulated an unprecedented societal demand for exotic foodstuffs and elaborate culinary preparations inconceivable on such a scale only a few decades earlier. As the systematic, socially valorized pursuit of culinary excellence, gastronomy is a modern pursuit, the gastronome a modern social status, and the restaurant the exemplary site for both practice and practitioner. Tied both to an older sensibility and to a newer commercial tradition, the restaurant evolved over the nineteenth century as the paradigmatic urban institution. The modern consumer frequented public restaurants rather than private banquets, and restaurants ended up operating a sea change in the fundamental modes of conspicuous consumption. No longer were the diners who patronized this modern eating establishment guests jockeying for dishes at a banquet or boarders who had to accept the menu of the day. Nor were they customers of a specialized food shop with a necessarily limited selection or travelers who had to take whatever fare the innkeeper might scare up. A number of specifically modern features set restaurant dining apart from other areas of food consumption and stamped it with the seal of the modern: a certain rationalization of dining (fixed prices, a written menu with standardized nomenclature); an anonymous yet public dining experience that set diners apart both from one another and from the restaurateur; and, finally, the personalized service that produced single meals of the diners' choosing.

Individuation of dining in the restaurant brought conspicuous consumption into modern times. At the same time that the restaurant reduced the scale of the exhibition, it diffused the discipline of consumption. Dining became more than ever a matter of savoir-faire. As Brillat-Savarin taught us, we all eat, but a far smaller number realize the higher accomplishment of eating knowledgeably and hence well. Like the other manifestations of conspicuous leisure analyzed so mordantly by Thorstein Veblen, flaunting one's savoir-faire signified power. The particularized performance of consumption was pressed into class service. Although Veblen did not fix on dining as a status marker, consumption of food supports his argument that the prominence of consumption changes the stakes and the nature of the social game. In the century since Veblen published *The Theory of the Leisure Class* in 1899, the mass media have made consumption incomparably more conspicuous. Although our own postindustrial, postmodern, globalized society has given it different roles to play, conspicuous consumption gives more than its share of support to the hierarchy of distinction.

As Veblen's analyses of upper-class behavior in late nineteenth-century America suggest, conspicuous consumption proposes an aesthetic and an ideology as well as a social strategy. The implications become clear when we consider what logic would lead us to call "inconspicuous consumption." Countering the very public spectacle of highly ostentatious repasts characterized by prodigality, inconspicuous consumption rests on an ethic of utilitarian modesty and an aesthetic of understatement. Associated with domestic consumption, that is, with private affairs that reject the flamboyant and the flashy, this ethic of moderation and discretion is the province of the traditional European bourgeoisie, the bourgeoisie that wore somber dress, ate soberly, lived discreetly; the bourgeoisie that kept to itself.

Inconspicuousness neither assumes nor requires invisibility. As discreet as we make it, this consumption, too, takes place in the public domain. A broad range of works in the eighteenth century, from the paintings of Chardin and Mercier's reporting on Paris eaters and eateries, to cookbooks such as the immensely and durably popular *Cuisinière bourgeoise* (The middle class cook [1746]), testifies to the visibility of such discreet consumption. For a good sense of the opposing aesthetics and rival ethics of private moderation and public display, we have only to confront the unpretentious workaday world portrayed by Chardin, with its ordinary kitchens and unadorned foods, with the worlds of elaborate display rendered by Watteau or Fragonard in that same France. Not that inconspicuous consumption was apolitical. To the contrary, inconspicuousness merely satisfied different needs and fulfilled other functions. The social and political roles engaged by inconspicuousness set its practitioners against conspicuous consumption and its practitioners, often aggressively so. Its censure made a powerful statement concerning society as a whole, a compelling judgment even when largely implicit. Divergent patterns of consumption expressed the fundamental antagonism between two conceptions of the social order. Bourgeois sobriety repudiated aristocratic extravagance just as the luxury of the nobility broadcast its disdain of middle-class moderation. Voltaire's verdict on the necessity of the superfluous ("Le superflu, chose très nécessaire") gave voice to the attitude and the values of an entire social class.

While it is easiest to identify in a highly coded, stratified society such as seventeenth- and eighteenth-century France, inconspicuous consumption remains part of the culinary scene. As in earlier times, inconspicuousness is a feature of public behavior. Sociologically speaking, whatever is not observable remains a dead letter, incapable of playing any role on the social scene. Hence what I have called inconspicuous consumption represents a choice among available modes of presenting the social self. Today, quite as much as in Ancien Régime France, though perhaps less noticeably, the choice between conspicuous and inconspicuous consumption presupposes resources to make those options real. Do we opt for the hominess of bistro "comfort" foods or for the lavishness of haute cuisine? The familiar or the culinary avant-garde? Do we prefer discretion over ostentation, sobriety over excess, prudence over profligacy? Or the reverse? Under what circumstances do we choose now the one, now the other? Our own habits and the temper of the times dictate behavior. As restaurateurs all over New York City will tell you, the excesses of the high-flying, big-spending 1990s yielded to post-9/11 restraint. In the wake of the devastating terrorist attack on the World Trade Center, New York diners flocked to neighborhood bistros.

Chefs, too, play the game of distinction, often flamboyantly so. Alternately parading and masking the enterprise, now advancing into the public arena with all flags flying and trumpets at the ready, now sounding a retreat from that world, cooking has joined the culinary spectacle. One of the most notable developments in modern times has to be the chef's rise to cultural visibility, an ascension that the past quarter century or so has rendered positively vertiginous. When the kitchen moves center stage, as it is doing more and more, the culinary spectacle deserts the dining table.

Such celebrity is all the more noteworthy because it is so recent. In many, probably most aesthetic spheres, producers in clearly low-status artisanal oc-cupations were kept to a low profile. The product received the attention. This cultural inconspicuousness is a logical consequence of the low social status of the artisan/artist or chef relative to his employer. Beyond the status gap, con-spicuous consumption not only presumes, it emphatically requires inconspic-uous production. The rationale is clear. With production out of sight, the spot-light falls exclusively on the elite consumer. The absence of competing activity amplifies the role of the consumer—the goal of the traditional culinary spec-tacle. Indeed, the conspicuous consumer depended upon the inconspicuous producer. Painters embarked on a long journey to become accepted as the in-dividual artists they aspired to be rather than anonymous artisans defined as they had long been by manual labor. Working as they did with far less "noble" primary materials than painters and creating an ephemeral product destined for the body, cooks were further subordinated to the aesthetic stratification that reproduced and reinforced social stratification.

On the whole, cooks—including chefs—were neither seen nor heard in public dining until postmodern times. Inconspicuous production governed traditional culinary production. In seventeenth-century France, just as the magnificent gardens at Versailles concealed complex feats of engineering, ar-chitectural planning, and horticulture under the insistently natural landscape, so culinary production operated as far as practicable from the site of culinary consumption. Upper-class households generally situated the kitchen well away from the dining area, in a separate building altogether, in a semide-tached wing or, at the very least, in the cellar. This separation of cooking and dining contrasted markedly, and by design, with the peasant kitchen-hearth, where a common fire served for heat, for cooking, and for conviviality. The eat-in kitchen of the contemporary city apartment reverses the progressive segregation of dining and cooking.[2] Chefs existed on stage only through the finished meal. There is, to be sure, the often-cited exception of Vatel. Yet de-spite the predisposition of later commentators to gloss his suicide as a heroic devotion to culinary duty, it is significant that dereliction, not achievement, occasioned the comment. Absent such a dramatic incident, few of us would have any notion of the prince de Condé's steward. Fewer still know the names of Condé's or anyone else's cooks, a far less exalted position. Only a truly ex-traordinary action could bring production to the fore.

Conspicuous Cooking

Like other artisans who aspired to the status of artist, chefs eventually emerged from the nether regions of their craft.[3] Legitimation for chefs came slowly, more slowly than for other artisans dealing with more "noble" materials. Skilled, conscious of his claims to culinary authority, the chef all the same remained subordinate to the markedly higher-status consumer. Bit by bit, however, chefs began to make claims on their own. With his tireless promotion of his culinary practice and his exalted conception of cuisine, Carême marked a turning point in the early nineteenth century, though cooking took a good long time to live up to the fervent proclamations of professional pride and singularity. *Gosford Park,* Robert Altman's film from 2001, gives us a recent exploration of this world in the English country estate. Staff, and that included the cooks, were servants, present through their work, not their persons. Their invisibility appeared all the more "natural" when the cooks were women.

The exclusion of women from the most public, upper reaches of the culinary world effected by professionalization over the nineteenth century is by no means entirely a thing of the past. Its hold remains particularly strong in elite French-oriented restaurants in France and wherever the French model supplies the standard. As a general rule and despite undeniable change, the "haute-er" one gets, the fewer women one finds.[4] The association of cooking with women and domesticity was a hindrance to professional status. Escoffier notes that when he started on the path to culinary glory in the mid-nineteenth century, elite society took little notice of the chef, whom they classed among the domestic servants. The incongruity of a man doing "women's work," the associations of cooking with filth both moral and material—all of these elements combined to keep the cook, albeit metamorphosed into a professional chef, well down the social scale from his customers.

The restaurant did not alter the relative positions of cook and consumer, at least not immediately. As readers of George Orwell's *Down and Out in Paris and London* (1933) will remember, cooking remained literally and figuratively "below stairs" in the fanciest of restaurants. Orwell found when he signed on to wash dishes that the faint of heart need not apply. His graphic descriptions depict the kitchen as an underworld of dirt, grease, and unbearable heat. From temperamental cook to lowly dishwasher, this world ran largely on drink, and those who toiled there rarely saw the light of day. How much things have changed is a matter for dispute. Orwell, one surmises, would feel quite at home in the culinary "underbelly" that the New York chef Anthony Bourdain has drawn of at least some contemporary eating establishments. On the other hand, one of the chefs whom I interviewed, Michael Romano of Union Square Cafe, claimed that reading Orwell determined him early on to have a very different kind of kitchen. No more than the customers in the restaurant where Orwell worked in the 1920s do diners in upscale restaurants think much about the conditions of food preparation.[5] Small wonder that Erving Goffman chose Orwell's depiction of the two culinary realms to illustrate the divide between front and back stage: the swinging door between kitchen and dining room sets an absolutely fixed boundary between two antithetical realms of darkness and light, production and performance.

> It is an instructive sight to see a waiter going into a hotel dining-room. As he passes the door a sudden change comes over him. The set of his shoulders alters; all the dirt and hurry and irritation have dropped off in an instant. He glides over the carpet, with a solemn priest-like air.

Orwell is amazed at the rapidity with which the waiter goes not simply from one room to another, but from one self to another. After an incendiary, scabrous exchange with a waiter, the visibly enraged maître d'hôtel

> entered the dining-room and sailed across it dish in hand, graceful as a swan. Ten seconds later he was bowing reverently to a customer. And you could not help thinking, as you saw him bow and smile, with that benign smile of the trained waiter, that the customer was put to shame by having such an aristocrat to serve him.[6]

"Above stairs," in the dining room itself, the culinary spectacle focused on the product, on the crêpes Suzette flamed in a copper chafing dish at table-side, on the peach melba nestled on a bed of sculpted ice like the mythical swan from *Lohingren* (Escoffier's image), or my childhood favorite, Cherries Jubilee (flambé canned dark cherries over vanilla ice cream). Escoffier invented the dishes and saw to their preparation, but it was the maître d'hôtel who served it with the requisite panache. The chef's long partnership with César Ritz points up the division of culinary labor. Escoffier ruled the kitchen, while Ritz, ever the consummate host, worked the front room. Of the drudges laboring in the insalubrious kitchen, surrounded by dirt and worse, the diner had no inkling. The chef fared little better. The renown of Escoffier, like that of Carême, remained an exception; even so, his reputation was also, and perhaps primarily, a professional one. He boasted that the two thousand or so chefs that he had trained in his kitchens in Paris and in London were scattered all over the globe where their culinary progeny practiced what the master preached. Escoffier's books on French cuisine carried his cuisine further, and one of them continues to be a reference in cooking schools today, in the United States as well as in France.

Among the signs of the rising visibility and prestige of the chef, we can count the various systems established for rating culinary establishments. The twenty-seven volumes of Curnonsky and Rouff's *La France gastronomique* (1921–28) inventoried regional dishes and singled out the most notable establishments for these specialties. They offered readers especial recommendations for restaurants as well as a more inclusive list of "adequate meals" *(repas convenables)*.[7] But it was the *Guide Michelin* that made culinary rating the national affair that it remains today and the international affair that the annual publication has become. As the automobile opened the countryside to tourism, the Michelin company seized the opportunity to promote its tires by providing culinary guideposts to the territory through which motorists would likely pass. First published in 1900, when it was distributed with purchases of tires, the *Guide Michelin* came onto the open market in 1920. A few years later, in 1926, the *Guide* began awarding stars for especial culinary excellence. The addition of two and three stars in 1931 created a system of culinary stratification in the virtually independent country of "Michelin France."

In contrast with the anti-urban, anti-modern fulminations of Curnonsky and Rouff, who abhorred the cosmopolitan hotel as the last place to look for good cooking, the *Guide Michelin* established a national hierarchy in which the urban centers, with Paris in the lead, were especially prominent. Quite like the national exams in the French educational system, the *Guide* renders its verdicts through a corps of anonymous inspectors. Convinced that the heart of French cuisine lay in what Americans would call the heartland, Curnonsky and Rouff took each province on its own terms, with its distinctive dishes and traditions. The *Guide Michelin* construed the country as a whole.

This national culinary geography copied the map of France without duplicating it. If the two shared a capital, since Paris claimed the lion's share of three-star restaurants, "Michelin France" fixed its own landscape. It rewrote the geography of France with its placement of culinary centers in otherwise out-of-the-way places—three stars, after all, proclaim that the restaurant is "worth a trip," and two stars advise the motorist to take "a detour."[8] Such promotion, and incentive, made the personalization of the restaurant inevitable. Restaurants in the provinces in particular were rooted in specific locations even as they transcended local products and traditions. Touring diners wanted to know as much as possible about any establishment that took them out of their way, much less one that incited them to make a trip for the express purpose of dining. And so the *Guide Michelin* came to list the name of the restaurateur-chef along with the signature dishes of the restaurant. Gastronomes and gourmets in the 1940s and 1950s flocked to Vienne for Fernand Point and to Saulieu for Alexandre Dumaine just as they went in the 1960s and 1970s to Collonges au Mont d'or for Paul Bocuse, to Roanne for the Troisgros Brothers, and to Eugénie-les-Bains for Michel Guérard, as they now make their pilgrimages to Annecy for Marc Veyrat and to Monte-Carlo for Alain Ducasse.

This personalization of culinary establishments coincided with the nouvelle cuisine of the 1970s—that is, the latest nouvelle cuisine to date in a line that stretches to the mid-eighteenth century, when the term first appeared.

The triumph of late twentieth-century nouvelle cuisine through a band of young chefs has been told many times. Like other such labels, this one was bestowed by journalists, in this instance Henri Gault and Christian Millau. More than any other single source, the *Guide Gault et Millau* formed a consciously avant-garde system of culinary stars and a public that brandished the flag for culinary creativity. This substantially altered culinary economy eventually promoted the chef well beyond the cultural visibility attained by Carême, Escoffier, and a few others. For a convenient modern benchmark we may take the Legion of Honor awarded in 1975 to Paul Bocuse, the outspoken patron of nouvelle cuisine beginning in the 1960s. Several of France's most celebrated chefs catered the award dinner hosted by the president of France in Paris, and Bocuse created a dish for the occasion (truffled chicken soup V. G. E., named for President Valéry Giscard d'Estaing), which immediately took a place of honor on the menu at his restaurant. That same year Bocuse appeared on the cover of *Time* magazine, and later became the first chef to be immortalized in the Musée Grévin, the French version of Madame Tussaud's gallery of wax figures of celebrated personages, both historical and fictional.[9] And, perhaps the ultimate accolade, Paul Bocuse can point to a rose that bears his name.

To attain such celebrity, the great chef has to be a great cook. But if there are a lot of great cooks, there are few stars. Preparing fantastic meals no longer suffices to propel a chef into stardom. Like Carême only with incomparably greater assets in play, today's top chef has to be a cultural entrepreneur of the first order. One needs only to consult the now-obligatory Web pages for any famous restaurant to see the range of activities and products that the truly successful chef must undertake. Cooking may be the center of culinary activity, but peripheral concerns loom larger and larger, at times threatening to overwhelm the kitchen. Top chefs today more often than not have several restaurants, and they cater to an ever more international clientele as well as corporate gift programs. Most maintain their Web sites in several languages.

As with the banquets of old, powerful media project the meal beyond the diners: newspapers; guidebooks, which proliferated with the rise of tourism in the nineteenth century and the automobile in the twentieth; increasingly glossy magazines such as *Gourmet,* which began publication in 1941; and a host of more recent entries in the culinary sweepstakes. Television programs undoubtedly make the strongest bid for public recognition of production. Culinary television programs in the United States began with James Beard's in 1946, but it was Julia Child's now-classic program on Public Television in the 1960s that probably did the most to raise the culinary consciousness of the American middle classes. Today's 24/7 culinary programming on the Food Network offers an extraordinary variety of shows. Cooking thrives as well on local television channels. Great Britain boasts a cable food channel in addition

"Is there anyone here who specializes in stress management?"

High-Tension Haute Cuisine

Any account of restaurant life will confirm that the kitchen is a frenetic environment where the staff races against time to get the meal on the table in apparent calm. Diners, sharply separated from the traditional kitchen, sit shielded from the intense pressures that necessarily go into the preparation of a fine but timely meal. This cartoon, with its call for help, signals the breakdown of that great culinary divide. Cooking and cooks are now often on view in the postmodern world of conspicuous cuisine. Cartoon by Edward Koren, *The New Yorker,* January 18, 1993. © The New Yorker Collection 1993 Edward Koren from cartoonbank.com. All Rights Reserved.

---

to the programs offered by BBC 1 & 2, at least one of which airs on the Food Channel in the United States (*The Naked Chef,* with its hip, working-class chef who preaches simple, "naked" ingredients).

This updating of the culinary spectacle has fundamentally modified relations between producers and consumers. Given the shift of focus from the consumer to the producer, the would-be conspicuous consumer in the restaurant must henceforth compete with the conspicuous producer in the kitchen for the authority to define the culinary experience. Since the demise of the patronage system, the market—in this instance the restaurant—creates a tension between chef and diner that can never be completely resolved. The customer may or may not always be right. (A sous-chef at one top New York restaurant recounted that when a customer sent back an exquisite wild salmon because she mistook its strong flavor for spoiled fish, the celebrity chef simply ended the meal then and there. There was no charge for what had been consumed, but the diners were "invited" to leave. This public triumph of knowledge over ignorance, of bona fide culinary authority over the well-provisioned pocketbook, brought cheers from the staff.)

As production moved to the fore as a feature of the restaurant experience, architects put kitchens where customers can see what's going on and who is doing what. Far from toiling in obscurity, chefs today work the front room, write books, and engage in promotional activities ranging from charity dinners to television shows. More than the finished product, the actual processes of production are what create the spectacle. The practice of cooking trumps the experience of eating. Production comes right into our living rooms as TV cooks chop, stir, and talk away, striving mightily to convey their excitement along with their expertise. For the excellence of the actual food, we have to rely on their words or our eyes. Seeing and listening prevail over tasting.

Entertainment alone cannot validate these cookery programs, which justify their existence through their communication of production techniques. A megapersonality such as Julia Child in the past or Emeril Lagasse (Lagasse's *Emeril Live* reigns as the most popular program on the Food Network) draws viewers. Another current celebrity chef is Mario Batali *(Molto Mario)*, who is recognized all over New York.[10] Yet for all their glitz and gab, these programs remain fundamentally a "show-and-tell-how-to-cook" enterprise. The basic instrumentality, the aim of improving the skills of the amateur cook, is clear if sometimes obscured by interactions with the studio audience. The only cooking program that currently airs on French television fits squarely in this "classical" category: *Bon Appétit, bien sûr* airs six days a week, just before lunchtime. The twenty-five-minute segment features top chef Joël Robuchon with a guest chef who prepares a single dish from start to finish. Practicality and doability, not extravagance and excess, are the watchwords (the voice-over indicates the cost of the dish per person). To be sure, the celebrity of the presiding chefs supplies an essential ingredient of *Bon Appétit, bien sûr.* It is, after all, television in the twenty-first century. Yet there is no doubt that reproduction in the domestic kitchen remains the primary objective of professional production.

At the far end of the spectrum of culinary shows stands *Iron Chef*, a Japanese cooking program that started in 1993 in Japan and attained cult status in the United States soon after it first appeared on the Food Network in 1999.[11] The first cooking program to appear on primetime on Japanese television, the

French Cooking and American Popular Culture

The French chef, symbolized in the United States by the television personality and cookbook author Julia Child, has reached deep into pop culture. The musical preferences of the gluttonous character of "Sarge" in the comic strip *Beetle Bailey* are in fact culinary ones. Child's theme song is literally food to his ears. Mort Walker, *Beetle Bailey,* 1996. Reprinted with Special Permission of King Features Syndicate.

exuberantly flamboyant *Iron Chef* marked a major departure from the discreet culinary norms of Japanese cuisine. Everything about *Iron Chef* screams unrestrained performance. The show sets up a culinary "battle" instigated by the Chairman of the "Gourmet Academy" who is dressed, like the chefs themselves, in an exotic outfit of brightly colored and lavishly embroidered silks. He is played by Takeshi Kaga, a well-known Japanese stage actor whose running commentary whips the live audience and its vast television counterpart into a high-intensity frenzy over the race of chef against time. The Chairman pits one of "his" Iron Chefs (Japanese chefs representing French, Italian, Japanese, and Chinese cuisine) against a challenger, a restaurant chef who is usually although by no means always Japanese. For heightened drama, one Iron Chef will occasionally battle another. In the hour of show time allotted for preparation, each contestant prepares a four- or five-course meal in the amazing giant Kitchen Stadium complete with fan-filled bleachers. Each meal is constructed around a single ingredient that is announced with much fanfare only at the beginning of the show (though strongly hinted at to the participants well in advance). Each side brings supporters. The host breathlessly commenting on every step of the preparation sounds like nothing so much as a sports announcer: Is the challenger looking worried? What is that weird-looking ingredient he is slapping into the wok? What in heaven's name is the Iron Chef doing with that frying pan? A panel of four tasters votes and comments on each dish in the meal constructed and cooked by each chef. The judges are mostly "laity"—actors and actresses, particularly young and attrac-

Garfield ® by Jim Davis

Cooking-Show Fatigue

The contemporary television cooking show involves millions of viewers in the activities of food production. A compulsive eater, the comic-strip cat Garfield is notorious for grabbing food wherever he finds it. Here, in his gluttony, he has turned his vicarious association with participatory cooking into a nerve-wracking endurance contest. Jim Davis, *Garfield*. GARFIELD © Paws, Inc. Reprinted with permission of UNIVERSAL PRESS SYNDICATE. All rights reserved.

---

tive, along with artists and politicians. Perhaps one of the panel has culinary expertise of some sort.

If the style of presentation is heavily influenced by the heated voice-over commentary of Japanese comedy routines and sports activities and by the fast-moving pace of video games, the outlandish costumes evoke the mediae-val castle and the defining fiction of the show. Like the culinary extravagan-zas of old, *Iron Chef* operates under the sign of excess, that is, spectacle. But moving producer and production center stage has changed the stakes. There are no consumers save the judges, and the product—the food to be con-sumed—disappears in the flashy production. For the most part, the dishes, both ingredients and techniques, lie well beyond the capabilities of the ordi-nary kitchen and the average cook. (One program featured a species of pig found only in a particular region of northern China of which only twenty or so could be found in Japan. Before the program neither the Iron Chef nor the challenger had ever worked with this meat.) As in the traditional culinary per-formance, the visual obliterates the gustatory. Where the consumer once ruled, the producer now triumphs. Cuisine has turned into a spectator sport. In place of the intensely private sensation of taste that sustains the individual act of eating, the culinary becomes an action show, viewed from afar. Is it any wonder that the savvy producer of *Iron Chef* should put the eager American fans of his program in the same category as the spectators at a professional wrestling show? The popularity of the show among eighteen- to twenty-five-year-old males renders the association more credible still.

Iron Chef

From cult program on the Food Network to upscale magazine, the spectacle of *Iron Chef* has conquered America. Millions watch the show, and the terminology has entered the general domain. But, as this cartoon makes clear, the *Iron Chef* phenomenon remains a spectacle. An Iron Chef cooking in a home kitchen is a humorous contradiction in terms. "Home cooking" and the sociability of the everyday have little to do with the frenzied culinary contest. The French chef cooks for a gathering of discriminating diners; the Iron Chef cooks competitively onstage for a panel of tasters. Both are deliberately removed from the everyday by unfamiliar ingredients, the extraordinary nature of their preparations, and their deployment of tools rarely found in the home. Cartoon by Roz Chast, *The New Yorker*, October 7, 2002. © The New Yorker Collection 2002 Roz Chast from cartoonbank.com. All Rights Reserved.

In the highly dramatic, aggressive market economy of the twenty-first century, where a show like *Iron Chef* can elicit such a strong response, cuisine entertains. Culinary consumption and production compete. We conspicuously consume the ever-more-ostentatious production of culinary purveyors, from television chefs to slick magazine layouts of exotic or exoticized familiar foods. Glitzy production has turned us all into gastro-voyeurs. One may object that a man wrestling a live octopus on a cutting board (voted the favorite *Iron Chef* episode) is still and all a different enterprise from two men wrestling in the ring. No doubt, but Toshihiko Matsuo, the producer of *Iron Chef,* unquestionably knows what he is talking about when likening the program to a battle. For what does *Iron Chef* resemble if not a food fight? A hyper-aestheticized battle, to be sure, but a food fight nonetheless. (The delights of transgression surely explain why *Iron Chef* is the favorite program of a five-year-old in my circle.) If his provocative piece on all-out wrestling is any indication, Roland Barthes would surely have understood this world of excess and ritualized violence. We neither have our octopus nor eat it either. We have our violence, and escape danger. Such spectacular food fights sublimate the aggression that lurks behind our most primitive desires, the aggression that attends our most apparently civilized behavior.

II. Identifying Cuisines

All of these developments take food further and further out of the kitchen. Because television and the Internet pay no mind to boundaries, they encourage cultural entrepreneurs, the Carêmes of the twenty-first century, "chefs without borders," so to speak, to operate on as wide a scale as possible. When the most celebrated chefs routinely set up a number of restaurants in addition to their starred flagship establishments; when young chefs apprentice back and forth across the Atlantic and the Pacific and seasoned chefs make the trips regularly as well; when a Japanese cooking program becomes a cult show in the United States; when we can find Maine lobsters in our local supermarket and order up foie gras from the Internet, we can hardly avoid confronting the global nature of contemporary culinary culture.

What, then, do we make of the new culinary identities? Where, and how, do we find French cuisine? Does culinary Frenchness exist with integrity today? What about the international prestige of French cuisine that once went without saying? From the seventeenth through the mid–twentieth century, great cuisine spoke French. Now it would seem to be no more than one of many culinary languages. Should we conclude, as many do, that French cuisine is no longer ascendant? That its glory days are gone forever? That its in-

"When you're on their flowers, you're a snail. When they want to eat you, suddenly you're an escargot."

French Culinary Hegemony

The French language defines the passage from raw to cooked. Here, as in so many other venues, the culinary *is* French. Language distinguishes between the ordinary and the exotic. Cartoon by Peter Steiner, *The New Yorker*, November 17, 1997. © The New Yorker Collection 1997 Peter Steiner from cartoonbank.com. All Rights Reserved.

---

ternational standing has slipped irremediably, never to be regained? Certainly, we hear no end of lamentation on this score.[12] In France as elsewhere in the postindustrial world, traditional foodways seem to be fighting a rear-guard action against successive invasions of snack and fast foods and genetically engineered foodstuffs along with national and supranational regulations. Observers of the culinary scene routinely cite the supposed destruction of tradition from the promiscuous mixing of culinary styles. The much-touted fusion cuisine of the 1990s, these critics complain, amounts to confusion cooking. Where is one to take one's stand?

The beginnings of modern French culinary culture provide some answers. Counterintuitive no doubt, the connections across two centuries should give us pause. For now as then, the internationalization and nationalization of French cuisine proceed apace. Then as now, national investment in culinary matters, both private and governmental, promotes a commitment with the aim of integrating culinary traditions into contemporary culinary culture in France. We will better understand the dilemmas in which French cuisine finds itself today when we understand the circumstances that laid the foundations for a new cuisine and the new culinary culture to go with it. Gastronomy came to the fore in the early nineteenth century under conditions that are not without parallels today. It would be astonishing if culinary culture did not change today as it did then.

The first parallel is the increased diffusion and the democratization of prosperity. Unprecedented economic growth beginning in the 1960s pushed French society into modern affluence. More and more people had access to the fruits of that affluence, and, given the prominence of the culinary in French society, cuisine and the culinary figured among their choices for leisure expenditures. As in the nineteenth century, urbanization continued to bring into city centers people and their foodways from near and far. Today, the transportation system that made Parisian gastronomy possible has expanded and accelerated as air freight and special messenger services join trains and refrigerated trucks to move produce ever more quickly from farm or fishing vessel to table.

As for the cuisine itself, the entrepreneurial activities that set a chef such as Carême apart now engage the profession as a whole—at least the part of the profession that aspires to greatness. In the highly competitive and aggressively international market of the twenty-first century, chefs simply cannot afford to stay in the kitchen. The genius of Paul Bocuse, like that of Carême, lay in his ability to promote at one and the same time himself, his cuisine, and his profession. Any chef with an eye on the culinary big time has to be heavily involved in promotional activities, from participating in international culinary competitions to publishing books, editing newsletters, writing newspaper columns, appearing on television, and taking part in charity events. It is imperative to maintain cultural visibility. For the losing no less than the winning contestant, an appearance on *Iron Chef*, for example, gives a big boost to the chef's restaurant. Challengers regularly add their *Iron Chef* meal to their restaurant menu. And finally, as in early nineteenth-century France, culinary texts and images multiply at an accelerating rate. If this proliferation of representations spreads the culinary good news, by the same token, the sheer volume of these representations intensifies competition, prompting more representations, more images, and more texts. Contemporary culinary culture is nothing so much as an intense media force field. It is symptomatic of the pres-

sures on high-profile chefs and their dependence on the media that the suicide of Michelin three-star chef Bernard Loiseau in 2003 prompted a debate
over the undue effect of criticism from well-placed gastronomic critics.[13]

These conditions, which were concentrated in France in the nineteenth
century, now span the globe. Consequently, an international culinary culture
has emerged whose contours are constantly shifting because its populations
are on the move. Unlike traditional cultures, culinary and otherwise, this one
is not tied to, or necessarily associated with, a particular time and place. On
the contrary, culinary culture today proves exceptionally mobile. Raw materials and finished products, producers and consumers alike all move about
with a notable absence of restriction. "What's regional? What's local?" chef
Charlie Trotter asks, and proceeds to answer his own question. "It's irrelevant.
Should Charlie Trotter's, this Chicago restaurant, be serving anything from
the ocean? . . . I don't know, but if you can get the stuff. I defy anyone from
Maine to serve better swordfish from Maine than we can. I don't care if
they're right there. We get the stuff 24 hours out of the water. I get fish faster
from Maine than I do from Wisconsin."[14] This mobility should not lead us
down the garden path of globalization. What we are confronting here is not
globalization so much as it is internationalization. All too many commentators
apply *globalization* indiscriminately for all trans- or supranational markets, so
much so that the term functions as shorthand for modern markets. There is a
world of difference between globalization proper, that is, the (re)production
of an identical product in a vast range of countries in the world, and what I
prefer to label *internationalization,* for the marketing and consumption of a
singular product from a particular location across national lines. Whereas
McDonald's supplies the paradigmatic example of globalization for the food
industry, it has nothing to do with the marketing of the local and the singular
by culinary entrepreneurs all along the line, from the farmer to the chef.

A top French chef, Alain Passard, supplies the operative term of explanation—passport. In 2001 with a good deal of fanfare, he announced that he
would no longer serve meat at L'Arpège, his (Michelin) three-star restaurant
in Paris, and henceforth would work solely with the fruits of the land and the
sea. Passard's concentration on less marked, more delicate tastes requires
more sustained attention to the foodstuffs. We chefs, Passard explained, work
with identities. Every product, not excluding the lowly carrot, has an identity,
and we need to know that identity in order to cook creatively. Just as the label on every bottle of wine declares its origin, so we need a passport of origin
for that carrot. The chef needs to know where it is from, where it has been,
and under what conditions. Like many other chefs, Passard knows most of his
suppliers personally. He knows their products, conveys his requirements to
them, and urges them to alter production on occasion. Ten years earlier,
Daniel Boulud in New York made the point that the issue for a chef was not

how much to create but how to obtain quality products and know the origins of these products. To assure himself and guarantee the diners at L'Arpège of the exactitude of this origin, Passard cultivates the local to the point of going himself on the boats that supply his fish. Well beyond specifying that the sole comes from the Atlantic off the coast of France, he can pinpoint the specific part of the Atlantic where the fish was caught. In other words, he verifies the sole's passport. Passard is by no means alone in this attention to the details of provenance. Eric Ripert, the executive chef at New York's Le Bernardin (four stars from the *New York Times*), has his own farm on Long Island that supplies him and several other chefs in Manhattan with organic produce. David Bouley, another acclaimed Manhattan chef and uncommon culinary entrepreneur, visits his suppliers by private plane and once envisaged selling organic produce retail.[15]

It will be objected, quite correctly, that only a high-profile chef with a substantial bank account can afford such obsession with the local. But the local, the authentic, and the singular sell well beyond the exploits of chefs on the culinary cutting edge. It is impossible to count the Web sites and catalogues, magazines and newspapers that peddle the authenticity of produce or the singularity of the product. From cheeses to flavored vinegars, from baked goods to cured meats, these goods purport to reattach us to the local or to the artisanal and personal. The sea salt from France carries the name of the salt gatherer *(saulnier)* responsible for the little box on the counter. McDonald's markets invariability—a Big Mac is a Big Mac is a Big Mac—in contrast with advocates of the local, who accept and for that matter extol the vagaries in nature and human agency.[16] Clearly, that variability has its limits, and culinary products and producers take their stand along a continuum that runs from reproducibility to unicity. A totally singular creation would take us into the realm of high art. Hence the artisan promises to deliver consistent quality, somewhere between the uniform and the unique. The importance here lies in consistency promised and produced.

All cooks position themselves and their work on the same continuum of reproduction and production. There can be considerable variation within a single meal that may well mix prepackaged, canned, and frozen foods mixed in with made-from-scratch dishes. Who these days doesn't make use of canned Italian plum tomatoes? Where does one draw the line? Carême himself was proud of making the culinary enterprise easier with any number of innovations, and surely no one is about to impugn either his commitment or his creativity. American cookbooks have come a long way from the first edition in 1931 of *The Joy of Cooking,* with its liberal use of canned soups to make complicated sauces. As committed as we are to fresh, "natural," "authentic" ingredients, no cook operates without shortcuts of some sort.[17] Every chef, every cook, moves back and forth along the continuum. Celebrity chefs themselves expand their expertise into domains that are far removed from the singularity that sustains their reputation, venturing into the land of prepackaged foods. Like Carême, who boasted of his time-saving stock concentrates, and Escoffier, who marketed bottled sauces under his name, chefs today look to the kitchens beyond their restaurants. Do the vacuum-packed meals marketed in French supermarkets by top chefs Paul Bocuse and Joël Robuchon betray their culinary ideals? Or are they a means for diffusing at least some of the qualities of haute cuisine to a population who will never dine in their restaurants? Remember, too, that Carême wanted every citizen "in our beautiful France to be able to eat delicious food." The answer to the question necessarily is both. The cuisine of shortcuts and convenience foods is not at all the same as what is presented in a top restaurant. Nor does it claim to be. Yet both cuisines, both sets of culinary practices, operate in the same universe. To be sure, they occupy different places in that universe, but the geography is known to all.

In transporting people and products across borders so readily, modern means of communication and transport have fashioned an international coterie of gastronomes attentive to the local product and the creative chef. The transnational reach of gastronomy is not new. The luxury hotels that developed in the mid-nineteenth century already catered to an international clientele. Nelly Melba, the soprano for whom Escoffier invented Peach Melba, was Australian. It was just this international culinary culture that prompted Curnonsky and Marcel Rouff to write twenty-seven volumes on gastronomy in the provinces, far away from the extravagances associated with the complicated, contrived cuisine of fancy hotels catering to a sophisticated clientele. The international gastronomy of today differs from its ancestor in its relatively broad diffusion of gastronomic practices. One does not have to be a ravishing soprano to move about in exalted culinary circles (although, as Renée Fleming can attest, it doesn't hurt).[18] The dissemination of haute cuisine keyed to the increase in prosperity in postwar Europe and America led more and more people to travel both more frequently and farther from home. The resulting expansion of culinary horizons and increase in the means to indulge one's fancies in turn produced a demand for quality. In France, for example, the consumption of better wines (the *appellations contrôlées*) has increased significantly over the past half century.

For Americans in particular, such demand for culinary quality represents a real shift in cultural priorities. We have come vast distances since Benjamin Franklin exhorted his countrymen to abjure the pleasures of the table and set their minds on higher things. Franklin's father conceived of dinner as a pedagogical opportunity. The pleasures of the palate did not enter into the equation.

At his table he liked to have, as often as he could, some sensible friend or neighbour to converse with, and always took care to start some in-genious or useful topic for discourse which might tend to improve the minds of his children. By this means he turned our attention to what was good, just, and prudent in the conduct of life; and little or no notice was ever taken of what related to the victuals on the table—whether it was well or ill dressed, in or out of season, of good or bad flavour, preferable or inferiour to this or that other thing of the kind.

Quite predictably, this negative culinary education resulted in a lifelong lack of concern about food. Franklin boasts of this indifference, which, pre-sumably, allowed him to focus on more important, intellectual pursuits.

I was brought up in such a perfect inattention to those matters as to be quite indifferent what kind of food was set before me, and so un-observant of it, that to this day I can scarce tell a few hours after din-ner of what dishes it consisted. This has been a great convenience to me in travelling, where my companions have been sometimes very unhappy for want of a suitable gratification of their more delicate, be-cause better instructed, tastes and appetites.[19]

The quasi-iconic status that Franklin's *Autobiography* long enjoyed in Amer-ican society gives this attitude more than individual interest. He was presented as a model for Americans, who were to turn their thoughts to serving their country, not satisfying their desires. The pleasures of civilization could wait.[20] What, one wonders, did Franklin make of French dining during his time in Paris negotiating the Treaty of Paris in the 1780s?

The sensual pleasures were habitually associated with France and with the aristocratic society that the young United States worked diligently to best. Americans with experience of France—Thomas Jefferson offers the prime ex-ample of rampant francophilia among the Founders—would judge the Amer-ican culinary scene rather differently. James Fenimore Cooper, the immensely popular author of the Leatherstocking tales, lived in France from 1826 to 1833 and had this to offer about his fellow countrymen's foodways:

There is a familiar and too much despised branch of civilization, of which the population of this country is singularly and unhappily ignorant: that of cookery. The art of eating and drinking, is one of those on which more depends, perhaps, than on any other, since health, activity of mind, constitutional enjoyments, even learning, refinement, and, to a certain degree, morals, are all, more or less, connected with our diet. The Americans are the grossest feeders of any civilized nation known. As a nation, their food is heavy, coarse, ill prepared and indigestible.[21]

When we recall that the France that Cooper knew was the country of Carême, Brillat-Savarin, and Grimod de la Reynière, the France where Fourier promoted gastronomy to the higher realm of gastrosophy, and the Paris of elegant restaurants, we have a sense of the implied comparison of Cooper's appraisal with the gulf separating America and France. It is surely revelatory of his distance from his native land that Cooper refers to Americans in the third person ("their food").

The country that made so little of culinary achievement and lived by Franklin's culinary indifference does not lie so very far in the past. Chefs who arrived in New York from France in the 1950s and in the 1970s are clear that the supposedly sophisticated culinary enclave of Manhattan had little recognition of what fine French cuisine was all about. For André Soltner of Lutèce, who had worked in Paris restaurants in the late 1950s, New York was "like the desert." For him, as for many others, the biggest change in the culinary scene in the subsequent thirty years was the sophistication of the public, which now understands and appreciates, among other things, the difference between fresh and frozen sole. David Bouley, who had worked with top chefs in France before starting in New York, saw a big difference between New York and France in culinary matters as recently as 1991. When he began working in New York restaurants in the 1970s, Bouley affirmed categorically, the distance was immense. He wasn't even convinced that the executive chef at Le Cirque at the time had eaten in a Michelin three-star restaurant, much less worked in one.

Times clearly have changed. The United States has come a long way since Cooper consigned Americans to the culinary lower depths and André Soltner was laboring to create an oasis in a culinary desert.[22] If contemporary international culinary culture in many respects obscures once characteristic national traditions, does that mean that these no longer exist? Can we assume that the Americans who consume Hudson River foie gras with delight do so in the same way as the French who eagerly await the Christmas season marked by the arrival of fresh foie gras in Paris markets? Nothing is less clear. For Americans, foie gras, even when locally made, remains an exotic product. For the French, the same dish belongs to the national culinary patrimony, a tradition of consumption that marks the season.

Just like nationalism generally, culinary nationalism continues to flourish in the twenty-first century. There is not only the sentiment of difference, of pride in indigenous traditions, but also very real differences in the practices themselves. The French difference has less to do with the quality of food or the level of culinary creativity than it does with the investment that the country makes in the culinary. Governmental intervention usually amazes the American observer, who acknowledges disease prevention and the balance of trade as proper reasons for governmental regulation of food, but most likely judges the French concern with regulating quality puzzling at the very least. Unquestionably, economic motives drive a goodly share of governmental investment. Thus, the wine growers' call to showcase their wines at the World's Fair in 1855 led to the classification of Bordeaux red wines that, with a slight amendment in 1973, we consult today. Louis Pasteur's *Études sur le vin* (1861) responded to an official commission from a Napoleon III worried about falling wine exports to Great Britain. Instituted in 1905, the elaborate system of Appellations d'origine contrôlées was revised considerably over the years to become more precise guarantees of quality as well as origin. Although the control is most evident and most elaborate in the case of wine, foodstuffs, too, fall under this surveillance of quality.[23] Since the 1920s, the annual and extremely competitive Meilleur Ouvrier de France (Best craftsman in France) competitions have created an aristocracy of talent in a range of culinary activities such as pastry, cheese, and other components of the meal. More recently, consciousness of the threats to indigenous traditions posed by globalization and modernization more generally has prompted private and public initiative and the establishment of culinary manifestations such as the Semaine du goût (Week on taste), the Centre National des Arts culinaires (National center for the culinary arts), and the Patrimoine culinaire/Sites du goût (Culinary patrimony/Places of taste), which identifies culinary landmarks—for example, the site where Roquefort cheese is made—worthy of preservation.

It is true that cuisine in its many forms is a significant French export. But French investment in the culinary reaches well beyond its tangible return. Although cuisine in France carries economic capital, it also, and more importantly, carries considerable symbolic capital. Like literature, cuisine is an elite pursuit, and these elite associations, again like literature, turn cuisine in its higher forms into an acknowledged cultural value. Recognition follows: Paris named a street for Carême near Les Halles (it disappeared with urban expansion and renewal in the twentieth century), another for Brillat-Savarin, another for Escoffier. The square in front of the Troisgros Restaurant in Roanne bears the name of Jean Troisgros, one of the two brothers who transformed their father's small local restaurant into a temple for gastronomes, inaugurated by President François Mitterrand, noted for his interest in food in general and fidelity to French cuisine in particular. (Charlie Trotter reported that when Mitterrand came to San Francisco in the 1980s, the Michelin three-star chef Alain Chapel came for a week just so the French president could have proper French cuisine; and when Mitterrand died, his favorite foods and restaurants figured prominently in the obituary spreads.) Like several top chefs today, Escoffier was named to the Legion of Honor—a recognition that is no more than just, given his conception of the culinary arts as "one of the most useful forms of diplomacy."[24]

Although contemporary French chefs may not express themselves in the same way, they, too, consciously serve their country. Alain Passard cited his appearance on *Iron Chef* as a means of representing France on the international scene. Daniel Boulud initially worried about opening his own restaurant in New York, because he wanted it to be worthy of his country. He wanted to do "something prestigious, something very French," because he considered it his role to "defend France here." And for Boulud, defending "the glory of one's country" means not becoming Americanized but staying "very French" and getting "as close as possible to the prestige that gastronomy is in France by doing it in New York."

III. Tasting France

Omnivores are anxious eaters.

—Diane Ackerman, *A Natural History of the Senses* (1990)

For us both as individuals and as collectivities, food choices matter enormously. Because we are omnivores—*homo sapiens* can eat any food—we have a daunting range of comestibles from which to choose, and it is a plethora of which few of us have any idea. Such a cornucopia of possibilities creates its own dilemmas. Among other things, choice makes us anxious eaters. Food, we know from experience, can be poison. So we worry whether the mold on the cheese will do us in or if the chocolate brownie that we crave contains the nuts that set off a life-threatening allergic reaction. As one astute and rather disabused observer of restaurant kitchens observed, eating is an act of faith. Perhaps what should surprise us is just how much faith we have, and how readily we put our lives on our forks.[25]

Despite the importance that health concerns have for us as individuals (and for governmental watchdogs), food anxieties turn out to be as cultural as they are physiological. We may agonize if our convictions forbid us to consume what is before us on the plate. We may also wonder how our food choices affect the environment, from the small-time farmer to the multinational corporation. We cannot avoid this disquiet; we do, after all, need to eat. At the same time, malaise in face of the unknown has its flip side. For though diet holds dangers, it also promises delight, and it is precisely this promise that turns omnivores into eaters that are as hopeful as they are apprehensive. Across class and national boundaries, we eagerly await the pleasures of the familiar food and excitedly anticipate unknown tastes. On the whole, it is striking that we consume so many foods so readily—looking forward to something wonderful prevails over the fear of something dreadful. Whether or not we actually verbalize our relationship to food, we concede with Brillat-Savarin that the pleasures of consumption touch us all: "The pleasure of the table is for people of every age, every condition, every country, and for every day." [26]

If we as a species have the capacity to eat any food, as individuals we cannot do so. It is not just that we omnivores are able to choose our foods, it's that we must do so. We are obliged to pick and choose, express preferences, compare foods, reject some, and accept others. Practical considerations limit those choices. Only a certain range of foods is actually available at any given moment, partly because of the vagaries of food supply and, even more so, because of what our culture defines as good to eat. More than the foods available, those assessments, the judgments about what is edible and what is not, determine the selections that we make. These choices shape our individual and collective selves. The array of food choices open to each of us supplies a cultural space in which we see ourselves and our difference from others. Every mouthful constructs as it performs culinary identity. A linguistic analogy helps sort out the levels on which we operate simultaneously. Our idiosyncratic culinary identity is somewhat like a culinary "idiolect" that designates the very particular ways each of us "speaks" food and our food choices.

Beyond this individual food discourse or idiolect we also belong to many groups, and each of these has its way of speaking food; that is, it is a culinary sociolect. Typically families speak, or practice, more or less idiosyncratic culinary sociolects. The local setting also connects with regional and national culinary languages. The fate of distinctive culinary languages and of the foodways that put those languages into practice is very much a concern today. How, then, do we sum up culinary France today? What distinguishes French culinary culture in the twenty-first century? Do French culinary traditions hold their own against the uniformity threatened by globalization, and if they do, how do they do so? How do the developments discussed above—conspicuous culinary production, the internationalization of the culinary—affect the traditions handed down from the nineteenth and twentieth centuries?

An Art of the Everyday

If not as exotic or as fabulous as it once appeared to many outsiders, culinary France remains a place apart. It is a place that we readily identify as French.

What we might call the culinary personality of France has to do with a noteworthy ideal of French culinary culture: the incorporation of culinary excellence into everyday life. The tension between the two terms of the equation—haute cuisine and everyday cooking—pits knowledge against practice; it sets *savoir* against *savoir-faire*. Cuisine is an art, and nowhere more insistently than in France; but, as Michel de Certeau put it, it is at the same time an art of the everyday, an art of making do.[27] Exclusive as haute cuisine may be—and exclusivity is, after all, part of the definition—it belongs to the same culinary culture as the neighborhood open-air markets available to all comers. High and low are first and foremost concerned with quality, which means that both do battle against culinary mores that put quality at risk.

Gourmets around the world look to French culinary culture for its insistence on cuisine as at once an art, a craft, a profession, and a way of life. There is perhaps no better example of this multifaceted culinary ideal than the central event of Marcel Rouff's *La Vie et la Passion de Dodin-Bouffant-Gourmet* (The passionate epicure [1924]). Conceived by Rouff as an homage to Brillat-Savarin, Dodin-Bouffant (*bouffer* means "to eat up") comes to us as the consummate gourmet, an individual who lives to eat and to eat extraordinarily well. He is most assuredly, as the title of the English translation confirms for us, a passionate epicure whose reputation for culinary intelligence has spread far beyond the small provincial town where he consumes legendary meals with the few friends who have passed gastronomic muster. One day, a foreign prince and would-be gastronome appears in the town and has the temerity to invite Dodin to dinner. It is something of a challenge, a disciple laying a bet that he can outdo the acknowledged master. The prince serves a repast that is both extraordinarily lavish—it takes almost four full pages to detail the many dishes and the wines (thirty-three in all) proposed for each course—and highly complex. It epitomizes the elaborate international cuisine found in "les palaces" avoided at all costs by Dodin's creator. Dodin judges the meal very severely. "Abundant, rich, but without light and without clarity," the repast has "no air, no logic, no line, . . . no rules, a parade, but no order." Even more appalling are "certain shocking solecisms in the composition of dishes and the order of succession of flavors." It becomes clearer with every morsel Dodin tastes that the prince's "desire to shine" patently takes precedence over a "sincere search for harmony." The uniformity of overly complicated "criminal" sauces has stifled "the divine perfumes of nature." Dodin's final judgment is categorical. He goes so far as to doubt that this meal could call itself cuisine. "For Iroquois, for princes, for Germans. Not for us."[28]

Dodin decides to give the prince a lesson. Accordingly, he serves a "simple" menu of dishes emblematic of French cuisine, dishes that emanate from the land, dishes that have been lovingly prepared by his incomparable cook, a woman who knows the land intimately. Eight lines suffice to detail the six dishes and five wines; their simple names contrast starkly with the high-sounding dishes served by the prince. The soup, "very complex and thought through," recalled the charms of a painting by Greuze, and then again the strong tones of Ribera, along with an "unexpected tenderness" that evoked Leonardo da Vinci. Rouff finds another analogy for the arrangement of this soup in the development of a sonata, "where each theme keeps its own identity and taste fused in the power and harmony of the whole." Almost as an afterthought, he gives us the ingredients: beef and vegetable bouillons to which has been added a mixture of mushroom and asparagus, a bit of chicken bouillon, beaten egg yolks, and, floating on top, artichoke hearts stuffed with a mixture of carp roe and mushrooms in cream. Crowning the soup are tiny croquettes made of shrimp tails and melted cheese.

As centerpiece to the meal, Dodin proposes a pot-au-feu, plain, ordinary boiled beef. The friends in attendance are thunderstruck by his audacity in offering such a quotidian dish to such an exalted personage, while the prince in his turn wonders how to take the insult of being served a dish that, in his household, would not have left the servants' hall. Of course, the boiled beef that Dodin serves the prince is neither plain nor ordinary, and, like the soup, it is definitely not simple. It is the touchstone of what cuisine should be all about.[29] Neither is the meal excessive, although contemporary readers may well find the descriptions of the dishes far more complex than their culinary experience can comprehend. Within the novel, however, culinary excess marks the prince's meal, not Dodin's. The point is that everything comes together in the repast that Dodin puts together. Nothing is an add-on merely for show. Slowly, as the meal unfolds, the prince comes to understand the errors of his culinary ways, and, for the first time, dining brings him the contentment of being not a prince but "simply a man." Unlike the extravagant dinner that he had served, featuring dishes with no roots that came from everywhere and belonged nowhere, his host serves dishes of French cuisine, true French cuisine, tied to the earth from which it came. "French cuisine came out of the old gallo-latin soil, the smile of its fertile countryside."

Rouff's choice of pot-au-feu as the sublime dish that wins the culinary battle of the century is hardly innocent. For, although boiled beef is found in many cultures, its French version, the pot-au-feu, stands for France itself.[30] In this tale published in the aftermath of World War I, Dodin's dinner defends the country. The culinary nationalism that Rouff articulates most clearly in the preface—which he significantly calls a "Justification"—surfaces throughout the book. Thus, the wine of Châteauneuf-du-Pape that accompanies the soup sonata "blew into the soul . . . all the sunshine it had stolen, all the fervor of that baked earth of the Rhône Valley, its spiritual homeland."[31] The soup proposes an ideal for the country, where the parts sustain and are subordinated to a national identity even as they retain their distinctive qualities. "There was a single taste, but each part of this taste kept its individual and natural taste."

When obliged by his doctor to take a strict cure at a German spa, Dodin and his cook, now his wife, find the food in Baden-Baden utterly inedible, an affront to French sensibility and physiology. Dodin does not mince words, and Rouff only somewhat facetiously entitles the chapter "Dodin among the Barbarians." The French soul and body alike reject the heavy German dishes smothered in viscous sauces or overwhelmed with acrid cabbage. When the author of a work with the incongruous title of *Metaphysics of Cooking* declares that the Ideal of Cooking alone counts and that his goal is to pull cooking out of "the rut of materiality" and set it on the path to a Platonic Idea, Dodin vehemently dissents. He does so in the defense of the most fundamental principles of French cuisine. Cuisine, Dodin believes with every fiber of his being, is a physics, not a metaphysics. The "nobility," the "grandeur," and the "luminosity" of French cuisine are fixed in the real, not the ideal; in the material, not the ethereal. Of course, little is needed for culinary nationalism to veer into culinary chauvinism. More directly than the comeuppance that he administered to the prince, Dodin's lesson to the Germans reassures the France of 1924 that, whatever the losses sustained in the war, France remains whole, its cultural integrity entire, its culinary superiority not only unchallenged but unchallengeable.

The ascendancy of French culinary culture and its historical grounding are made perfectly clear in Rouff's portrait of Dodin-Bouffant, the man who consumes correctly. To be correct, the gastronome must first understand the law of the stomach—*gastronomie*. Knowledge of eating depends less on the moment of pleasure in the act of tasting and much more on the conception of what taste should mean. As Dodin puts the matter, this knowledge requires logic, line, rule, and order. It requires, in sum, a regulated cuisine that is understood by all parties. Moreover, the total effect of Dodin's lesson mimics the course of French history. An aristocratic desire to "shine" on the part of the ignorant guest must give way to the "sincere search for harmony" of republican culture. Even more to the point, monarchical proclivities for opulence and display must give way to an enlightened understanding of true enjoyment. Dodin's meal converts the guest who is just learning how to eat from a prince into "simply a man," but a "knowing" man. To those who understand, like Dodin and his model Brillat-Savarin, the meal realizes the republican ideal of liberty, fraternity, and equality.

Here and elsewhere, French cuisine succeeds because it reaches for a standard in "contentment of being" that everyone can recognize. But Rouff's story of Dodin-Bouffant also contains warnings that mirror the anxieties of French culinary culture. The gastronome in this tale is not entirely well and must travel for his health, and when abroad, he raises a vital issue: is French culinary culture exportable? Dodin's triumphant pot-au-feu comes out of "the smile of [France's] fertile countryside"; it belongs to "the old gallo-latin soil." And yet Dodin is angry rather than fatalistic when he rejects the heavy dishes of his German spa. French cuisine *is* exportable even if French culinary culture remains fixed in time and place. The Germans of the story are "barbarians" because they lack a cuisine to support their own culinary culture. Where logic, line, rule, and order are missing, wretched excess takes over. The German dishes are "smothered" and overwhelmed precisely because no cuisine controls preparation. The result is disaster and not just because the Germans fall far short of Dodin's standards. The largest suggestion of French cuisine bespeaks those shining republican norms that come after the revolution of 1789 and that have triumphed in the victory of 1918. The finest meal properly served and properly understood is not about ostentation but about the equal fraternity of diners who understand how food can bring contentment around a table.

The culinary superiority that Dodin arrogates to the French lies in his insistence on a bond between cook and consumer, a relationship characterized by intimacy on the one hand and equality on the other. In spite of having spent his career in the employ of titled and exceptionally wealthy patrons, Carême insisted that great cuisine was a collaborative venture in which chef and host operated on an equal footing. This intimacy and equality need not obtain outside the culinary relationship. They most often do not, as the example of Carême makes clear; surely no one considered him the equal of Talleyrand or the baron Rothschild. But insofar as that connection is concerned, there is an ideal of rights and responsibilities for both parties. It requires, among other things, that diners eat with understanding. As Brillat-Savarin decreed long ago, intelligence is, or should be, a prime ingredient of culinary consumption. The relationship expressed most forcefully by Carême is, in fact, a fundamental assumption of French culinary culture: the diner's *savoir-manger* both corresponds and responds to the chef's *savoir-faire* just as the chef is dedicated to the customer's pleasure. And once again, this fundamental assumption is grounded in an evolving French relation of rights and responsibilities in republican society.

Dodin-Bouffant's saga makes an especial point of the affective nature of the bond uniting culinary artist and public. Dodin's incomparable cook is not a professional chef. Rouff tellingly transforms Carême's exemplary male culinary duo of chef and patron into a conjugal couple. A country woman of good peasant stock, Adèle Pidou has only her culinary intelligence to recommend her. Nonetheless, Dodin does not hesitate to call her a genius, and to acknowledge that his culinary visions could not be realized without her. Although the Prince's Dinner had been of his devising, he is well aware that its material realization depended on this "handmaiden of his thought," as the English translation brings out the gender implications of the French *auxiliare* (auxiliary or aide). In truth, these two make the perfect culinary couple because Adèle is, in fact, rather like Dodin himself, unremarkable except for everything touching on food. So vital is she to his very being that when the decidedly ungrateful prince offers her a princely sum to quit Dodin and cook for him, the confirmed bachelor meets the challenge by taking the plunge and proposing to his cook.

Marriage symbolizes the perfect culinary relationship of cook and gastronome, production and consumption. If Rouff highlights Adèle's lack of other personal attractions—her heavy thighs, double chin, and faded hair, her "somewhat vulgar countenance" and rustic speech—it is because he wants to address the significance of the culinary bond—a bond with sensual undertones of its own. True affection here springs from a shared love of food; the competing sensuality of sex does not, apparently, distract the culinary couple. That this one passion suffices becomes clear when Dodin, after "fifteen years of devotion and not one failed meal" with Adèle, almost succumbs to the advances of a luscious young widow who is also an exceptional cook. When the moment of amatory decision arrives in the middle of a succulent repast, Dodin abstains precisely because the meal is so wonderful. He has no right, he tells the crestfallen lady, to take this genius of the culinary away from her vocation, and so he takes his leave, having yielded to the food alone. Culinary devotion brooks no rival.

Culinary attachment is not a romantic passion where the intense flame burns for only a moment. Dodin joins Brillat-Savarin in viewing gastronomic pleasure by reason, order, and rule rather than fervor: "Gourmandise is an act of our judgment by which we prefer things that please our taste over those that do not have this quality." The bond between the culinary couple cannot be a sometime thing; it calls for a continuity that is all the more imperative, because this relationship is a true collaboration. The secrecy and furtiveness of an illicit passion would undercut the mutual trust and the collaboration of cook and diner that alone guarantee culinary creativity. Just as important for French culinary culture, a passion that contravenes social norms undermines the ideal of equal sociability that presides over the meal. For Dodin as for Brillat-Savarin, dining brings people together.

Of course, no more than Carême and his titled employers are Adèle and Dodin on anything like an equal footing. The undeniable intimacy of culinary collaboration notwithstanding, inequality characterizes the relationship in the hierarchy of production and consumption. Reproducing the hierarchy of the patriarchal household, this traditional model of culinary relations keeps women cooking in private and away from "chefing" in public. Professional chefs could make a case for equality and even superiority because the patronage model of social relations no longer held in the rapidly transforming culinary universe of the twentieth century. They could also reinforce their claims to superior status by working very hard to distinguish themselves from women cooks in the domestic kitchen, and they did so with great diligence. This professionalizing context suggests that, along with the pot-au-feu that Dodin serves up for his country, the culinary couple of Dodin-Bouffant and Adèle Pidou offers a seductive argument for the "good old days." Marrying up does not make Adèle presumptuous. How could it when Rouff keeps her in the kitchen? To be sure, promoted to the respectable estate of spouse, Adèle dines with her husband and his friends. It is abundantly clear, however, that the kitchen is where she belongs.

The Culinary Contract

Cookery . . . is a choice work that requires much love.[32]

—Dodin-Bouffant

What do the aphorisms of a Brillat-Savarin in the early nineteenth century or the culinary imagery of Dodin-Bouffant in the early twentieth possibly have to tell us about the globalized, internationalized culinary world of *Iron Chef,* McDonald's, and mad-cow disease? Has the twenty-first century moved beyond such traditional models? The best answer to both questions is both no and yes. No, we are not altogether beyond traditional models, and, yes, the spirit of Brillat-Savarin and Dodin-Bouffant still regulates aspects of French culinary culture today. The trademark sociability, the understanding between producer and consumer, the precision and aestheticization of the culinary in everyday life, the passion for the culinary—these features of French culinary culture remain in place.

We can conjecture that if *Iron Chef* does not appear on French television, it may be because this show has little connection to culinary practice in everyday life, little resonance in a culinary culture that makes much of exactly that connection and of the particular brand of sociability that it prizes. The trademark excess of the Japanese show contests the ideals of moderation and harmony in French cuisine. Not that culinary spectacle is absent from French culture. From the Ancien Régime to Carême and beyond, conspicuous production proves quite as French as it is American, and in many respects more so. Conspicuity simply plays differently in the two cultures. French culinary display, in its modern versions, is often less spectacular or more subtle than American counterparts.

The frenetic exhibitionism that has Japanese and American television viewers in thrall breaks the contract between cook and consumer—the contract by which the two parties acknowledge their respective responsibilities as well as their rights and trust each other to perform in a predictable, orderly way. There is no need for a culinary contract with *Iron Chef* because competitive cooking makes no connection between the parties. Few of the exotic ingredients and none of the dishes prepared in the immense Stadium Kitchen of the *Iron Chef* studio will ever find their way to the viewer's table. And this is precisely the point. The exotic, the massive, and the dramatic take *Iron Chef* out of the everyday just as surely as Roland Barthes' all-out wrestlers transport their spectators onto a different plane of existence. For the everyday cook as for the everyday diner, *Iron Chef* provides culinary escapism, magnifying, dramatizing, and exoticizing the familiar gestures of the everyday. The truncated competition that never ends in consumption takes cuisine out of everyday life altogether.

This kind of competition takes *Iron Chef* away from the serious business of cooking for real consumers. The colossal culinary spectacle wrenches food from its culinary context of cooking and eating. Competitive cooking of this sort has no place in the culinary everyday because it is all about cooking, not about eating and still less about dining. The tasters judge the dishes, but they do not dine. They have no connection to each other and none to the chef. There is no meal because each dish is judged, and graded, separately, and there are two such sets of dishes. In fulfilling its obligations to the television audience and meeting the viewers' expectations, *Iron Chef* abrogates the culinary contract.

At the opposite end of the culinary spectrum, competitive eating nullifies the culinary contract just as surely as spectacular competitive cooking. There is even less need for an understanding between cook and diner, since it is not at all a question of quality. Quantity alone decides the outcome in competitive eating contests. The knowledgeable eater that Brillat-Savarin held up as an ideal has no place at the groaning board set before the competitive eater. For a consumption parallel to the production of excess by *Iron Chef*, we can look to Coney Island, where an annual hot dog–eating contest has been held on the Fourth of July ever since Nathan Handwerker set up his hot dog stand in 1916. The 2002 winner of The Mustard Yellow Belt, a Japanese man weighing in at a mere 112 pounds, consumed 50 ½ hot dogs in just 12 minutes.[33]

It would be comforting for my characterization of French culinary culture and the image of the French as Brillat-Savarin's knowledgeable eaters if we could consign as totally un-French the extravaganzas of competitive eating. Unfortunately, French moderation does not stand up across the board. In France as elsewhere, eating contests are one more manifestation of the carnivalesque and, as such, part of popular culture. The excesses of competitive eating transgress the norms in any culinary culture, and France is no exception. One need only recall Pierre Bourdieu's analysis of lower-class eating habits in France and its focus on the expressive photograph of a young man with stuffed cheeks facing a huge plate of beans in an eating contest in the south of France. No more than for the food served on *Iron Chef* does the food consumption at an eating contest partake of everyday life and the sociability that sustains French culinary culture. Competitive eating is indifferent to the product. As with the hot dogs, that product is usually quite ordinary and may be, as with the beans in France, a local specialty.[34] The balance has shifted from the exceptional producer of competitive cooking to the extraordinary consumer of competitive eating. Both reflect another choice of the omnivore, the capacity to eat what, when, and however much one wants.

These digressions from the norm notwithstanding—and this is Bourdieu's point—the ideal of French cuisine and the norms of French culinary culture, anchored in the bourgeoisie, represent measure as value and as norm. If eating to excess is everywhere transgressive to a certain degree, sheer quantity is particularly so in France, where haute cuisine retains its elite connotations. One would not likely find a French restaurant advertising a "Belly Buster" dinner as did one roadside restaurant in upstate New York that I passed recently. Competitive eating cancels out the culinary contract and also flouts the presumption of quality that French culinary culture holds up as an ideal. Daniel Boulud is categorical on this matter: only in France is there an "obsession for quality," whether for the food, the service, the setting, or the level of cleanliness. "It's not quantity that counts, it's quality, especially in France." Not unexpectedly, especially in his early years in New York, Boulud saw his mission as pushing for just such culinary quality in New York. Charlie Trotter recounted the mind-boggling and totally different standards of culinary quality that he found in top restaurants on his first trip to France.

Eating and cooking contests alike contravene the sociability and the attendant formalization of production and consumption that so marks French culinary culture. Sociability in general acts to moderate the aggression contained in eating. Sustained by the formalization of manners and dining etiquette, this sociability concerns communication about food as well as, perhaps as much as, its actual consumption. The most celebrated of Brillat-Savarin's famous aphorisms, the one with which this book began—Tell me what you eat, and I'll tell you what you are—both assumes and requires a dialogue. As I have argued in chapter 3, that communication, especially when written, lays the foundation for a culture of consumption. Not for nothing did he consider the lone diner something of a menace to society. Eating is a question of conviviality—a bringing together. Solitary pleasures of any sort threaten the social fabric by eliminating fellowship from the equation.

The special rapport among diners as between the diners and the host is of-

ten cited as a prime ingredient of a good meal. Escoffier cited a tradition of sociability or conviviality as one element of a good cuisine. The ultimate goal of
cuisine is achieved when people appreciate the pleasures of a good meal with
friends. The pleasures of food are to be shared, and since one cannot actually
share one's food, the only possibility is to commune, communicate, converse—in other words, to create a community through and in the communication of pleasure. Here, indeed, is the nexus where cuisine joins consumption. This is not a French monopoly by any means. Only a few miles from the
"Belly Buster" meal in upstate New York is Wally's Diner, whose motto could
apply to hundreds if not thousands of local restaurants and neighborhood
diners across America: "Good Food, Good Friends, Good Gossip" promises the
cooking, the conviviality, and the conversation that are fundamental to the
culinary contract as Brillat-Savarin defined it for a different time and a different place.

The culinary contract is also special because it is so enmeshed in the intimacy of a bodily connection between food prepared and ingested. These material, corporeal connections implicate the self in the preparation and the consumption of food, and these connections establish a personal relationship. At
the end of my interview with him, New York chef Jean-Michel Bergougnoux
said that the absolutely essential quality of any chef was the generosity of chef
to customer, of cook to diner: "To do this job," he emphasized, "you have to
want to live well, you have to like to eat, you have to like to drink. And
you have to like taking care of people." Neither Brillat-Savarin nor Dodin-
Bouffant could have put it better.

And this is the ultimate principle of *Accounting for Taste*. Cuisine is neither
food, nor recipes, nor yet cooks and consumers, but the ideal of a self inextricably bound up with pleasure given and received. Well beyond the "service
and hospitality" rubric under which the U.S. government classifies restaurants, the model of excellent eating envisions an ideal world. Like any other,
French culinary culture teaches practices as it realizes norms and values. More
explicitly than most others, it also speaks about a belief system and creates
myths that reach beyond France. We tell ourselves these culinary tales to help
us understand what we eat—and what we are.

In the world of lawyers and clients, a contract is not a tale of identity but the
consequence of a willed decision to regulate a given affair. The parties to the
contract affix their signatures to confirm acceptance of the provisions spelled
out in the document. In contrast, the culinary contract depends on a very dif-

ferent sort of commitment. Unlike the explicit, and therefore written, provisions of legal contracts, its requirements are implicit. Its authority comes not from the state but from shared norms and common values.

French culinary culture is constructed from these commonalities, reliances, and acceptances, many of which it shares with other cultures. French cuisine has echoed around the world, but however widespread these beliefs and practices, they are not universal. French culinary nationalism would have us think so, but there are dissenters, outsiders, those who do not accept the French culinary contract because they are not part of the contract community. Examples of such dissent are not hard to find. Only across the Channel, the English have long been entwined in a love-hate relationship with French cuisine. But few have disputed French culinary culture as vigorously as a Moroccan scholar who visited Paris in the 1840s. In the very middle of the great development of gastronomy, the professionalization of cooking, the period of great restaurants and flourishing gastronomic discussions, Muhammad As-Saffar judged the shortcomings of French food and conviviality as not simply wanting but a failure. Note that he agrees about the importance of conviviality for the Arabs as well as the French. Where he disagrees is in the relationship to food. It is as if the French did not live up to the precepts of Brillat-Savarin:

> They [the French] linger at the table for more than two hours, because it is their custom to stretch out the talk during the meal so they can overindulge in food. The Arabs say that perfect hospitality is friendliness at first sight and leisurely talk with one's table companions. But we detested the arrival of mealtimes because of the endless waiting, nor did we understand their conversation.

The foods fared little better. Most of it did not agree with our traveler, who found the meat extremely fatty and the menus lacking in variety. The spice of life, as it were, was missing, the spices of his life, most certainly:

> They are not creative in varying their menus with different things. Even if they have just eaten [something], they bring it on the next time. In general, their food lacks flavor, and even salt and pepper.

Culinary Paris held few charms for this foreigner, who nevertheless seemed to accept the hardship with equanimity. After all, travelers can't be choosey about their food. "But he who has no choice can make do; of necessity, one can stay alive on it." This puncture to the prideful Gallic balloon makes it clear that the French culinary contract articulates the norms and values and standards of a particular, bounded time and place.[35]

But since complete outsiders seldom make direct contact with the host culture, such categorical rejection is rare. More to the point and more revelatory is the indirect connection that Simmel identified in the relationship to the community of the figure that he called the Stranger *(Der Fremde)*. Structurally part of the community and foreigner to it, the Stranger is at once at home and abroad. *Babette's Feast,* a film by a Danish filmmaker based on a novella written in English by a Danish author, dramatizes the understanding given to those who come from elsewhere. In that community, like Simmel's Stranger, Babette, the exiled Frenchwoman, plays an essential role. Structurally part of the community to which she does not belong, Babette is, as Simmel puts it, the potential wanderer who redefines that community. This cinematic fable testifies to the power of French cuisine in foreign lands; to the capacity of the French culinary contract not simply to express but to create community; and, finally, to the good that the Stranger brings to that community through a very complicated act of creation.

Babette's Feast: A Fable for Culinary France

In the never-ending competition of sight and taste, *Accounting for Taste* can end with a film, and no ordinary film at that. Among the many films that center on food at the end of the twentieth century, *Babette's Feast* (Babettes Gaeste-bud) stands out for its reach and for the subtlety of its sensuality. For this film depicts far more than food and foodways; it shows more than the sensuality of food in our lives. Paradoxically, this Danish film tells an exemplary tale of French cuisine. Its portrayal of a French cook far from France evokes the French culinary landscape even more than the Danish countryside where it is set.

Surely it is appropriate that the cinema supply the iconic culinary text of the twentieth century. Film captures, as a photograph cannot, the interactive process that culinary art requires. More immediately than print and like cuisine itself, film conveys a sensory awareness that embraces the viewer as the more intellectual medium cannot. Just as the written recipe can only suggest the sensory, so words inevitably fail to convey the comprehensive, all-enveloping sensuality of taste. The immediacy achieved by the moving narrative raises *Babette's Feast* to iconic status well above the short story by Isak Dinesen from which it is drawn. Through its exploitation of the sensory, the film transforms a "story from the human heart," as Dinesen puts it in the narrative frame of the original story, into an emblem of French culinary culture.[1]

Brought to the screen in 1987 by the Danish director Gabriel Axel, *Babette's Feast* arguably inaugurated what the past twenty-five years or so have consecrated as a veritable cinematic genre—the food film. From the exuberantly sexual foreplay of the couple devouring a turkey leg in *Tom Jones* (1963) to the Taiwanese *Eat Drink Man Woman* (1994) and the fluffy paean to the senses, *Chocolat* (2000), with many films in between, the food film has become a staple in the cinematic larder, another sign of the salience of food in the larger culture today.[2] We all have our favorite from this lengthy roster. Indeed, based on the sheer number of food films, it would seem that just about every group that lays claim to a cuisine now has a film to tell the world about it.

Babette's Feast shares many characteristics with other food films. First and foremost, it lovingly details the many pleasures of food, though unlike many others it does not equate the sensory with the sexual. More than others, however, and conspicuously more than Isak Dinesen's short story, it celebrates the senses. It invests cuisine—very pointedly *French* cuisine—with incomparable transformative powers. The spectacular repast that crowns the film conjures up a vision of spiritual well-being created by the transcendent artistry of a chef who sacrifices all for her art and, through that art, recreates her country. This restitution of place and resurrection of time makes the most powerful case yet for the intimate drama of culinary metamorphosis.

I.

Babette's Feast takes place in a remote seaside village in Jutland, the site of an especially strict Lutheran sect. The beautiful young daughters of the founder of the sect renounce suitors from the outside world who would have taken them away from their father, their village, and their religion. Martine (named for Martin Luther) rejects an aristocratic, worldly army officer, and Philippa (named for Luther's friend Phillip Melancton) turns down the offer of Achille Papin, a visiting French opera star, to sing in Paris, where he promises to make her a star. Years pass; neither sister marries. The two devote their lives to good works and keeping their now-dead father's spirit alive.

One evening some thirty-five years later, in September 1871, in the midst of a driving rainstorm, a bedraggled and visibly exhausted woman appears on the doorstep of the two sisters, who are now in late middle age. The stranger bears a letter of introduction from Achille Papin, who remembers his idyll in rural Denmark as a very special, because so very different, time and place in his life. He asks the sisters to take in the woman, a refugee from the civil war raging in Paris in which her husband and son were both brutally killed "like rats."[3] She herself, his letter informs them, barely escaped with her life. Babette Hersant has lost her family, her country, her language, and, as it turns out, her art. She is beaten, desolate, and desperate to be taken in.

Such is the simplicity of the sisters' life that they scarcely know what to do with a servant, even one who will work for no wages. Nevertheless, they take her in, and Babette—played by the luminous Stéphane Audran—soon becomes indispensable to them and to those whom they succor. The slight but significant touches that she brings to the daily fare make the food more palatable—and even, in a term that seems foreign to this strict Protestant sect, pleasurable. Babette insists on the quality of foodstuffs as she bargains in rudimentary but effective Danish with the grocer and the fishmonger, both of whom she astounds with her insistence on superior vegetables and absolutely fresh fish. It is clear that no one else gives such care to the quality of material ingredients or makes use of the herbs that she gathers in the fields overlooking the sea and hangs in her kitchen.

When Babette leaves for a time and the sisters return to their task of dispensing their own unappetizingly brown ale-bread soup to the poor, one old man testily throws his spoon down when served the meal that had been perfectly acceptable before Babette's arrival. Once good taste is learned, there is no return. Another ends his prayers with thanks to God for sending Babette. The sisters sense rather than actually know that food tastes better, although they know for sure that their financial state has greatly improved since this foreigner came to them. Into this world disdainful of earthly delights, Babette subtly presses claims for the life around us. In a telling aesthetic gesture that sets her apart from the rest of the villagers, she washes the windows of the cottage to let the light and beauty of the outside world into the dark interior.

Fourteen years pass. The sisters make plans to celebrate the one-hundredth anniversary of their father's birth. This celebration comes at a crucial moment: like many other sects after the loss of a charismatic founder, the disciples have fallen to squabbling and backbiting. The sisters hope that the simple repast that they envision will make whole what time and travail have sundered and thus will restore the spiritual harmony of their early church. At this point, Babette receives a letter from France with the news that she has won ten thousand francs in the state lottery. A child of misfortune, she has quite suddenly been made fortunate. After much thought, she requests permission to prepare the commemorative feast for the sisters and the community of believers, but she wants to do so on her own terms, as a "real French dinner." She also insists on paying for it. The sisters reluctantly grant her request. They assume that this will be the last meal she will make for them before she returns to France a rich woman. After a journey to marshal supplies that she has ordered from France, Babette returns at the head of a great procession of foodstuffs, including gleaming candelabra and silverware, elegant china and table linens, cases of wine, a calf's head, several quails in a cage, and an enormous live turtle that gives Martine nightmares.

Horrified at what they fear will turn into a "witches' Sabbath," the sisters warn the community, begging forgiveness in advance. Like the early Christian martyrs, they determine to meet the presence of evil with resignation, in silence, with their minds on heaven, not earth. No one will think about the food. "It will be as if we never had the sense of taste," says one of the disciples. The sisters' apprehension only increases as Babette sets about preparing the meal. "Surely that isn't wine?" Martine asks in fear and trembling. "No, that isn't 'wine,'" Babette replies indignantly. "It's Clos de Vougeot 1845," the strange name only enhancing Martine and Philippa's sense of foreboding. With the help of a young boy engaged for the occasion, Babette slaughters, cooks, sifts, bakes, stirs, irons, polishes, burnishes. The dinner brings an unexpected guest, Lorens Loewenhielm, the army officer and suitor of Martine from years before, who is now a general. As before, he is visiting his aunt nearby and will accompany her to the celebratory dinner.

The general is an essential figure for the culinary narrative, because he knows, as the others do not, what he is eating. The bubbly drink that one disciple reckons a kind of lemonade, he recognizes as a Veuve Cliquot 1860. More and more astounded as the meal proceeds, Loewenhielm comes to the realization that the only place that could have produced such a repast was the renowned Café Anglais in Paris whose signature dishes included the very "entombed quail" *(cailles en sarcophage)* that they are now consuming.[4] As a young man posted to Paris, he had been honored at a memorable dinner at the very place. In the course of that dinner, his host, General Galliffet, recounted the surprising story of the extraordinary chef of this superb restaurant who, "quite exceptionally," was a woman. This incomparable chef had the great gift of transforming a dinner into "a kind of love affair" that "made no distinction between bodily appetite and spiritual appetite." The entombed quail were her invention.[5]

General Loewenhielm never seeks to learn how this dish, which he determines to be absolutely authentic, has appeared in such an unlikely venue. Under the circumstances, his silence is appropriate: explanation is neither necessary nor significant. Like the other guests, Loewenhielm accepts this manna from heaven as a sign of grace to be received without question and with boundless gratitude. The twelve at table, with Babette in the kitchen preparing the transformative red wine and bread, make this pointedly a last supper. Even the quail in their tombs suit a dinner where death is so present.[6] The guests are themselves very elderly, and their thoughts turn frequently to the fate that awaits them in the hereafter, the punishments that will be meted out for past sins. The hymn that Philippa sings after dinner poignantly invokes the end of life, when all will be reconciled: "The sand in our hourglass will soon run out / The day is conquered by the night / The glories of the world are ending / So brief their day, so swift their flight / God, let thy brightness ever shine / Admit us to Thy mercy divine."[7]

Unmistakably, that reconciliation has already occurred around the dinner table, where Babette has indeed worked magic. Her feast has renewed friendships, restored love, and revived the harmony of the community. No one, in the end, can ignore the transcendent power of taste correctly rendered. General Loewenhielm comes to the realization that "in this beautiful world of ours, all things are possible." The other guests become just tipsy enough to open themselves, quite against their will, to the wonder of the material world and to corporeal pleasure. One guest rejects the water that is served late in the dinner, reaching avidly instead for the wine that she first tasted with such visible foreboding. Smiles on the erstwhile dour faces translate an inner well-being, the contentment of simply being. Poignantly, the departing congregants join hands to sing one final hymn as they dance in a circle under the stars in a crystal clear sky: "The clock strikes and time goes by: / Eternity is nigh. / Let us use this time to try / To serve the Lord with heart and mind. / So that our true home we shall find. / So that our true home we shall find." It is, after all, the Christmas season, and the birth of their founder on December 15th precedes by only a few days the birth of their Savior.

Babette remains in the kitchen during the entire dinner. The serving boy moves between the dining room and the kitchen as he follows Babette's careful instructions about what and how much to serve whom in which glass. The camera cuts back and forth between these two rooms, dwelling lovingly on close-ups of the dishes being prepared and being served, the wine poured and sipped. In other words, the cinematic observer sees everything in the harmony of production and consumption. Babette is joined in the kitchen by one guest, the general's coach driver, to whom she serves every dish. In an addition that is at once authentic and comic, his frequently voiced response— "that's good"—expresses the deep satisfaction that the vow of silence will not allow the other guests to express. Only toward the end of the meal does Babette allow herself to savor the magnificent old burgundy that she has dispensed so prodigally. Only at the very end does she eat the incomparable meal that she has prepared (even then she remains standing). When the guests leave, Martine and Philippa come to the kitchen to compliment her on the meal and prepare to say good-bye. Babette quietly reveals that she was the head chef at the Café Anglais to whose artistry the general paid such eloquent testimony.

She also stuns her employers in another way: she will not return to France—ever. There is no place for her there; everyone dear to her has died, the world she knew has disappeared. Besides, she has no money. The sisters are dumbfounded to learn that Babette spent her entire lottery winnings on the dinner—just what a dinner for twelve would cost at the Café Anglais, she states matter-of-factly. The sisters are taken aback at her sacrifice. "It was not just for you," Babette responds. She has proven her powers, performed her art. She has made her guests happy just as she had at the Café Anglais. "That's what Papin knew"—an artist himself, the opera singer recognized their kinship, their common pursuit of artistic excellence, their fulfillment in bringing pleasure. She subscribes to Papin's pronouncement that "Throughout the world sounds one long cry from the heart of the artist: Give me the chance to do my very best." Babette has had a last chance to give of her very best, so that, contrary to what Martine fears, she cannot be poor: "an artist is never poor." For the first time, Philippa embraces her servant in an act of love that at once acknowledges the claims of the artist and her right to sacrifice. Babette will reap one final reward. In this film that balances visions of the hereafter with sights of the here and now, Philippa, the other artist as singer, admits Babette to the paradise of the righteous. Though a Catholic—Papist, in the sisters' lexicon—Babette will dwell in the New Jerusalem promised in the opening hymn and toward which the disciples yearn.[8] In heaven, with its promised meeting of righteousness and bliss, Babette's art will "delight the angels!" Echoing the words that Achille Papin had written to her fourteen years before, Philippa assures Babette that in heaven she will be the artist God meant her to be.

Not surprisingly, the commentary that *Babette's Feast* has occasioned sets those who are interested in the food against those who engage the religious dimensions of the film. Among the former, beginning with the Copenhagen restaurateur who supervised the presentation of food in the film, we can count the cooks who set out to turn the fabled repast into a real dinner. One of the most prominent French gastronomic critics criticized the film on just this score, condemning the pretentiousness of the feast and the egregious historical error of making a woman head chef in a restaurant such as the Café Anglais.[9] Academic commentary, on the other hand, has delved into the religious interpretation, a topic on which French film critics seem to have had little to say. Perhaps the pietistic Lutheranism of the film is as alien for the largely Catholic French as Babette's cuisine was for her Lutheran guests. No one, however, not even the foodies who have made *Babette's Feast* a cult film, has seriously explored the film as a paradigm for French cuisine, and specifically what that cuisine stands for in the late twentieth century. For it is not the single repast, however glorious, that speaks to French cuisine today; rather, it is that meal within the larger conception of food and the proper relations in the culinary contract that ties cook to producers and to consumers. "I made them happy," Babette says with pride. That happiness is the accomplishment of great art and of great love, of the material with which the artist works, and of the public that she serves.

Its everydayness sets the culinary apart from other arts. Cuisine is a practice of everyday life, to invoke Michel de Certeau a last time—or even better, as the French title of his book has it, cuisine is an art of "making do" *(les arts de faire)*. Babette is an artist of the everyday, but one who also, when given the opportunity, moves in the more exalted public circles of the spectacular. More obviously humble, the cook works with what is available; the spectacular appears in the parallel transformation wrought by the great artist-chef. This dialectic of everyday life confronting extraordinary spectacle plays out in so many circumstances and assumes so many guises as to be constitutive of French cuisine. The connection between the everyday and the spectacular also controls the continuum between cooking and chefing. The culinary roles of cook and chef imperfectly coincide with the status designations of *cook* and *chef.* Thought to be *a* cook and actually *the* cook for thirteen years, Babette reveals herself to be a great chef. Just as clearly, her "chefing" depends on the cooking that also informs the everyday life of the community.

That Dinesen defied historical accuracy to promote a woman to the official, public status of chef has, I think, to do with a desire to emphasize the connection between culinary extremes. Haute cuisine and everyday cooking lie at different ends of the same continuum. *Babette's Feast* makes the same point about music. The hymns that provide most of the music in the film articulate and express the faith of the community, just as the duet from Mozart's *Don Giovanni* that Achille Papin teaches Philippa signifies her situation with him. The seductiveness of the music reinforces the scene of seduction that Papin and Philippa perform and then begin to experience.[10] Philippa, apparently fearful of her growing involvement with Papin, chooses to discontinue her lessons. She refuses a life on the stage, as Babette chooses not to return to France. Yet like Babette, Philippa, Papin's "beautiful soprano of the snows," continues to illuminate the humbler setting. The wonderful, immensely satisfying world of music includes hymns as well as Mozart. Papin is sure that he will hear Philippa's voice in paradise. Both women use their gift in lesser settings to make people happy, to express joy, to illuminate everyday life. It is then altogether fitting that Philippa should be the one to pay homage to Babette as an artist, repeating to Babette the very words that Papin had written her so many years before.

A second article of faith in *Babette's Feast* is the certainty of the instantaneous and direct power of art. Like grace, like the mercy invoked by the pastor early in the film and the general at the end, art touches individuals of every station, even against their will. Surely it is not stretching things too far to see this story as Dinesen's contribution to the debate over mass culture that was raging in the 1950s when she wrote "Babette's Feast." Against the contemnors of so-called mass society, the film, like Dinesen's short story, proposes an overwhelmingly optimistic, consistently elevated view of art, artists, and society. Against virtually all that we know about the socialization of taste— just ask anyone who has urged a child to try something new—*Babette's Feast* affirms the immediate accessibility of new and strange foods. The artist creates for the untutored no less than for the connoisseur. The young Philippa, Papin promises, will sing for the emperor but also for the young working girls from the poor neighborhoods. The general articulates his pleasure; his coachman in the kitchen says no more than "that's good," while the others say nothing at all. If the first appreciation is the more knowledgeable, the transformation of the silent diners offers the more eloquent testimony to the power of culinary art.

So, too, the viewers of the film do not need to have experienced "a real French dinner" to fall under the spell of the feast that Babette prepares. Nor do we need to recognize the hymns or identify the works by Mozart and Rossini to be moved by the music and to grasp its significance for the film. These two performing arts, music and cuisine, speak to the senses directly; their effect is all in the moment. Critical appreciation enhances the experience by increasing understanding, but the senses make the primal connection. The film works so well because it joins taste (food) and hearing (music) to the conforming and informing power of sight. Each becomes greater in the presence of the others—much as a fine meal requires companionship and presentation as well as perfect consumption.

Babette's Feast illuminates the connection between culinary production and the act of consumption. Not only is each a function of the other, neither can be conceived without the other. The truism that links production and consumption aside—food exists to be consumed—works about food and about cuisine, like works throughout literary and cinematic history, tend to focus on the one at the expense of the other. Notably, this film appeared as adventurous chefs were capturing the attention of the media in France and abroad. Babette's promotion, or, better yet, her elevation, is appropriate in an increasingly international food culture. To be sure, this feast is Babette's, the Christ figure who sacrifices for the spiritual good and material contentment of the community. Nevertheless, and like the Last Supper on which it is loosely modeled, this feast is all about public participation. Cuisine, this film tells us as it continually cuts back and forth between the kitchen and the dining room, is a social relationship.

II.

The incongruity of Babette's cuisine in isolated Jutland is dramatized in this film of many distances. The Danish director worked with a short story set in Norway written in English by a Danish author. Jutland itself is distant from any world that we know. It exists in a world unto itself out of historical time. Yet the concerns of the villagers—to live a righteous life, to dedicate the self to God—are eternal and timeless. Drama enters this self-contained community when outsiders intrude, however momentarily. The aristocratic army officer from the Danish court who has spent time in Paris, the French opera singer, and Babette, the French refugee, insert this tale into history, mark it as a modern fable, and, most important, connect it to the larger world of politics and of art. These outsiders situate the film not vaguely, in a nineteenth century that differs little from the seventeenth, but in the midst of a century wracked by social, economic, and political change. The politics that the film barely hints at—as we shall see, Dinesen's text is much more explicit—make *Babette's Feast* also a tale of France. In addition, if the political resonance is muted, the artistic context is very much present, through the opera singer from Paris and most of all through Babette's accomplishment in French cuisine.

In contrast with the timelessness of the religious community, the French chronology is remarkably precise. Babette arrives in September 1871. In his letter of introduction, Papin recalls that he had been in Jutland thirty-five years previously, that is, in 1836. Assuming that the sisters were born in the 1820s, they would be in their mid-sixties when Babette makes her festive meal fourteen years after her arrival, thus in 1885. Although thirty-five years places the younger Papin's previous stay in Jutland during the July Monarchy (1830–48), the period that he evokes so lovingly, the era that acclaimed his art, is the Second Empire (1852–70). The regime of Napoleon III went down in humiliating defeat to the Prussians in 1870 and set the scene for the Commune of 1871 that the Third Republic (1870–1940) repressed so cruelly, forcing Babette to flee.

Like Papin's beloved empress, Babette will spend the rest of her life in exile.[11] Her past is the Commune as well as the Café Anglais, the brutality of repression as much as the opulence of gastronomy. Her husband and son were executed. She can count herself fortunate to have gotten out of the country alive. She has lost everything except her art. The contemporary engraving shown briefly during Martine's reading of Papin's letter of introduction shows a firing squad at work. (Estimates of the number killed during this period range from 20,000 to 25,000.) The irony of Babette's situation becomes even greater when we realize that the man who proclaimed that the chef at the Café Anglais was the only woman worth fighting a duel for—in General Loewenhielm's narrative of his dinner at the Café Anglais—was General Galliffet, the man known in leftist circles as the "butcher of the Commune" because of his capricious brutality in executing Communards.[12]

Babette's Feast holds the viewer with the beauty of the here and now and especially with the pleasures of the flesh. It speaks to the senses. Sight and sound supplement the gustatory, for which, in the event, they necessarily substitute. We cannot taste the feast that Babette prepares and her guests consume. Yet though we cannot be moved directly by the foods as they are, we are seduced vicariously, through the vision and the music with which the film envelops the viewer. This focus on the sensual joys of the present defines the film and, I dare say, has everything to do with its original popularity and its subsequent cult status. Just how distinctive a feature this appeal to the sensory is in the film emerges from a comparison with Dinesen's story. At first glance a faithful rendering of the story, the film in fact diverges significantly from the original text. Its lessons differ, and the means of instruction differ as well. Gabriel Axel's film, quite unlike Dinesen's narrative, is a fable for the French, an iconic projection of and for French culinary culture. That Axel is not French only renders the homage to French cuisine all the more striking, all the more worthy of our notice. Its very foreignness allows *Babette's Feast* the greater testimony to the prestige that continues to accrue to French cuisine abroad as well as at home.

Distinct emphases appear on every level of the film, beginning with chronology. In contrast with the short story on which it is based, *Babette's Feast* ages the sisters by fifteen years or so, so that they are in their late forties when Babette arrives and in their mid-sixties for the final feast, not, as Dinesen's chronology would have them, in their mid-thirties and late forties respectively.[13] The advanced age of the sisters; the greater expanse of time separating youthful visions and hopes from trials and disappointments in the present; the visibly aged faces; Babette's spending fourteen years with the sisters before winning the lottery, not twelve; the presence of death and concern with the hereafter—all reinforce the elegiac quality of the film. The overpowering idea of life ending, the impulse to meditate on one's life course and the choices one has made, the anxious contemplation of the future—render the euphoria produced by the meal more dramatic, the prospect of rejuvenation more entrancing.

If Dinesen's disciples and even General Loewenhielm appear somewhat foolish, her Babette is both mysterious and forceful.[14] When Philippa reproaches Babette for giving away everything she had for their sake, Axel's Babette rectifies quietly and rather sadly, "It was not just for you." In reply to Martine's assertion that she will be poor henceforth, she observes simply, "an artist is never poor." By contrast, Dinesen dwells at length on the same sequence, which is both longer and stronger than in the film. Babette gives a look of perhaps "pity, even scorn," and replies categorically to Martine, "For your sake? . . . No. For my own." Then, not as a reply but as a claim to distinction, she twice declares, "I am a great artist." Appearances notwithstanding, she will never be poor: "A great artist, Mesdames, is never poor. We have something, Mesdames, of which other people know nothing." Thus, Dinesen depicts a forcefully assertive artist who proclaims her rights, affirms her superiority, and underscores her distinction from the sisters and, indeed, from their entire world. Artists, Dinesen impresses upon us, are a breed apart.[15] The common humanity of which the film makes so much figures minimally in the short story.

The assertiveness of Dinesen's Babette suits a brooding, passionate figure whose unplumbed depths frighten the fearful sisters and whose artistic persona is of a piece with her political personage. In fact, Dinesen makes much more of the political context than does the film. Her Babette comes not simply as a refugee from a civil war in which her husband and son were killed, but as herself an active participant in that war. Papin's letter introduces Babette as a Communard. Arrested as a Pétroleuse—the term used, Papin explains, for women who used petroleum to set fire to houses—she has "narrowly escaped the blood-stained hands of General Galliffet." The narrowness of her escape is even clearer if we recollect that the French army crushed the Commune at the end of May 1871. Babette arrives at the sisters' cottage the very next month, "haggard and wild-eyed like a hunted animal." Soon she was "held in awe" by them because of her bargaining prowess in the marketplace. For the disciples, she appeared "the dark Martha in the house of their two fair Marys." Speaking little of their language, she would sit brooding silently, "her dark eyes wide open, as enigmatical and fatal as a Pythia upon her tripod." Not surprisingly with such a comparison, the sisters are terrified by the notion that their trusted servant had been an incendiary.

Finally, Dinesen dwells at length upon the cosmic irony of Babette's serving a man who had dined with the very General Galliffet who was responsible for the deaths of her son and husband. The irony is all the greater given the reason that Babette did not return to Paris. All those whom she had served at the Café Anglais, the elite whom she battled so fiercely on the barricades of the Commune and whose names she gives, were gone. However cruel, however oppressive, "those people belonged to me, they were mine," because they alone had the understanding to appreciate what a great artist she was. Less than that will not do. She cites Papin: "it is terrible and unbearable to an artist to be encouraged to do, to be applauded for doing, his second best." She will not return to a world that will reward the also-ran. This is the "perspective of tragedy" that so moves the sisters, a tragedy that they sense without understanding. Until she tells them, the sisters have no idea of Babette's art. They can remember none of the dishes that they had eaten. They are most certainly not the ideal public that Babette craves.

Gabriel Axel's film softens Babette considerably, largely by muting her politics and assertiveness while strengthening her portrayal as artist. No mention is made of her past as a Pétroleuse, and since she arrives in Jutland in September, not June, Babette is more distanced from the bloody events of the Commune. General Galliffet's name is mentioned only once, by General Loewenhielm at dinner, and only in reference to his role as a consummate gastronome. (That Dinesen explains his role in the suppression of the Commune undoubtedly speaks to a sense that few readers would have any notion of General Galliffet.) The irony of Babette's serving Loewenhielm, who once dined with Galliffet, comes only in retrospect and with knowledge that the film does not give. Nor does she list the people who "belonged" to her, describe the world that has disappeared, or say anything about the insufferableness of doing one's second best. Because the film makes us privy to the power of her art, Axel's more self-effacing Babette has no need to tell us how great she is, for we see it. We see for ourselves the transformations that her feast has wrought: the faces illumined, the hearts transformed, the rancor buried, the good fellowship restored, the jubilation and the joy. Above all, this Babette is an artist who communicates with her public, however humble that public may be. She is, in a word, a culinary artist at her best.

Although we cannot actually taste Babette's feast, the film works to convey taste by proxy. In contrast with Dinesen, who details very little about the dishes themselves, no doubt wishing to avoid the pitfalls inherent in gastronomic overwriting, Axel suggests the sensuous pleasures of the gustatory through the equally sensuous enjoyment of sight and sound. The hymns that are sung throughout the film, the duet from *Don Giovanni*, the piano played by Philippa on different occasions—the music exercises a seduction all its own. The purity of sound draws us along just as Philippa's voice drew Papin to church.[16] By another route, visuals bring the viewer into the universe of the film. The multiple grays, the washed-out blues of the sea and the sky, and blacks dominate the narrative until the feast bursts forth with its brilliant and dramatic colors, the general's resplendent uniform and, most of all, the meal itself: the red of the wine, the deep purple of the ripe figs, the golden pineapple, the copper utensils in the kitchen, the gleaming silver, china, and glassware on the table.[17] It is again fitting that the film alters General Loewenhielm's conclusion, which comes as something of a benediction after his experience of grace at the feast. The realization that Dinesen gives him, that "in this world anything is possible," Axel amends simply but significantly to "in this *beautiful* world *of ours,* all things are possible." The beauty of this world here and now is to be seen and experienced by all of us. We do ourselves, and God, a disservice when we fail to take pleasure in the beauty that surrounds us. For this beauty dissolves conflict by putting us in touch with another, better world, a world that knows neither acrimony nor animosity.

Just as the meal in the film effaces the discord among the disciples, so, too, *Babette's Feast* uses the senses to illuminate and transcend the everyday. The film mutes the political because it takes us beyond conflict. We see not only the effects of consumption but also, and most importantly for my fable of French cuisine, the care of preparation. *Babette's Feast* is a food film because it follows the meal from beginning to end, from the trip to procure foodstuffs through the multiple activities of cooking and serving and the pleasures of dining. Consistent with the emphasis on the construction of beauty, the film

Babette in the Kitchen

Babette puts the finishing touches on the salad for the incomparable feast that she is preparing for the religious sect of her patrons. The cross that she wears identifies her visibly as a Catholic—a Papist in the eyes of a community of strict Lutherans. An outsider, she is also their servant, but the kitchen is her privileged spot; there she reigns supreme with an authority that is part skill, part tradition, and part the accomplished chef's intuition. Still from the film *Babette's Feast.*

glosses over the less appealing, destructive aspects of preparation. There is no hint of how the turtle actually ends up as soup. The closest we come to slaughter is a shot of the quail carcasses in a basket being taken to the garbage. Instead, the film focuses on preparation. The camera closes in on Babette's hands as she cuts the rounds of puff pastry dough, adds caviar and crème fraîche to the blinis, stuffs the quail with foie gras, and assembles it, with the head in place, on its pastry coffin. Walnuts are added to the endive salad, big rounds of hard cheese are cut into serving portions; the Nesselrode pudding is finished with whipped cream, glazed chestnuts, and chocolate sauce. We are almost at table level as each wine is poured into glasses that sparkle like a stained-glass window on a sunny day.

Axel's *Babette's Feast* shows us that cuisine is not simply the final product put on the table. The process of preparation that the film follows in loving detail makes it abundantly clear that cuisine operates within a vital web of social relations anchored by the cook. Reaching backwards in the culinary sequence to farmers and fishermen, both near and far, Babette's glorious dinner offers a striking illustration of the internationalization of food. Her insistence upon French products for a "real French dinner" makes "frenchification" the absolutely appropriate term. Then there are the men who transport the goods, the young boy who helps in the kitchen and waits on table (and, as in real life, those who clean up)—all the intermediaries who connect production and consumption. Then, and only then, do we encounter the diners at the far end of the culinary chain. Even though Babette remains out of sight in the kitchen, emerging to begin clearing the table only after the guests have departed, the camera cutting back and forth between kitchen and table calls attention to the connections between cook and consumer. The conversations that Babette overhears from the kitchen tell her that the meal is working its magic. Ultimately, the dramas of cooking frame the drama of dining: the end lies in the beginning just as the beginning implies the end. The theological reverberation of this statement is, of course, especially appropriate for a film that makes so much of beginnings and endings.

III.

By any criterion, *Babette's Feast* is a food film. More than that, it is a French food film, a film of French food, "a real French dinner" presented in amorous particulars. Still more than that, this is a French food film by virtue of the eating order that it represents and proposes for our delight, and that eating order is unequivocally French. Like Proust's *Recherche*, *Babette's Feast* resurrects a country that is no more, the France before 1870 that had already disappeared when Babette arrived in Jutland in 1871, was even more obscure when the tale was written in 1952, and had become positively prehistoric by 1987, when the film appeared. Culinary France is an ideal, and France is an idealized country that lives through its cuisine. *Babette's Feast* constructs something of a legend out of French cuisine, a narrative lived between history and myth, in that such cuisine restores the community of the faithful and resurrects a country. The very distance of the film from France, its foreign author and filmmaker, language and setting, heightens our awareness of the constructed nature of the country that is culinary France.

A glorious banquet allows Babette to give of her very best in her exile from France. It allows her to realize her artistic gift, and to make her public supremely, ineffably happy in a joy that seamlessly merges the spiritual and the corporeal. It also permits her to recall the country that she will never see again. The very names of the foods bring forth the land and its culinary art. From the wines, whose quality is guaranteed by a very particular wine seller in Paris (Chez Philippe, rue Montorgueil), to the quail, these foodstuffs are as talismanic as Proust's madeleine and as memorable. The gesture of reconstruction goes back in literature at least to Virgil's Andromache, Hector's widow whom Aeneas finds in a Trojan landscape that she has constructed in the Greece that holds her captive. Similarly, Babette conjures up the France that she knew and loved, the Paris of the Café Anglais whose patrons acclaimed her as "the greatest culinary genius." Her exile is all the more poignant because, like Andromache, she cannot go home again. As she tells the sisters, the France that she knew is no more. She brought it into existence once again if only for a moment—the utopian moment of her feast based on the stunning good fortune of winning the lottery.

As the madeleine dipped in a cup of tea gives inexpressible joy to Proust's narrator by resurrecting his childhood, so Babette's feast carries her and her guests to another, better world. We who watch this feast may also count ourselves among Babette's guests. It is not so much a lost France that the film offers the contemporary viewer as an idealized France that is called into existence by its cuisine. Babette is every French cook and every French chef, the vital link in the culinary chain that metamorphoses the raw to the cooked and the cooked to the miraculously pleasurable. The fable of French cuisine turns out to be a culinary tale for all times and places, for all those cooks who transform eating into dining, and for all those diners who come away from the table transformed.

Appendix A

Bibliography—Cookery Works by Date of Original Publication

Primary works referred to in text

1651. François Pierre de La Varenne. *Le Cuisinier françois, enseignant la manière d'apprêter & assaisonner toutes sortes de viandes grasses & maigres, légumes & Pâtisseries en perfections, &c.* Jean-Louis Flandrin, Philip Hyman, and Mary Hyman, eds. Paris: Montalba, 1983.

1665. Pierre de Lune. *Le Cuisinier,* in *L'Art de la cuisine française au xviie siècle.* Paris: Payot & Rivages, 1995.

1674. L. S. R. *L'art de bien traiter,* in *L'Art de la cuisine française au xviie siècle.* Paris: Payot, 1995.

1691. François Massialot. *Le Cuisinier roïal et bourgeois.* 1691. 3d ed., Paris: Charles de Sercy, 1698.

1692. Audiger. *La Maison réglée,* in *L'Art de la cuisine française au xviie siècle.* Paris: Payot & Rivages, 1995.

1735. Vincent La Chapelle. *Le Cuisinier moderne.* 5 vols. La Haye: n.p., 1742.

1740. *Le Cuisinier gascon.* Amsterdam: n.p., 1747.

1746. [Menon]. *La Cuisinière bourgeoise, suivie de l'Office à l'usage de tous ceux qui se mêlent de la dépense des Maisons. Contenant la manière de disséquer, connoître & servir toutes sortes de Viandes.* New ed., Bruxelles: François Foppens, 1759.

1747. [Desalleurs l'aîné]. *Lettre d'un patissier anglois au nouveau Cuisinier françois.* Pp. 197–231 appended to *Le Cuisinier gascon,* new ed. Amsterdam.

1759. [Menon]. *Le Manuel des Officiers de bouche. Ou le Précis de tous les Apprêts que l'on peut faire des Alimens pour servir toutes les Tables, depuis celles des grands Seigneurs jusqu'à celles des Bourgeois: Ouvrage très-utile aux Maîtres pour ordonner des Repas & aux Artistes pour les exécuter.* Paris: Leclerc.

1793. [Menon], trans. *The French Family Cook: Being a complete System of French Cookery. Adapted to the Tables, not only of the Opulent, but of Persons of moderate Fortune and Condition.* London: J. Bell.

1795. [Mme Mérigot]. *La Cuisinière républicaine qui enseigne la manière simple d'accommoder les Pommes de terre.* Paris: Chez Mérigot jeune. An III partially reprinted pp. 173–85 in Beatrice Fink, ed., *Les Liaisons savoureuses: Réflexions et pratiques culinaires au dix-huitième siècle.* St. Étienne: Publications de l'Université de St Étienne, 1995.

1806. Viard, Alexandre. *Le Cuisinier impérial, ou l'art de faire la cuisine pour toutes les fortunes.* Reprint, Nîmes: C. Lacour, 1993.

1811. Raimbault, A. T. [Cousin d'Avallon]. *Le Cuisinier étranger pour faire suite au Parfait Cuisinier. Contenant une Notice raisonnée de tous les mêts étrangers qu' on peut servir sur une table française.* 2d ed., Paris: Delacour.

1814. Beauvilliers, A. B. *L'Art du cuisinier.* 3d ed., Paris: Pillet, 1824.

1815. Carême, Antonin [Marie-Antoine]. *Le Pâtissier pittoresque.* 4th ed., Paris: n.p., 1842.

1815. ———. *Le Pâtissier royal parisien.* 3d ed., 2 vols., Paris: n.p., 1841.

1816. *Gastronomiana, ou Recueil d'anecdotes, Réflexions, Maximes et folies gourmandes.* Avignon: Jean-Albert Joly.

1817. Viard, A. *Le Cuisinier royal, ou l'art de faire la cuisine et la pâtisserie pour toutes les fortunes.* 9th ed.

1822. Carême, Antonin. *Le Maître d'hôtel français, ou Parallèle de la Cuisine ancienne et moderne selon les quatre saisons.* Paris: J. Renouard et Cie, 1842.

1827. *Code Gourmand, Manuel complet de Gastronomie contenant les lois, règles, applications et exemples de l'art de bien vivre.* Paris: Ambroise Dupont.

1828. *Le Gastronome français, ou l'art de bien vivre.*

1828. Carême, Antonin. *Le Cuisinier parisien, ou L'Art de la cuisine française au dix-neuvième siècle.* Reprint, Lyon: Éditions Dioscor, 1986.

1833. ———. *L'Art de la cuisine française au dix-neuvième siècle. Traité Élémentaire et Pratique suivi de dissertations culinaires et gastronomiques utiles aux progrès de cet art.* 2 vols. Paris: Chez l'auteur.

1836. ———. *French Cookery: comprising L'art de la cuisine française, Le Pâtissier royal, Le Cuisinier parisien.* Trans. William Hall. London: John Murray.

1909. Escoffier, Auguste. *A Guide to Modern Cookery* [original edition (1902) in French].

1913. Richardin, Edmond. *La Cuisine française du XIVe au XXe siècle—L'Art du bien manger.* Paris: Éditions d'art et de littérature.

1913. Pampille [Marthe Daudet]. *Les Bons Plats de France—Cuisine régionale.* Paris: Arthème Fayard.

1921–28. Curnonsky [Maurice Sailland] and Marcel Rouff. *La France gastronomique—Guide des merveilles culinaires et des bonnes auberges françaises.* 27 vols. Paris: F. Rouff.

Appendix B

Sample of Cookbooks

Bibliographie de la France, *1811–98**

1811 2 (*Bibliographie de l'Empire* in first year of publication) PHYSIQUE, CHIMIE, PHARMACIE
A. Viard, *Le Cuisinier impérial, ou l'art de faire la cuisine et la pâtisserie pour toutes les fortunes,* 6th ed., 2000 ex.
Magiron (homme de bouche), *Le Nouveau Cuisinier universel,* 2000 ex.

1821 7 AGRICULTURE, ÉCONOMIE RURALE, VÉTÉRINAIRE ET DOMESTIQUE
La Cuisinière bourgeoise[†]
La Cuisinière bourgeoise, new ed.[†]
La nouvelle Cuisinière bourgeoise[†]
La petite Cuisinière habile[†]
Le Cuisinier économe
Le Confiseur moderne
Le Confiseur royal

1825 9 AGRICULTURE, ÉCONOMIE RURALE, VÉTÉRINAIRE ET DOMESTIQUE
Le Cuisinier des cuisiniers
Le Cuisinier économe
Viart et al., *Le Cuisinier royal*
La Cuisinière bourgeoise[†]

---

* The *Bibliographie de la France* is the official record of modern French publishing. Volumes are presented by year of publication, total volumes published, category, and title; reissued titles count as a separate entry. Numbers in parentheses following a publication year denote books pertaining to cuisine.
† Coded feminine.
‡ Woman author.

La Cuisinière de la campagne[†]
Manuel du cuisinier et de la cuisinière[†]
Mme Gacon-Dufour, *Manuel du Pâtissier et de la Pâtisserie*[‡]
Nouveau Dictionnaire de cuisine
La Pâtissière de la campagne et de la ville[†]

1834 6 AGRICULTURE, ÉCONOMIE RURALE, VÉTÉRINAIRE ET DOMESTIQUE
La Cuisinière de la campagne et de la ville, 15th ed.[†]
————, 16th ed.[†]
La Cuisinière du Haut-Rhin[†]
Le Cordon bleu par Mlle Marguerite (Horace Raisson)[†‡]
La Nouvelle Cuisinière bourgeoise, 6th ed.[†]
La Nouvelle Cuisinière française, 7th ed.[†]

1839 3 AGRICULTURE, ÉCONOMIE RURALE, VÉTÉRINAIRE ET DOMESTIQUE
Le Cuisinier méridional
Le Cuisinier parisien
Mlle Catherine, *Manuel Complet de la Cuisinière Bourgeoise*[†‡]

1847 4 AGRICULTURE, ÉCONOMIE RURALE, VÉTÉRINAIRE ET DOMESTIQUE
Le Cordon bleu[†]
Beauvilliers and Carême, *La Cuisine ordinaire*, 4th ed.
La Cuisinière de la campagne et de la ville[†]
La Cuisinière des cuisinières[†]

1848 15 (4) SCIENCES ET ARTS: VI. ARTS UTILES B. ALIMENTS
Nouveau Manuel du Cuisinier
Manuel du pâtissier anglais (traduit en français par Dick Boston)
La Cuisinière des Cuisinières de la ville et de la campagne[†]
La Cuisinière républicaine par la Citoyenne Catherine, Cordon Tri-Colore Cidevant Cordon-Bleu
    (Pamphlet)[†‡]

1849 9 (5) SCIENCES ET ARTS: VI. ARTS UTILES D. ARTS ALIMENTAIRES (separate
    from Économie domestique)
Manuel de la Cuisinière[†]
Mlle Marion, *Le Restaurateur des Ménages, ou La Cuisine Bourgeoise*[†‡]
Le Parfait Cuisinier français moderne
La Cuisine parisienne

1850 12 (3) SCIENCES ET ARTS—ARTS ALIMENTAIRES
Almanach—Manuel de la Cuisinière[†]
La Cuisinière de la campagne et de la ville[†]
Mme Blancmesnil, *La Cuisinière du Bon Marché pour la Ville et la Campagne*[†‡]

1854 12 ÉCONOMIE DOMESTIQUE ET ARTS ALIMENTAIRES—CUISINE—PAIN, ETC.—VINS, ALCOOLS, ETC.

(45 total; also under the category Arts du vêtement)

Almanach des ménagères et des gastronomes[†]

Almanach des ménagères et des gastronomes, 2d ed.[†]

Almanach de la jeune cuisinière bourgeoise[†]

Almanach complet de la cuisine

Almanach-manuel de la cuisinière[†]

Manuelo del cocinero, cocinera[†]

Manuelo des cocinero, cocinera, 2d ed.[†]

La Bonne Cuisinière bourgeoise[†]

La Bonne et parfaite cuisinière[†]

Le Cuisinier perfectionné

Viart et al., *Le Cuisinier impérial de la ville et de la campagne*

La Cuisinière de la campagne et de la ville[†]

1871 6 (2) ARTS INDUSTRIELS: 2. ÉCONOMIE DOMESTIQUE

La Cuisinière assiégée, Ou L'art de Vivre en Temps de Siège; Par Une Femme de Ménage (36 pp.)[††]

La Cuisine pendant le siège. Recettes pour accommoder les viandes de cheval et d'âne et en préparer une nourriture agréable, suivies de conseils sur la conservation ou l'utilisation de diverses substances. Par M . Destaminil, chef de Cuisine (24 pp.)

1872 17 (9) ARTS INDUSTRIELS: 2. ÉCONOMIE DOMESTIQUE

Mme Blanquet, *La Cuisinière des Ménages*[††]

Breteuil, *Le Cuisinier européen*

Dubois, *La Cuisine de tous les pays*

Gouffé, *Le Livre de la pâtisserie*

La Cuisine de carême et des jours d'abstinence

Mlle Madeleine, *La Parfaite Cuisinière bourgeoise*[††]

Anonymous, *Nouvel Manuel de la Cuisinière bourgeoise*[†]

de Périgord, *Le Trésor de la Cuisinière et de la maîtresse de maison*[†]

Répertoire de Cuisine simplifiée

1880 17 (10) ARTS INDUSTRIELS: 2. ÉCONOMIE DOMESTIQUE

Album de la marmite

L. E. Audot, *La Cuisinière de la campagne et de la ville*[†]

Audot et al., *Supplément à la Cuisinière de la campagne*[†]

Mme R. Blanquet, *La Cuisinière des Ménages*[††]

Croisette, *La Bonne et parfaite Cuisinière*[†]

E. Dumont, *La Bonne Cuisinière française*[†]

C. Esséyric, *Les Secrets de la Cuisine*

Lambez, *Nouvelle Cuisinière bourgeoise*[†]
T. Provence, *La Cuisine de tous les jours*

1898 29 (7) [3 vols., 1 for tables] ARTS INDUSTRIELS: 2. ÉCONOMIE DOMESTIQUE
    (alphabetized; not above)
André-Valdès, *La Cuisine rationnelle et pratique*
L. E. Audot, *La Cuisinière de la campagne et de la ville, ou Nouvelle Cuisine économique*[†]
Cuisinier gascon—Le Meilleur Traité alimentaire
Mlle A. Ennery, *Le Nouveau Livre de Cuisine*[‡]
G. Garlin, *La Bonne Cuisine*
F. Grandi, *Deux cent cinquante manières d'apprêter les oeufs*
Mlle Jeannette, *La Nouvelle Cuisinière Habile*[††‡]

Appendix C

Research Notes

Although I first wrote about food and cuisine in 1975, my work on what was to become *Accounting for Taste* began in earnest when I moved to New York in 1989. The year before I had been asked by the American Sociological Association to organize its session about the sociology of culture for its annual meetings. After receiving four session papers dealing with food, I decided to devote the entire agenda to culinary affairs. One of those papers was by Sharon Zukin, professor of sociology at Brooklyn College and the Graduate Center of the City College of New York, who was then working on a larger project concerned with urban foodways. Sharon invited me to join her in interviewing chefs in Manhattan restaurants, and I accepted her invitation with alacrity. It was a wonderful way to reacquaint myself with New York City and to begin exploring the vibrant food scene in Manhattan.

Our interview sample was serendipitous. We were interested in comparing the perspectives of three groups of restaurant professionals: executive chefs who cooked in restaurants as employees, chef-owners, and owners who were not themselves chefs. We chose high-profile, culinarily adventurous chefs as measured by their celebrity in the general media, primarily *The New York Times,* as well as others with whom we had some personal connection. In addition, we made a particular point of looking for women, whose presence in the elite restaurant world is, to put it mildly, less than salient. We classified the cuisines that we sought as Elite French/Italian and Nouvelle American. Then, after making a preliminary list of interviewees, we wrote them (in French for the French chefs) to solicit the interviews. Our final list came to thirty-one interviews of individuals in twenty-three restaurants; of the people whom we initially contacted, only two refused to grant interviews. Where possible, we interviewed (separately) the owner and the executive chef (Sirio Maccioni and Daniel Boulud at Le Cirque, Danny Meyer and Michael Romano at Union Square Cafe, Drew Nieporent and

Deborah Ponzek at Montrachet). Some time later, I added other interviews, which were conducted in the United States, Canada, and France.

The interviews themselves followed a loosely structured questionnaire that focused on career patterns, kitchen organization, staff training, the conception of the restaurant's public, and the changing cuisine. With my focus on things French, I was particularly concerned to learn what French chefs working in the United States thought of producing French cuisine in restaurants that served Americans, employed Americans, and necessarily relied on American products. "What is French cuisine for you?" was, to me, the primary question. Perhaps the most useful question, all the more revelatory when the answer repeated a previous one, was, "Is there something that I should have asked but did not?"

With the exception of those from printed sources, the quotations in chapter 5 are from the interviews that I conducted, transcribed, and, in the case of the interviews in French, translated (Bergougnoux, Boulud, Jammet, LeCoze, Passard, Vongerichten). We sent copies of all the transcriptions to the interviewees; only two made comments or clarifications.

Most of the interviews took place in the summer and fall of 1991, generally in midafternoon between the lunch and dinner service as the only free time readily available. And, to answer the inevitable question, with two exceptions we did not eat at the restaurants when we conducted these interviews, though we were usually offered, and accepted, coffee. (We had previously or have subsequently dined in many of the restaurants.) Declining such an offer would have contravened the ethic of generosity that is so strong a trait of chefs. At Bouley's, seeing us standing there in his kitchen armed with our tape recorder and surrounded by food, the pastry chef sent over two scrumptious miniature raspberry-pear ganache-soufflés, along with the admonition to the sous-chef to whom we were talking that "you can't very well cook in front of them without giving them anything to eat." The exceptions to our no-dining rule were a lunch at Le Cirque for Sharon Zukin, which owner Sirio Maccioni insisted upon after her interview with him; and my meal in a private dining room at Le Bernardin with chef Gilbert LeCoze, who scheduled a lunchtime interview.

The interviews are, quite simply, marvelous documents. The interviewees were both very passionate about their work and extremely articulate about the issues that we were raising. They all expressed great interest in our project, and some even turned the tables to ask us about our own work. Consequently, the interviews are as illuminating as they are informative. Moreover, the interviewees were extremely generous with the time that they had in short supply; after all, academics had nothing particular to offer them or their restaurants. Even though his assistant had warned us that David Bouley couldn't give us more than twenty minutes, he ended up talking to us for an hour and a half, whereupon he invited us into the kitchen to see the dinner service in preparation and talk with the sous-chef.

Immediately following are the interviews that I conducted and from which I quote in the text; the interviewees' restaurants; and a brief career update since the time of the interviews. It is striking how the celebrated chefs of 1991 continue to dominate the restaurant scene in New York over a decade later. Next are all the interviews that were conducted, along with the name of the interviewer.

Cited interviewees (New York City unless noted) or chefs from printed sources

Jean-Michel Bergougnoux—Le Cygne, executive chef   July 24, 1991
A few weeks following my interview with Bergougnoux, Le Cygne closed after several years in the same location in central Manhattan. Bergougnoux moved to Raphaël that October. He is currently head chef at L'Absinthe, a French-style brasserie on Manhattan's East Side.
<http://www.labsinthe.citysearch.com/1.html>

David Bouley—Bouley, chef-owner   May 31, 1991
In 1996 David Bouley, one of the highest-profile chefs in New York, closed the flagship restaurant that he had opened in southern Manhattan in 1991 and announced plans for a mega-restaurant complex and for revamping a Manhattan landmark, The Russian Tearoom. The projects did not pan out. In 1997 Bouley opened Bouley's Bakery in southern Manhattan and the Austrian-inspired Danube in 1999. Because of the damage incurred after the September 11, 2001, terrorist bombing of the World Trade Center nearby, Bouley's Bakery and Danube closed, though David Bouley was in the forefront of efforts to feed rescue workers at Ground Zero. Danube soon reopened, and in February 2002, Bouley opened on the site of Bouley's Bakery.
<http://newyork.citysearch.com/feature/24826/>
<http://www.newyorkmetro.com/frame/set.htm?site=http://www.bouley.net>

Daniel Boulud—Le Cirque, executive chef   October 21, 1991
After Daniel Boulud left Le Cirque, he opened Daniel in 1993. When Sirio Maccioni reconceived Le Cirque as Le Cirque 2000 and moved it to another location, Boulud turned Daniel into Café Boulud in September 1998 and in January 1999 revamped the old Le Cirque into Daniel. Boulud has since opened a more informal restaurant, db Bistro Moderne, in Midtown (celebrated for its outrageously rich hamburger with foie gras and braised short ribs). In 2003 Boulud published *Letters to a Young Chef* (Basic Books) as well as a new cookbook, *Daniel's Dish—Entertaining at Home with a Four-Star Chef* (Filippacchi), and opened a second Café Boulud in Palm Beach.
<http://danielnyc.com/>
<http://starchefs.com/dboulud_bio.html>
See also Leslie Brenner, *The Fourth Star—Dispatches from inside Daniel Boulud's Celebrated New York Restaurant* (New York: Clarkson Potter, 2002).

Georges Briguet—Le Périgord, owner   July 22, 1991
Briguet continues to run Le Périgord, carefully choosing the chefs who will maintain its tradition of elegance and fine dining.
<http://www.leperigord.com/>

André Jammet—La Caravelle, owner   September 16, 1991
André Jammet continues the traditions of La Caravelle, now in its forty-first year in New York. Since 1988 Jammet has run La Caravelle, which is invariably cited for the excellence of its chefs. He supervises the restaurant very closely, to the point of shopping for produce himself.
<http://www.lacaravelle.com/welcome.asp>

Gilbert LeCoze—Le Bernardin, chef-owner   June 7, 1991
Gilbert LeCoze died unexpectedly of a heart attack in 1994 at the age of 48. Le Bernardin, the restaurant that he and his sister, Maguy LeCoze, opened in New York in 1986, reprised the name and the seafood cuisine of his Michelin two-star restaurant in Paris. Since LeCoze's death, Le Bernardin has been run by Maguy LeCoze and chef Eric Ripert. It continues as the premier seafood restaurant in Manhattan, known as well for the particular excellence of its service.
<http://www.le-bernardin.com/>

Michael Noble—Diva at the Metropolitan Hotel, Vancouver, B.C.   February 12, 2001
At the Vancouver restaurant Diva, Michael Noble was named Chef of the Year in 1999/2000 by the Canadian Federation of Chefs and Cooks and participated as a challenger on *Iron Chef* (potatoes were the required ingredient for his contest dishes). He later returned to his hometown of Calgary, where he opened a seafood restaurant, Catch, in the fall of 2002. Noble also serves as coach and manager for the Bocuse d'Or team.
<http://www.calgaryplus.ca/profile/674739/>

Alain Passard—L'Arpège Paris, chef-owner   March 13, 2001
At the time of my interview, Alain Passard had a three-star Michelin rating, which has continued, even after he eliminated meat from his menu in January 2001.
<http://www.alain-passard.com/>

Marta Pulini—Le Madri, executive chef   July 23, 1991
Marta Pulini has continued to work in various consulting capacities for the culinary enterprises of Pino Luongo.

Michael Romano—The Union Square Cafe   May 30, 1991
After a stint as the first American chef at André Jammet's La Caravelle, since 1988 Michael Romano has made The Union Square Cafe restaurant a favorite among New

Yorkers. Rather than change the highly successful formula of this restaurant, the owner, Danny Meyer, chose to open other restaurants in Manhattan, including Tabla (nouvelle Indian), 11 Madison (new American), and Grammercy Tavern.
<http://starchefs.com/mromano/html/index.shtml>

André Soltner—Lutèce   May 24, 1991
The elder statesman of French chefs in Manhattan, André Soltner started his American career as chef at Lutèce in 1961. He bought the restaurant in 1972 and sold it in 1995. Now a master chef at the French Culinary Institute in New York, Soltner consults and gives cooking demonstrations across the United States

Charlie Trotter—Charlie Trotter's-Chicago   November 9, 1991
Charlie Trotter celebrated the fifteenth anniversary of his restaurant in August 2002.
<http://www.charlietrotters.com/home.asp>

Jean-Georges Vongerichten—JoJo's   July 29, 1991
Jean-Georges Vongerichten has continued to expand his culinary empire. In addition to the bistro JoJo's (1991), which he had recently opened at the time of our interview, he opened Vong, a "Euro-Thai" restaurant (1991, New York; 1995, London; 1997, Hong Kong; 1999, Chicago), the Lipstick Café (1992), Jean-Georges, a temple of haute cuisine at Columbus Circle in Trump Towers (1997), the Mercer Kitchen (1998), Prime Steakhouse-Bellagio, Las Vegas (1998), Dune-Bahamas (2000), and 66 (2003). Like his peers, Vongerichten has a number of cookbooks to his credit. Taking up what must be the ultimate challenge, he opened a restaurant in Paris (2001).
<http://www.jean-georges.com/#>
<http://www.cuisinenet.com/glossary/chfvong.html>

FULL SAMPLE

Interviewee	Restaurant	Interviewer*
Chefs (9)		
Jean-Michel Bergougnoux	Le Cygne	PPF
Daniel Boulud	Le Cirque	PPF
Tom Collichio	Mondrian	SZ
Bobby Flay	Mesa Grill	JP
Judy Mancini	Rogers & Barbero	JP
Charles Palmer	Aureole	SZ
Debra Ponzek	Montrachet	JP
Marta Pulini	Le Madri	PPF
Michael Romano	The Union Square Cafe	PPF, SZ
Sous-chefs (5)		
Lou Amdur		JP
Romi Doratan	Le Bar Bat	JP
Girard	Nick & Eddie's	JP
Chris Heimer	Le Madri, Coco Pazzo	JP
John Lee	Chanterelle	JP
Chef-owners (9)		
David Bouley	Bouley	SZ, PPF
Larry Forgione	An American Place	SZ
Peter Hoffman	Savoy	SZ
Gilbert LeCoze	Le Bernardin	PPF
Charles Palmer	Aureole	SZ
Anne Rosensweig	Arcadia	SZ
André Soltner	Lutece	PPF, SZ
Jean-Georges Vongerichten	JoJo's	PPF
David Waltuck	Chanterelle	JP
Owners (8)		
Kalil Ayoubi	Cal's	JP
Georges Briguet	Le Périgord	PPF, SZ
André Jammet	La Caravelle	PPF
Sirio Maccioni	Le Cirque	SZ
Danny Meyer	The Union Square Cafe	SZ
Drew Nierporent	Montrachet, Tribeca Grill	JP
Pat Rogers	Rogers & Barbero	JP
Peter Stephan	Café Luxembourg	SZ

*Interviewers: PPF, Priscilla Ferguson; SZ, Sharon Zukin; JP, Jennifer Parker (Talwar).

Notes

Prologue

1. Louis Veuillot, "Metz perdue," *L'Univers*, November 1, 1870; reprinted in *Paris pendant les deux sièges* (1871), *Oeuvres complètes* (Paris: P. Lethielleux, 1928), 13:167. Here as throughout this book, translations are mine unless otherwise indicated.

Chapter One

1. The *Oxford English Dictionary* cites *cook* as originating in 1380 and *cookery* (favored by British usage) in 1393, imports from Old, then Middle High German. *Cuisine*, another import referring to either a kitchen or a style of cooking, and *cuisinier*, referring to a French cook, make their appearance in 1483. *Cooking* turns up in 1645, with no less an authority than John Milton ("Man's perverse cooking hath turn'd this bounty of God into a Scorpion"). The last quotation points to the negative connotations of cooking as a "dressing up" and falsification of a work. Cf. the American expression for illegal financial manipulation, "cooking the books," and the French variation, *cuisine* or *cuisiner*, to refer to shady manipulation of various sorts (as in "la cuisine politique"). The French language adopted *cuisine* from Latin at the end of the twelfth century for both the kitchen and food preparation.

2. See Françoise Aubaile-Sallenave, "La Méditérranée: Une cuisine, des cuisines," *Information sur les sciences sociales* 35, no. 1 (1996): 139–94; and Sidney W. Mintz, *Tasting Food, Tasting Freedom: Excursions into Eating, Culture, and the Past* (Boston: Beacon Press, 1996), chap. 7, "Cuisine: High, Low, and Not at All," pp. 92–105. See also Amy Trubek, "Terroir: From Local Knowledge to National Discourse," paper presented at the Society for French Historical Studies meetings, Milwaukee, April 2003.

3. Taking something of a contrarian tack, Alberto Capatti and Massimo Montanari argue for a "gastronomy of hunger," in which the very restriction of resources spurs

culinary invention. In *La Cuisine italienne—Histoire d'une culture* (1999), trans. Anna Colao with Mino Colao (Paris: Le Seuil, 2002), pp. 20–21. It is nonetheless true that greater resources allow greater scope to the culinary imagination.

4. Thomas McNamee, "Dinner in Tuscany," *Saveur* 54 (November 2001): 47; and Molly Turner, "Vermont Chicken Pie," ibid., p. 61. McNamee also states that "Tuscan food, whether of yeoman or aristocrat, is not about innovation, surprise, complexity or 'elsewhereness.' The gnocchi exemplify its ideals: a sense of the earth, an expression of the place of origin, a clarity of flavor, and a faithfulness to historical type. *Typico* is a word of high praise here" (p. 47).

5. See Mark Kurlansky, *Cod—A Biography of the Fish That Changed the World* (New York: Walker & Co., 1995), pp. 252–56.

6. Herman Melville, *Moby-Dick* [1851], ed. Harrison Hayford and Hershel Parker (New York: Norton, 1967), chap. 15, pp. 64–65.

7. Julie Dulude, "Chowders Do Battle for Red Stocking," *Vineyard Gazette*, December 19, 1997, p. 8a. For the record, the contest, sponsored by a local business association, raised some $2,000 for children's Christmas gifts. There were two categories of chowder, quahog (clam) and Island (seafood); winners were chosen by ballots cast by attendees. Most entrants were local restaurants, but one man brought out an old family recipe modernized with the use of bay leaf.

8. Norbert Elias, *The Civilizing Process—Part 1, The History of Manners* (1939; trans. E. Jephcott, Oxford: Blackwell, 1994), p. 3.

9. Jean Anthelme Brillat-Savarin (1755–1826) was a provincial lawyer elected to the National Assembly in 1789. Later appointed to various positions in the judiciary, then elected mayor of his hometown in 1793, Brillat-Savarin found it prudent to leave France under the Terror. He settled in New York, where he earned his living giving French lessons and playing in a theatrical orchestra. Returning to France under the Directory, he once again occupied various judicial posts in Paris. Besides the *Physiology* he wrote judicial works, including an *Essai historique et critique sur le Duel* (1819). He died of pneumonia caught during the anniversary service of the execution of Louis XVI in the Cathedral of Saint Denis (the traditional burial place of French royalty). See the "Notice sur l'auteur" by le baron Richerand in Brillat-Savarin, *Physiologie du goût* (1826; Paris: Charpentier, 1839).

10. What sounds like a proverb was formulated well after Brillat-Savarin, by the materialist philosopher Ludwig Feuerbach in *Die Naturwissenschaft und die Revolution* of 1850, as "Der Mensch ist, was er isst." M. F. K. Fisher, in her translation of Brillat-Savarin's *Physiology of Taste* (1949; reprint, Washington, D.C.: Counterpoint, 2000), p. 5, claims that the connection between being and eating was not original to Feuerbach, but she provides no anterior citation other than Brillat-Savarin.

11. See the report of the Abbé Grégoire to the Convention, "Rapport sur la nécessité et les moyens d'anéantir les patois et d'universaliser l'usage de la langue française" (1794), reprinted in Michel de Certeau, Dominique Julia, and Jacques Revel, *Une politique de la langue—La Révolution française et les patois: L'enquête de Grégoire* (Paris: Galli-

mard, 1975), pp. 300–317. Basing his conclusions on questionnaires sent to government officials in the provinces, Grégoire estimated that fully half the French could not speak French at all, and only 3 million of some 20 million inhabitants could speak it more or less fluently. Successive governments worked diligently to impose French as a truly national language on the linguistic patchwork of the French provinces. For the nineteenth-century estimate, see Eugen Weber, *From Peasants into Frenchmen* (Stanford, Calif.: Stanford University Press, 1976), p. 70.

12. Quoted by John Cooper, *Eat and be Satisfied: A Social History of Jewish Food* (Northvale, N.J.: Jason Aronson, 1993), p. 85. See also pp. 107, 198.

13. The ambassador, Jérôme Lippomano, and Brantôme, quoted by Alfred Franklin, *La Cuisine* (Paris: Plon, Nourrit & Cⁱᵉ, 1888), pp. 106–8.

14. Marcel Rouff, *La Vie et la Passion de Dodin-Bouffant-Gourmet* (1924; Paris: Le Serpent à plumes, 1994), pp. 11–12.

15. See Barbara Ketchum Wheaton, *Savoring the Past: The French Kitchen and Table from 1300 to 1789* (Philadelphia: University of Pennsylvania Press, 1983), esp. chap. 7, "The Court Festivals of Louis XIV." For the connections between culinary creativity and the flourishing luxury industries (porcelain, linen, silver, etc.), see Gérard Mabille, "1690–1800—La Table à la française," in *Histoire de la table—Les arts de la table des origins à nos jours,* by Pierre Ennès, Gérard Mabille, and Philippe Thibaut, pp. 125–91 (Paris: Flammarion, 1994). For a close look at the running of a princely household, see Dominique Michel, *Vatel et la naissance de la gastronomie* (Paris: Le Grand Livre du mois, 1999). Audiger's *Maison réglée et l'art de diriger la maison d'un grand seigneur tant à la ville qu'à la camopagne* (1674), reproduced in Gilles Laurendon and Laurence Laurendon, eds., *L'Art de la cuisine française aux dix-septième siècle* (Paris: Payot & Rivages, 1995), devotes a chapter to each functionary in an aristocratic household, from the chaplain to the gardener.

16. See Wheaton, *Savoring the Past,* p. 292.

17. François Massialot, *Le Cuisinier roïal et bourgeois,* 3d ed. (Paris: Charles de Sercy, 1698); Bonnefons from Wheaton, *Savoring the Past,* p. 125; L. S. R. here and below from Gilles Laurendon and Laurence Laurendon, eds., *L'Art de la cuisine française au dix-septième siècle* (Paris: Payot & Rivages, 1995), pp. 22–23.

18. *Almanach perpétuel des Gourmands, contenant Le Code Gourmand et des applications, règles et méditations de gastronomie transcendante,* 6th ed. (Paris: Barba, 1830), p. 6. Stephen Mennell, *All Manners of Food: Eating and Taste in England and France from the Middle Ages to the Present* (Oxford: Basil Blackwell, 1985), p. 74, notes the connections between classicisms in different realms, though without elaborating the institutional connection. Alain Girard points to the codification and rationalization, the prestige of the written word over oral discourse, the ties to science as factors in connecting the emergent cuisine to elites in "Le Triomphe de *La Cuisinière bourgeoise:* Livres culinaires, cuisine et société aux xviie et xviiie siècles," *Revue d'histoire moderne et contemporaine* 24 (October–December 1977), pp. 518–19.

19. Between 1480 and 1800 Philip Hyman and Mary Hyman count only 50 sepa-

rate cookbooks, but these yielded 472 separate editions. "Imprimer la cuisine: Les livres de cuisine en France entre le xve et le xixe siècle," in *Histoire de l'alimentation,* ed. J-L Flandrin and M. Montanari (Paris: Fayard, 1997), pp. 643–45.

20. *Le Pâtissier françois,* quoted by ibid., pp. 652, 650.

21. See Girard, "Le Triomphe de *La Cuisinière bourgeoise,*" pp. 497–523. Hyman and Hyman, "Imprimer la cuisine," p. 653, identify 62 editions between 1746 and the end of the century, which would represent some 93,000 copies in circulation over the half century. In total, they have located 122 editions between 1746 and 1866. Mary Hyman and Philip Hyman, "Livres et cuisine au XIXe siècle," in *À table au XIXe siècle* (Paris: Flammarion, 2001), p. 89. The nineteenth-century figures are taken from my sample of fourteen years in the *Bibliographie de la France* from 1811, its first year of publication, to 1898. See appendix B of the present text.

22. Quotations in this and the next two paragraphs are taken from the nonpaginated preface of [Menon], *La Cuisiniére bourgeoise, suivie de l'Office a l'usage de tous ceux qui se mêlent de la dépense des Maisons. Contenant la maniére de dissequer, connoître & servir toutes sortes des Viandes,* new ed. (Bruxelles: F. Foppens, 1759). The translation appeared as *The French Family Cook* (London: J. Bell, 1793), with the explanatory subtitle that, even more than the French title, stresses the dual nature of the work, which, despite its comforting, homey title, nonetheless aims fairly high on the social scale: *Being a complete System of French Cookery. Adapted to the Tables, not only of the Opulent, but of Persons of moderate Fortune and Condition . . . Necessary for Housekeepers, Butlers, Cooks, and all who are concerned in the Superintendence of a Family.*

23. Wheaton, *Savoring the Past,* p. 161, contends that French cooks actually exercised considerable influence on everyday life of *cuisine bourgeoise* in their country through the foreign dishes they introduced upon their return to France. See chap. 9, "French Cooks Abroad." As in France, haute cuisine was beyond the means of most kitchens and consumers. On the foreign editions of La Varenne, see p. 292 of Wheaton.

24. Girard, "Le Triomphe de *La Cuisinière bourgeoise,*" emphasizes the exclusion of the urban lower classes as well as the peasantry from the evolving culinary patrimony (pp. 508–10) and the ideological dependence of the bourgeoisie in culinary affairs. On peasant diets, see Jean-Louis Flandrin, "L'alimentation paysanne en économie de subsistance," in *Histoire de l'Alimentation,* ed. Jean-Louis Flandrin and Massimo Montanari (Paris: Fayard, 1997), pp. 597–627.

25. See Christiane Mervaud, *Voltaire à table—Plaisir du corps, plaisir de l'esprit* (Paris: Éditions Desjonquères, 1998), pt. 1. Voltaire's personal abstemiousness makes all the more striking the luxury of the table he felt constrained to have.

26. Jérôme Lippomano, cited by Franklin, *La Cuisine,* p. 108.

27. Louis-Sébastien Mercier, *Tableau de Paris,* 2 vols. (1788; reprint, Paris: Mercure de France, 1994) vol. 1, chap. 10, p. 46.

28. Reynald Abad, *Le Grand Marché: L'approvisionnement alimentaire de Paris sous l'Ancien régime* (Paris: Fayard, 2002). Abad makes effective use of local government officials' complaints about the primacy of the Paris market.

29. [Desalleurs l'aîné], *Lettre d'un patissier anglois au nouveau Cuisinier françois*, appended to *Le Cuisinier gascon*, new ed. (Amsterdam, 1747), p. 199.

30. Le Grand d'Aussy, P. J. B., *Histoire de la vie privée des français depuis l'origine de la nation jusqu'à nos jours*, 2 vols. (1782; reprint, Chilly-Mazarin: Éditions SenS, 1999–2000), 1:27–29. See Julia Csergo, "Avant-Propos," ibid., 1:11–25.

31. Le Grand d'Aussy, *Histoire de la vie privée des français*, vol. 1, chap. 1, p. 36.

32. See Julia Csergo, "La Constitution de la spécialité gastronomique comme objet patrimonial en France (fin xviiie–xxe siècle)," in *L'Esprit des lieux—Le patrimoine et la cité*, ed. Daniel J. Grange and Dominique Poulot (Grenoble: Presses Universitaires de Grenoble, 1997), 183–93.

Chapter Two

1. M. Audiguier, "Coup d'oeil sur l'Influence de la cuisine et sur les ouvrages de M. Carême," cited in Antonin Carême, *L'Art de la cuisine française au dix-neuvième siècle*, 2 vols. (Paris: Chez l'auteur, 1833), vol. 2, pt. 3, pp. 299–316; quotation is from p. 311. References to this edition will be cited as *L'Art* (1833). Although the modern edition of this work, edited by Gilles and Laurence Laurendon (Paris: Payot & Rivages, 1994), lacks the prefatory material, aphorisms, and sundry observations that are so revelatory of Carême's obsessions, it is more useful for the analysis of the cuisine. It will be cited as *L'Art* (1994). The other citations to Carême are to *Le Pâtissier royal parisien* [1815], 3d ed., 2 vols. (Paris, 1841); *Le Pâtissier pittoresque* [1815], 4th ed. (Paris, 1842); *Le Cuisinier Parisien* (1828; reprint, Lyon: Éditions Dioscor, 1986); and *Le Maître d'hôtel français*, 2 vols. (1822; Paris: J. Renouard et Cie, 1842). All translations are mine unless otherwise indicated.

2. See Stephen Mennell's insightful discussion of Carême's cuisine as a paradigm of French professional cooking, with paradigm taken in the sense of Thomas Kuhn's *Structure of Scientific Revolutions* (1962): *All Manners of Food: Eating and Taste in England and France from the Middle Ages to the Present* (Oxford: Basil Blackwell, 1985), pp. 148–49.

3. Dumas is cited from the *Grand Dictionnaire de cuisine* (1873; Paris: Phébus, 2000), p. 212; and from *Propos d'art et de cuisine* (Paris: Calmann Lévy, 1877), p. 29. Auguste Escoffier, *A Guide to Modern Cookery* (1909; London: Studio Editions, 1994), p. vi.

4. Jean-Claude Bonnet, "Carême, or the Last Sparks of Decorative Cuisine," pp. 155–82 in *Taste Nostalgia*, ed. Allen S. Weiss (New York: Lusitania Press, 1997); Georges Bernier, *Antonin Carême 1783–1833: La sensualité gourmande en Europe* (Paris: Grasset, 1989), pp. 223–24, notes how little place Carême occupies in a larger culinary consciousness, an observation that my own experience in France has confirmed many times over.

5. "Une page des Mémoires de Carême," in *Les Classiques de la table*, by Justin Améro, new ed. (Paris: Firmin-Didot, 1855), 2:214. Other unidentified quotations from Carême are cited from this source.

6. The political opportunism of Charles-Maurice de Talleyrand-Périgord (1754–1838) was only slightly more notorious than his love of fine food, allegedly leading a political opponent to remark that the only master Talleyrand never betrayed was Brie cheese. Christian Guy, *Une histoire de la cuisine française* (Paris: Les Productions de Paris, 1962), p. 119. Carême categorically affirmed his gastronomic supremacy (*L'Art* [1833] 1:xiii–xvi). The gastronomically uninterested and untutored Napoleon left his minister of foreign affairs in charge of much of the official entertaining. Talleyrand very likely served as the gastronomic as well as the political model for the wily prime minister of Russia, to whom Oscar Wilde attributes the aspiration to culinary immortality quoted in the epigraph at the beginning of this chapter.

7. Lady (Sydney) Morgan, *France in 1829–30,* 2d ed. (London: Saunders and Otley, 1831), 2:411–12. See the whole discussion, with liberal excerpts from Carême's *Maître d'hôtel,* pp. 402–20.

8. Ibid., 2:415–16. Commenting on this passage, Bernier (*Antonin Carême 1783–1833,* p. 220) criticizes not only the French translation in *Les Classiques de la table* but Lady Morgan's gastronomic competence. The implied comparison (pickles, cayenne, allspice), he argues, is undoubtedly more relevant to the cooking of Lady Morgan's native Ireland than to anything that passed for haute cuisine in France. Morgan was, of course, writing for an English audience of presumed inveterate pickle eaters. See Carême's recipe for the fish soup served at this dinner (*L'Art* [1994], pt. 1, chap. 13, pp. 115–16), which he subsequently baptized *Potage anglais de poisson à la Lady Morgan.* The account cited above also makes a point of discussing the elegance of the table setting. On table settings, etc., see Pierre Ennès, "1789–1848—Naissance de la table moderne," in *Histoire de la table,* ed. Pierre Ennès, Gérard Mabille, and Philippe Thiébaut (Paris: Flammarion, 1995), pp. 193–251.

9. For general assessments on the orientation of Carême's cuisine, see Philip Hyman, "Culina mutata, Carême et l'Ancienne cuisine," in *L'Art culinaire au XIXe siècle—Antonin Carême* (Paris: Délégation à l'action artistique de la ville de Paris, 1984), pp. 63–69, translated as "Culina mutata, Carême and l'ancienne cuisine," pp. 71–82 in *French Food: On the table, on the Page, and in French Culture,* ed. Lawrence R. Schehr and Allen S. Weiss (New York: Routledge, 2001).

10. See Julia Csergo, ed., *Pot au feu—Convivial, Familial: Histoires d'un mythe* (Paris: Éditions Autrement, 1999). On the domestic science cookbooks, see Nancy J. Edwards, "The Science of Domesticity: Women, Education and National Identity in Third Republic France, 1880–1914" (Ph.D. diss., University of California-Berkeley, 1997), xviii.

11. William Hall, trans., *French Cookery: Comprising L'Art de la cuisine française, Le Pâtissier royal, Le Cuisinier parisien* (London: John Murray, 1836), pp. 4–5.

12. There are also 108 lean variants of the 358 sauces, ragoûts, garnitures, and essences. Of the 129 names, 83 are French. Of the 123 identified names, 16% represent the military (17 men plus 3 battles), 43% the aristocracy (53 individuals), 13% (16) royalty, 36% (44) arts, letters, and sciences; 13% (16) are connected with gastronomy as hosts (Apicius, Brillat-Savarin, Grimod de la Reynière, Lucullus, Roth-

schild, and so on), as chefs or maîtres-d'hôtel (Laguipierre, Robert, Vatel, Vincent La Chapelle), and as supposed inventors of the sauce in question (béchamel, magnonaise [mayonnaise]). The considerable overlap in these categories, especially for the aristocracy and the military, explains why the total is not 100%.

13. From *Le Cuisinier françois* in 1651 with famous names for only .02% of its recipes, to Massialot's *Le Cuisinier roïal et bourgeois* (1691) with 10.2%, and Menon's *La Cuisinière bourgeoise* (1746) with 14.5%, an astonishing 68.67% of the recipes in Carême's *L'Art de la cuisine française* (1833) (808 recipes out of 1,347) carry celebrated names. By 1914 this nominatory proliferation required publication of a handbook for ready reference. See Edmond Neirinck and Jean-Pierre Poulain, *Histoire de la cuisine et des cuisiniers: Techniques culinaires et pratiques de table, en France, du Moyen-Age à nos jours* (Paris: Éditions Jacques La noire, 2000), pp. 61–63.

14. Jean Anthelme Brillat-Savarin, *Physiologie du goût* (1826; Paris: Charpentier, 1839), preface, pp. 33–35.

15. Avertissement (preface), A. T. Raimbault, *Le Cuisinier étranger pour faire suite au Parfait Cuisinier. Contenant une Notice raisonnée de tous les mets étrangers qu'on peut servir sur une table française*, 2d ed. (Paris: Delacour, 1811). Notice the promise of the subtitle to present all the foreign dishes that might conceivably find a spot on a French table!

16. Mary Hyman and Philip Hyman, "Livres et cuisine au XIXe siècle," in *À table au XIXe siècle* (Paris: Flammarion, 2001), p. 81.

17. A. Viard, *Le Cuisinier impérial* (1806; Nîmes: C. Lacour, 1993), dedicatory preface, author's preface; A. B. Beauvilliers, *L'Art du cuisinier* (Paris: Pilet, 1814), dedication, "Discours préliminaire," p. xii.

18. See in particular Honoré de Balzac, *La Comédie humaine*, 12 vols. (Paris: Gallimard-Pléiade, 1976–81), *Splendeurs et misères des courtisanes* [1845], 6:442, 484, 518; *La Cousine Bette* [1846], 7:319, makes an extensive comparison of doubtful taste between the seductions of the courtesan and those of Carême's cuisine. See Dumas, *Grand Dictionnaire de cuisine*, p. 74. Brillat-Savarin devotes a short chapter to Beauvilliers. Brillat-Savarin (*Physiologie du goût*, meditation 28, chap. 143, pp. 327–28) argues for the originality of *L'Art du cuisinier* in "exactness and method." Writing post-Carême, Eugène Briffault, *Paris à table* (Paris: Hetzel, 1846), p. 147, consideres Beauvilliers an exceptional restaurateur but an ordinary chef.

19. See Kimberly Stevens, "A 24-Karat Wedding Cake with Diamonds You Eat," *New York Times*, 23 March 2003, sec. 9, col. 1, p. 15; archived at <http://www.nytimes.com/2003/03/23/fashion/weddings/23FIEL.html?ex=1049975181&ei=1&en=98c52a700 b6a87ba> . One cake was in the form of a pyramid; one, for the marriage of two psychoanalysts, a reproduction of Freud's couch; and yet another, baked Ferragamo, Jourdain, and Blahnik shoeboxes topped with a fire-red stiletto-heel Blahnik slingback formed from edible hand-sculptured sugar. Although Carême might have rued the blatant commercialism, he most certainly would have appreciated the architectural confections.

20. Regina Schrambley, "That New Brightness of the Plate: Chefs Translate the Classics," *New York Times,* October 10, 2001, pp. F1, F4. "Just as Billy Joel is dabbling in classical music these days, contemporary chefs are taking new cues from that old guy, Escoffier." Behind Escoffier lies Carême: "Clearly, chefs are acknowledging that the mother sauces codified by Carême dominated cooking for centuries for a reason."

21. In their study of nouvelle cuisine as a social movement, Hayagreeva Rao, Philippe Monin, and Rodolphe Durand stress the crucial importance of theorization in prompting chefs to abandon classical cuisine for nouvelle cuisine. "Institutional Change in Toque Ville: Nouvelle Cuisine as an Identity Movement in French Gastronomy," *American Journal of Sociology* 108, no. 4 (January 2003): 795–843. One might speculate that the French proclivity for theorization generally—which we have seen beginning in the seventeenth century for culinary matters—makes the theoretical a necessary engine of social and cultural change.

22. My connection of the chef and the artist is inspired by Pierre-Michel Menger's insightful analysis of artistic occupations, *Portrait de l'artiste en travailleur: Métamorphoses du capitalisme* (Paris: Le Seuil, 2002). Menger sees the artist as an exemplary figure for the new economic order of contemporary capitalism that prizes innovation, creativity, and flexibility of work, and also of the "spectacularization" that creates a highly skewed market. Menger calls on sports for telling comparisons, but as chapter 5 will propose, the culinary world today would serve equally well. For the argument that places cuisine among the fine arts, see Allen S. Weiss, *Feast and Folly: Cuisine, Intoxication, and the Poetics of the Sublime* (Albany: State University of New York Press, 2002).

23. The following discussion draws on the now classic formulation of Benedict Anderson, *Imagined Communities: Reflections on the Origin and Spread of Nationalism* (London: Verso, 1983); and Michael Billig, *Banal Nationalism* (London: Sage, 1995), especially chaps. 1–2. Anderson argues that unlike states, which are defined by authority, nations require an act of the imagination to think of a given territory as a whole. Billig refers to "banal nationalism" not for the articulated ideologies or philosophies justifying nationalism but for the ingrained, largely unconscious ideological habits that make nationalism part of everyday life. I explore the place of French literature in defining France in Priscilla Parkhurst Clark, *Literary France—The Making of a Culture* (Berkeley and Los Angeles: University of California Press, 1987).

Chapter Three

1. *Gastronomie* first appeared in French in 1623 as a translation from the Greek of the (lost) poem of the Epicurean philosopher and culinary sage Archestratus. *Gourmand,* first cited in 1354 as a synonym for *glutton,* takes as its modern meaning what English gives to *gourmet,* that is, someone who is particular about food. In the fifteenth century, *gourmet* designated the "servant of a wine merchant," which evolved into a "wine taster." The modern sense of an individual who appreciates culinary refinement

dates from the eighteenth century. It is worth noting that although the French have officially been *gourmands* since the fourteenth century and modern *gourmets* since the eighteenth, not until the nineteenth century did they became *gastronomes*. *Nouveau petit Robert* (Paris: Dictionnaires Robert, 1993).

2. Hans-Jurgen Teuteberg and Jean-Louis Flandrin, "Transformations de la consommation alimentaire," in *Histoire de l'alimentation*, ed. Jean-Louis Flandrin and Massimo Montanari (Paris: Fayard, 1997), pp. 725–726; "progress of our culinary art," Antonin Carême, *Le Pâtissier royal parisien*, 3d ed., 2 vols. (Paris, 1841), xxxii; Eugène Briffault, *Paris à table* (Paris: Hetzel, 1846), pp. 180–81; "cosmopolitan whole," Jean Anthelme Brillat-Savarin, *Physiologie du goût* (Paris: Charpentier, 1839), meditation 28, p. 329; sixteenth-century visitor cited in Alfred Franklin, *La Cuisine, La vie privée d'autrefois . . .* (Paris: Plon, Nourrit et Cⁱᵉ, 1888), pp. 106–108; cf. *supra*, chapter 1.

3. "three thousand restaurants," Jean-Robert Pitte, "Naissance et expansion des restaurants" in *Histoire de l'alimentation*, ed. Jean-Louis Flandrin and Massimo Montanari (Paris: Fayard, 1997), p. 773; and "set every cook to work," Brillat-Savarin, *Physiologie du goût* (1839), meditation 28, p. 324. On the development of the modern restaurant as a response to incipient modernity, see Rebecca Spang, *The Invention of the Restaurant: Paris and Modern Gastronomic Culture* (Cambridge, Mass.: Harvard University Press, 2000).

4. "successive upheavals of civilization," *Code Gourmand, Manuel complet de Gastronomie* (Paris: Ambroise Dupont, 1827), preface; "distinction between cooks and diners," A. B. de Périgord [Horace Raisson], *Nouvel Almanach des Gourmands servant de guide dans les moyens de faire excellente chère* (Paris: Baudoin Frères, 1825), p. 12; "heroes of gastronomy," Brillat-Savarin, *Physiologie du goût* (1839), pp. 324–26.

5. Edmond Goblot, *La Barrière et le niveau—Essai sur la bourgeoisie française moderne* (Paris: Presses Universitaires de France, 1967).

6. The other six are avarice, anger, envy, pride, lust, and sloth *(avarice, colère, envie, orgueil, luxure, paresse)*. The seven sins were codified in the sixth century as deadly, or, as French has it, "capital" sins, since these dispositions (rather than acts) were at "the head of," and therefore responsible for, a multiplicity of sinful acts (anger, for example, leading to murder). This code offers a brilliant instance of ideological control, for if it is relatively easy to determine whether a given act has been committed, where does one draw the dividing line for these sinful dispositions? Where does gluttony begin, or end? One is always at risk.

7. See Jean-Claude Bonnet, "Le Système de la cuisine et du repas chez Rousseau," *Poétique* 22 (1975): 244–67 and "Le Réseau culinaire dans *l'Encyclopédie*," *Annales E.S.C.* 31, no. 5 (1976): 89–94. For the other side of the culinary debate, see Christine Mervaud, *Voltaire à table—Plaisir du corps, plaisir de l'esprit* (Paris: Éditions Desjonquères, 1998).

8. See appendix B and chapter 4 below. On the development of the parallel professional track beginning in the 1860s with the publication of journals and the development of trade associations and the accompanying strategies of distinction, see Amy

Trubek, *Haute Cuisine—How the French Invented the Culinary Profession* (Philadelphia: University of Pennsylvania Press, 2000), chap. 6, esp. pp. 94–109.

9. See Priscilla Parkhurst Ferguson, *Paris as Revolution* (Berkeley and Los Angeles: University of California Press, 1994), chap. 2, "Mapping the City," and chap. 3, "The Flâneur: The City and Its Discontents." Though better known as the librettist for Rossini's *Guillaume Tell* and *Moïse,* Jouy (Victor-Joseph Étienne) styled himself as the Hermite de la Chaussée d'Antin who sallied forth into Paris and even the provinces. The multiple volumes of his urban explorations first appeared in the *Gazette de France* from 1811 to 1814.

10. A. B. L. Grimod de La Reynière, *Journal des Gourmands et des Belles, ou L'Épicurien français* (Paris: Capelle et Renaud, 1806), 1:23.

11. Julia Abramson, "Grimod's Debt to Mercier and the Emergence of Gastronomic Writing Reconsidered" (*EMF: Studies in Early Modern France* 7 [2001]: 141–62) stresses the continuity between the old and the new gastronomic regimes. Rebecca Spang in *The Invention of the Restaurant* sees the *Almanach* as a full-scale satire of the new empire, arguing that usual readings of this self-contained world of excess have missed the point. Even if she is correct in identifying a satirical component, it nonetheless remains true that the "straight" readings have significantly shaped the collective sense of gastronomy in France. See also Michael Garval, "Grimod de la Reynière's *Almanach des gourmands:* Exploring the Gastronomic New World of Postrevolutionary France," in *French Food: On the Table, on the Page and in French Culture,* ed. Lawrence R. Escher and Allen S. Weiss (New York: Routledge, 2001), pp. 51–70; and Julia Abramson, "Legitimacy and Nationalism in the *Almanach des Gourmands* (1803–1812)," *JEMCS [Journal of Early Modern Cultural Studies]* 3, no. 2 (2003): 101–35.

12. Spang, *The Invention of the Restaurant,* chap. 6, makes much of connections between the culinary codes laid down by Grimod de la Reynière and those imposed on French society by Napoleon I in the First Empire (1804–14), precisely the period in which Grimod was publishing the *Almanach.*

13. In the following section, Brillat-Savarin is quoted from *Physiologie du goût* (1839); the appropriate aphorism or meditation reference is given in the text.

14. The irregular publishing history of Fourier's work makes his contribution to culinary discourse more conjectural than that of the others. Although his first work appeared in 1808 *(Théorie des quatre mouvements et des destinées générales),* his last stayed in manuscript until 1967 *(Le Nouveaux monde amoureux).* Nevertheless, Fourier's ideas were known well before the (fragmentary) edition brought out by his disciples in the mid-1840s.

15. Quotations in this section are from the *Oeuvres complètes,* 12 vols. (Paris: Anthropos, 1966–68): "happiness superior to your desires," 1:170; "gastro-âneries," 6:255 n. 1; gastrosophy, 8:283; "theory of social equilibrium," 4:130; "equilibrium of the passions," 6:258; material abundance, 1:77; "travesty of nature," 6:255–56; life expectancy of 144 years, 1:180, n. 1. See also Rolande Bonnain-Merdyck, "Fourier,

gastrosophe," in *Actualité de Fourier: Colloque d'Arc-et-Senans,* by Henri Lefebvre et al. (Paris: Anthropos, 1975), pp. 145–80.

16. Quotations to the end of this section are from Honoré de Balzac, *La Comédie humaine,* 12 vols. (Paris: Gallimard-Pléiade, 1976–81): *Eugénie Grandet* (3:1148); *Cousin Pons* (7:495, 492–93); *l'Auberge rouge* (11:90–91); *La Fille aux yeux d'or* (5:1050); and *Physiologie du mariage* (11:930).

17. Claude Lévi-Strauss, "Social Structure" (1952), in *Structural Anthropology* (Garden City, N.J.: Doubleday-Anchor, 1967); my corrected translation.

18. Pierre Bourdieu, *The Field of Cultural Production* (New York: Columbia University Press, 1993), pp. 162–163. See also Priscilla Parkhurst Ferguson, "A Cultural Field in the Making: Gastronomy in 19th-century France," *American Journal of Sociology* 104, no. 3 (November 1998): 597–641.

19. However clear an idea we may have about how certain fields operate, we know rather less about how they became fields. Bourdieu's own empirical analyses tend to map the field as constituted, since they mostly draw the larger societal and intellectual consequences in order to identify the mechanisms and the logic by which the field reproduces itself. *Homo academicus* begins with the postwar university field and gives relatively little consideration to the conditions out of which the field emerged. Although the subtitle of *The Rules of Art—Genesis and Structure of the Literary Field*—indicates the goal of tracking the emergence of the literary field in mid-nineteenth-century France, the title belies the theoretical scope. Moreover, Bourdieu focuses on the structure and logic of the literary field and its evolution in the last half of the century rather than on the conditions out of which the field emerged in the first half.

20. See Michael Freeman, "Sung," in *Food in Chinese Culture: Anthropological and Historical Perspectives,* ed. K. C. Chang (New Haven, Conn.: Yale University Press, 1977), pp. 141–76. On the suppression of gastronomy by the Communist government, see the novel by Lu Wenfu, *Vie et passion d'un gastronome chinois [Meishiija],* trans. A. Curien and Feng Chen (Arles: Éditions Philippe Picquier-Unesco, 1988).

21. See Sidney W. Mintz, *Tasting Food, Tasting Freedom—Excursions into Eating, Culture, and the Past* (Boston: Beacon Press, 1996), pp. 117–22; and Marion Nestle, *Food Politics* (Berkeley and Los Angeles: University of California Press, 2002).

22. Howard Becker, *Art Worlds* (Berkeley: University of California Press, 1982), p. x.

23. Cf. the striking absence of such connection to the larger cultural arena in the restaurants studied by Gary Alan Fine, *Kitchens: The Culture of Restaurant Work* (Berkeley and Los Angeles: University of California Press, 1996), pp. 133–37, in a medium-size urban setting (Minneapolis-Saint Paul). Fine relates these thin networks to the fragmented economic organization of the restaurant industry (each restaurant producing its own, singular product) and the structures of restaurant kitchens. That this world of restaurants is far from a restaurant world is clear from the speculation of a reader Fine cites about what would be necessary to turn the world of these restaurants into an art world (p. 264). Sharon Zukin, *The Cultures of Cities* (Oxford: Blackwell,

1995), chap. 5, confirms this picture in a study of a range of midlevel restaurants in New York City.

Chapter Four

1. I retain the shortened French title of *À la recherche du temps perdu* for the work that entered English in C. Scott Moncrieff's translation as *Remembrance of Things Past*. As Proust himself objected, the static *remembrance* of the Shakespearean title fails to convey the active, never-ending seeking of *recherche* that structures the novel; *things* eliminates the structuring relationship to time; and *past* is eminently more benign, less poignant than *lost*. After an outcry when the Terence Kilmartin retranslation in 1982 kept Moncrieff's title, a more recent issue (1992) finally made the title faithful to the original, with *In Search of Time Lost*. Still, Moncrieff and his title set Proust in anglophone culture. References to *À la recherche du temps perdu* will be to the four-volume French edition of 1987–89 published by Gallimard-Pléiade, indicated by volume and page number. Although the translations are largely my own, I have indicated in italics the corresponding passage in the three-volume revised translation of C. Scott Moncrieff retranslated by Terence Kilmartin (New York: Vintage, 1982).

2. For subtle readings of the particular configuration of literature and the culinary at the end of the nineteenth century, see Marie-Claire Bancquart, *Fin-de-siècle gourmand 1880–1900* (Paris: PUF, 2001).

3. Julia Csergo, "La modernité alimentaire au XIXᵉ siècle," in *À table au XIXe siècle* (Paris: Flammarion, 2001), p. 66, emphasizes this nostalgia for a lost proximity to the foods consumed, which, thanks to faster transportation and more reliable means of conservation, came increasingly from greater distances.

4. Here, too, the ephemeral nature of the artistic creation raises the analogies with music. With the white flowers in the salon and her white outfit, Odette composes her own "symphony in white major" (1:624/*1:683*), in Proust's nod to the poem by Théophile Gautier. Handed Odette's jacket to carry, Marcel discovers in the lining a "thousand details of execution" destined to go unnoticed, "like those orchestral parts to which the composer gave all his care even though they would never reach the ears of the public" (1:627/*1:686*). Like the writer, Odette manipulates time and subjugates space. The connections between aesthetic product, time, and space on which Proust insists historicize this art in contemporary society. Unlike the other arts, or more obviously than the others, fashion is fixed in space and in time: "her clothes were tied to the season and to the hour by a bond that was necessary and unique" (1:626/*1:685*); "she was surrounded by her garments as by the delicate and spiritualized apparatus of a whole civilization" (1:608–609/*1:667*). Odette wears the Belle Époque.

5. See the remarkable analysis by Jean-Pierre Richard, "Proust et l'objet alimentaire," *Littérature*, no. 6 (1972), 3–19.

6. In contrast with other European countries that hark to an originary national literary figure—Italy with Dante, Spain with Cervantes, England with Shakespeare, and Germany with Goethe—French literature recognizes no single foundational figure but, rather, oppositional and complementary pairs (Corneille/Racine, Montaigne-Pascal/Pascal-Voltaire/Voltaire-Rousseau, etc.). See Priscilla P. Clark, *Literary France— The Making of a Culture* (Berkeley and Los Angeles: University of California Press, 1987), chap. 5. Within a long literary tradition, Proust occupies a very different historical niche from early writers of other traditions, though one could see him as a foundational figure for modernism. There is, in any event, no figure of comparable stature in French literature whom Proust confronts.

7. Jacques Ozouf and Mona Ozouf, *"Le tour de France par deux enfants:* The Little Red Book of the Republic" (1984), in *Realms of Memory—The Construction of the French Past,* ed. Pierre Nora and trans. A. Goldhammer (New York: Columbia University Press, 1997), 2:125–48.

8. Marcel Rouff, *La Vie et la Passion de Dodin-Bouffant-Gourmet* (1924; Paris: Le Serpent à plumes, 1994), introduction.

9. See Eric Hobsbawm, "Inventing Traditions" and "Mass-Producing Traditions: Europe, 1870–1914," in *The Invention of Tradition,* ed. Eric Hobsbawm and Terence Ranger (Cambridge: Cambridge University Press, 1983). On the efforts in France, see the multivolume collection edited by Pierre Nora, *Les Lieux de mémoire,* 7 vols. (Paris: Gallimard, 1984–92). A study of Breton elites leads Caroline Ford to conclude that by 1900 the republican Left and the nationalist Right paradoxically began to define the nation in similar terms by emphasizing culture as a central component of French national identity: *Creating the Nation in Provincial France—Religion and Political Identity in Brittany* (Princeton, N.J.: Princeton University Press, 1993), p. 11.

10. On professionalization see Stephen Mennell, *All Manners of Food: Eating and Taste in England and France form the Middle Ages to the Present* (Oxford: Basil Blackwell, 1985), chap. 7; and Amy Trubek, *Haute Cuisine—How the French Invented the Culinary Profession* (Philadelphia: University of Pennsylvania Press, 2000), chap. 6. Trubek argues that culinary journals before 1870 were the work of and for gastronomes, that is, leisured and monied consumers, in contrast with the instrumental publications aimed at producers, both the professional and the domestic market. Alberto Capatti argues that these technological advances spelled the end of traditional French cuisine. For culinary pessimists, it was as lost as Proust's childhood. Capatti, *Le Goût du nouveau—Origines de la modernité alimentaire* (Paris: Albin Michel, 1989), pp. 17–32, 61–86.

11. Eugène Briffault, *Paris à table* (Paris: Hetzel, 1846), chap. 1. Quotes are from p. 5.

12. A. Viard, *Le Cuisinier impérial, ou l'art de faire la cuisine pour toutes les fortunes* (1806; facsimile reprint, Nîmes: C. Lacour, 1993), p. xi. The requirements of French taste are from A. B. de Périgord [Horace Raisson], *Nouvel Almanach des Gourmands* (Paris: Baudoin Frères, 1825), pp. 107–08.

13. See the insightful discussion in Regina Bendix, *In Search of Authenticity—The For-*

mation of Folklore Studies (Madison: University of Wisconsin Press, 1997), esp. chap. 1. Bendix relates the search for the authentic to the craving for an unmediated experience of another culture.

14. On culinary provincialism see Julia Csergo, "L'Émergence des cuisines régionales," in *Histoire de l'alimentation,* ed. Jean-Louis Flandrin and Massimo Montanari (Paris: Fayard, 1997), pp. 823–41; and "La Constitution de la spécialité gastronomique comme objet patrimonial en France (fin xviiie–xxe siècle)," in *L'Esprit des lieux—Le patrimoine et la cité,* ed. Daniel J. Grange and Dominique Poulot (Grenoble: Presses Universitaires de Grenoble, 1997), pp. 183–93. Csergo analyzes the redefinition of cultural diversities and complementarities after the French Revolution. After the mediaeval attention to regional differences, the Ancien Régime elaboration of a national prestige cuisine relegated local dishes to a peripheral role. In cookbooks as in travel literature, they turned up infrequently and then most often associated with peasant fare, of possible ethnographic interest but devoid of gastronomic appeal.

15. On the dependence of wine production on scientific normalization, see Harry W. Paul, *Science, Vine and Wine in Modern France* (Cambridge: Cambridge University Press, 1996). On cheese, see Pierre Boisard, *Le Camembert—Mythe national* (Paris: Calmann-Lévy, 1992). Including Camembert with soldiers' rations in World War I did much to identify this cheese as a national rather than a local product. Unlike Roquefort, for example, whose production, like that of wines, must follow legal prescriptions of the *appellations contrôlées,* there are no legal requirements for Camembert.

16. Nancy Edwards, "The Science of Domesticity: Women, Education and National Identity in Third Republic France, 1880–1914" (Ph.D. diss., University of California-Berkeley, 1997). In the introduction and chapter 4, Edwards argues that domestic science classes for girls created a feminine niche in the national patrimony, a means for bourgeois women to internalize the lessons of republicanism. See also Edmond Richardin, *L'art de bien manger* (1913), p. 211 n. The work of Marie Ernest Edmond Richardin (1850–1917) included several editions of *La Cuisine française du XIVe au XXe siècle* (1903, 1906, 1913), *La Bonne Cuisine pour tous d'après les vieux préceptes de la grand'mere Catherine Giron et les formules modernes des meilleurs cuisiniers,* and *La Géographie des gourmets au pays de France* for the Touring Club de France.

17. Catherine Bertho Lavenir, *La Roue et le stylo—Comment nous sommes devenus touristes* (Paris: Odile Jacob, 1999), pp. 233–39, explores the culinary implications of tourism. Regional gastronomy depended significantly on the efforts of tourist professionals to meet the culinary expectations of urban tourists. See Curnonsky [Maurice Sailland] and Marcel Rouff, *La France gastronomique—Guide des merveilles culinaires et des bonnes auberges françaises,* vol. *Le Périgord* (Paris: F. Rouff, 1921), p. 21. Curnonsky and Rouff saw tourism as supporting fragile culinary traditions.

18. On the political functions of official commensality in republican France, see Joselyn George, "Le Banquet des maires ou la Fête de la Concorde républicaine," in *Les Usages politiques des fêtes aux XIXe et XXe siècles,* by Alain Corbin et al. (Paris: Publications de la Sorbonne, 1997), pp. 159–67; and Olivier Ihl, "De bouche à oreille: Sur les pra-

tiques de commensalité dans la tradition républicaine du cérémonial de table," *Revue française de science politique* 48, nos. 3–4 (1998): 387–408.

19. Marthe Allard Daudet (1878–1960), second wife of Proust's good friend, Léon Daudet, who was responsible for the culinary and fashion pages of the right-wing *L'Action française*, of which Daudet was also director. Albert Capatti places Pampille within the nostalgic, politically conservative, indeed reactionary regionalist current that became so prominent in the 1920s: *Le Goût du nouveau*, pp. 139, 160, and especially pp. 23–227. For a translation of, introduction to, and useful commentary on Pampille and on *Les Bons Plats de France*, see Shirley King, *Pampille's Table* (Boston: Faber & Faber, 1996), which also adapts the recipes for a modern American kitchen.

20. Joseph d'Arçay, *La Salle à manger du Docteur Véron* (Paris: Alphonse Lemerre, 1868), p. 43.

21. Pampille [Marthe Daudet], *Les bons plats de France—Cuisine régionale* (1913; Paris: Arthème Fayard, 1934), pp. 5–6.

22. See Priscilla Ferguson and Sharon Zukin, "The Careers of Chefs: 'French' and 'American' Models of Cuisine," in *Eating Culture*, ed. Ron Scapp and Bryan Seitz (Albany: State University Press of New York, 1998), pp. 92–111; Ann Cooper, *"A Woman's Place Is in the Kitchen"—The Evolution of Women Chefs* (New York: Van Nostrand Reinhold, 1998); and Trubek, *Haute Cuisine*.

23. Barbara Ketchum Wheaton, *Savoring the Past: The French Kitchen and Table from 1300 to 1789* (Philadelphia: University of Pennsylvania Press, 1983), chap. 4. By the eighteenth century some two dozen food guilds were in existence, supplying foodstuffs (butchers, fishmongers, poulterers, charcutiers, grain merchants, gardeners) and prepared foods (bakers, pastry cooks, sauce makers, charcutiers again, rôtisseurs, cook-caterers [*cuisiniers*]). There were frequent disputes as to who got to sell what.

24. Louis-Sébastien Mercier, *Tableau de Paris* (1788; Paris: Mercure de France, 1994), 2:1060 (bk. 5, chap. 383—"Cuisiniers").

25. Mennell, *All Manners of Food,* chap. 5.

26. Pierre Hamp, *Mes Métiers* (Paris: Gallimard-Éditions de la Nouvelle revue française, 1930), p. 20 ff.

27. Châtaillon-Plessis and Gilbert cited by Maguelonne Toussaint-Samat, *Histoire de la cuisine bourgeoise du moyen âge à nos jours* (Paris: Albin Michel, 2001), pp. 176–77. See also Trubek, *Haute cuisine,* chap. 6, on the concerted efforts to separate chefs from workers and to define cooking as a profession rather than a trade.

28. In her analysis of immigrant foodways in the United States at the end of the nineteenth and early twentieth centuries, Hasia Diner makes a similar point for the Italians, who, unlike the Irish, had a range of culinary contacts across class lines before they emigrated. The urban setting multiplied those contacts many times over. See Hasia R. Diner, *Hungering for America: Italian, Irish, and Jewish Foodways in the Age of Migration* (Cambridge, Mass.: Harvard University Press, 2001).

29. Culinary historian-detectives Mary and Philip Hyman uncovered Raisson hiding under Mlle Marguerite's skirts. See "Livres et cuisine au XIXe siècle," in *À table au*

XIXe siècle (Paris: Flammarion, 2001), p. 85. The term *cordon bleu* dates from 1814, taken from the *Cordon bleu* (blue sash) worn by members of the royal Order of the Holy Spirit. Irony surely played an important part in the promotion of the lowly cook to an exalted status to which no woman, much less a cook, could aspire. See Toussaint-Samat, *Histoire de la cuisine bourgeoise,* p. 177.

30. In Mary and Philip Hyman's more extensive survey, of "named" editions over the nineteenth century, 58 carried the designation of *cuisinière*, against 46 for *cuisinier*. See Hyman and Hyman, "Livres et cuisine au XIXe siècle," p. 85. The Hymans located 122 editions of the *Cuisinière bourgeoise* between its original publication in 1746 and 1866 (p. 89).

31 Auguste Escoffier, "Why Men Make the Best Cooks," *The Epicure* 13, no. 2 (1902): 9. Thanks to Amy Trubek for unearthing these wonderfully revelatory quotations (*Haute cuisine,* p. 125).

32. Auguste Escoffier, *Souvenirs inédits—75 ans au service de l'art culinaire* (Marseille: Éditions Jeanne Lafitte, 1985), p. 172. We should not imagine that Louis XIV and his retinue went hungry. On the contrary, "Everyone ate very well, had lunch, had supper, walked about, played games, went hunting." Mme de Sévigné, *Correspondance,* 3 vols. (Paris: Gallimard-Pléiade, 1972) 1:234–36 (26 April 1671). Vatel was "praised and blamed" in equal measure, though the king did express regrets over his fate. One senses from Mme de Sévigné's account that Vatel's military-style suicide was out of place for a commoner.

33. Escoffier, *Souvenirs inédits,* p. 191.

34. Quotes from Curnonsky and Rouff, *La France gastronomique,* vol. *Le Périgord* (1921), p. 22; vol. *L'Alsace* (1921), p. 21.

35. For this argument in detail, see Edwards, "The Science of Domesticity."

Chapter Five

1. See the 1867 painting by Henry Baron, reproduced on pp. 96–97 in Anthony Rowley, *À Table! La Fête gastronomique* (Paris: Gallimard, 1994); see pp. 96–97 and passim for examples of gastronomic extravagance in Europe from the Middle Ages to the present. See also John H. D'Arms, "Performing Culture: Roman Spectacle and the Banquets of the Powerful," in *The Art of Ancient Spectacle,* ed. Bettina Bergmann and Christine Kondoleon (New Haven, Conn.: Yale University Press, 2000), p. 132; and Barbara Ketchum Wheaton, *Savoring the Past: The French Kitchen and Table from 1300 to 1789* (Philadelphia: University of Pennsylvania Press, 1983), p. 142.

2. Carême wrote movingly of the literally infernal conditions of the upper-class kitchen, where burning wood (later coal) ovens brought on all kinds of lung diseases and contributed to the generally high level of stress. Battle metaphors continue to supply a favorite topos of chefdom. See Anthony Bourdain, *Kitchen Confidential* (New York:

Bloomsbury, 2000), an exposé-cum-memoir evocatively subtitled *Adventures in the Culinary Underbelly* (currently being made into a movie).

3. For the trajectory followed by painters, see Nathalie Heinich, *Du peintre à l'artiste: Artisans et académiciens à l'âge classique* (Paris: Minuit, 1993); and by writers, Priscilla Parkhurst Clark, *Literary France—The Making of a Culture* (Berkeley and Los Angeles: University of California Press, 1987), esp. chaps. 2–4.

4. See the profile of Christine Massia in Annie Lorenzo, *Profession? Cuisinier-Restaurateur* (Paris: Charles Massin, n.d.). Quite like Escoffier (see chapter 4), three-star chef Joël Robuchon notes the paucity of women chefs, whom he finds less exacting and less creative, though they have a greater professional conscience and greater application. See Joël Robuchon and Elisabeth de Meurville, *Le Carnet de route d'un compagnon cuisinier* (Paris: Payot, 1995), pp. 86–87. On the positive side, in the United States, see Beverly Russell, *Women of Taste—Recipes and Profiles of Famous Women Chefs* (New York: John Wiley and Sons, 1997). Alice Waters (Chez Panisse, Berkeley) is undoubtedly the best-known woman restaurateur in the United States, and it is telling that she began her restaurant in California.

5. As Gary Fine argues in his study of restaurant workers, even today, "doing dirt" is what kitchens are all about. *Kitchens: The Culture of Restaurant Work* (Berkeley and Los Angeles: University of California Press, 1996), p. 32 ff.

6. Erving Goffman, *The Presentation of Self in Everyday Life* (New York: Doubleday, 1959), pp. 121–22, quoting George Orwell, *Down and Out in Paris and London* (1933; reprint, New York: Harcourt, Brace, Jovanovich, 1961), chap. 12, p. 68.

7. Curnonsky [Maurice Sailland] and Marcel Rouff, *La France gastronomique—Guide des merveilles culinaires et des bonnes auberges françaises*, vol. *Le Périgord* (Paris: F. Rouff, 1921). They found four restaurants of note in the Périgord, for example, and forty adequate meals.

8. Claude Fischler speaks of the Michelin "Galaxy" in *L'Homnivore—Le goût, la cuisine et le corps* (Paris: Odile Jacob, 1990), chap. 9, pp. 237–64. With some 10% of the population of metropolitan France, according to the *Guide Michelin,* Paris retains and has in fact strengthened its dominance of haute cuisine in recent years:

	Three stars	Two stars	One star
1990	26% (5/19)	23% (21/90)	19% (78/398)
1997	28 % (5/18)	27% (20/74)	13% (55/423)
2002	39% (9/23)	26% (20/76)	13% (55/421)
2003	40% (10/25)	———	———

9. See <www.bocuse.fr>. At the time of his suicide in 2003, Bernard Loiseau (three stars, Saulieu) had three additional restaurants in Paris and a range of corporate activities, and was listed on the French stock exchange (his Web site provided investment instructions). Along with food related products, the "shop" on his Web site sells table

linens, bath gels, and beauty products! Alain Ducasse (three stars, Monte Carlo; three stars, Paris) has a restaurant in New York; Joël Robuchon (three stars in Paris until he retired at the age of 51) has a restaurant in Tokyo which he runs jointly with Claude Vrinat, the owner of Taillevent (three stars in Paris), and in 2003 opened a new bistro-style restaurant on the Left Bank.

10. On Batali see Bill Buford, "The Secret of Excess," *New Yorker*, August 19 and 26, 2002, pp. 122–41.

11. In the United States, *Iron Chef* first aired on local cable stations in the Bay Area in Japanese-language programming blocks. Subtitled versions appeared in 1997, and the international version was first broadcast on the Food Network in July 1999. Although victory is weighted toward the Iron Chefs, the outcome is never a foregone conclusion. The well-known New York chef Bobby Flay, from the restaurant Mesa Grill, lost his first battle with Iron Chef Japanese, Masaharu Morimoto (at that time also a highly regarded chef in New York), in New York on June 25, 2000, but won the rematch in Tokyo on December 22, 2000 (broadcast on U.S. television in June 2001). Some 960,000 households watched the first show, and CNN interviewed Flay on the second occasion. For the rematch Flay and Morimoto entered the set accompanied by horses, trumpeters, and one hundred chef-supporters. See <http://www.ironchef.com> for show history, the list of the battles, and chefs, along with ingredients. See the official Web site <http://www.ironchef-fujitv.com> and also Fuji Television, Inc., *Iron Chef— The Official Book*, trans. Kaoru Hoketsu (New York: Berkley Books, 2000). Better yet, for the full flavor, catch the program.

I am very grateful to Yuiko Fujita for her research on *Iron Chef* in Japan and in the United States, notably her persistence in obtaining a remarkable interview with producer Toshihiko Matsuo of Fuji Television.

12. Patric Kuh, *The Last Days of Haute Cuisine—America's Culinary Revolution* (New York: Viking, 2001), traces the broadening of American culinary sensibilities through chefs in high-end restaurants.

13. Paul Bocuse accused the demotion of Loiseau's restaurant in the *Guide Gault et Millau* in February 2003, a severe critique in the national daily newspaper, *Le Figaro*, and rumors of a loss of his third star in the *Guide Michelin* as contributing factors to his suicide. Loiseau had in fact suffered from depression for a number of years. William Echikson, "Death of a Chef: The Changing Landscape of French Cooking," *New Yorker*, May 12, 2003, pp. 61–67.

14. Here as below, unless otherwise indicated, references to interviews are to those that I, often with my colleague Sharon Zukin, conducted with the chefs listed in appendix C. See our article, "The Careers of Chefs: 'French' and 'American' Models of Cuisine," in *Eating Culture*, ed. Ron Scapp and Bryan Seitz (Albany: State University Press of New York, 1998), pp. 92–111; see also appendix C below.

15. For one two-star chef's ambition of obtaining a third Michelin star, a crucial element was the quality of local products. For his frenetic and ultimately successful pur-

suit, see William Echikson's book on Bernard Loiseau, *Burgundy Stars—A Year in the Life of a Great French Restaurant* (Boston: Little, Brown & Co., 1995). For the same genre (top-star-in-the-making) applied to the equally competitive culinary New York, see Leslie Brenner, *The Fourth Star—Dispatches from inside Daniel Boulud's Celebrated New York Restaurant* (New York: Clarkson Potter, 2002). (Four stars is the top rating given by the *New York Times*.)

16. Jacinthe Bessière, "Local Development and Heritage: Traditional Food and Cuisine as Tourist Attractions in Rural Areas," *Sociologia Ruralis* 38, no. 1 (1998): 21–34.

17. Gary Fine (*Kitchens*, pp. 23–30) draws useful distinctions among *shortcuts* (accessible to anyone who knows the task, as with convenience foods), *approximations* (taking recipes as suggestions rather than rules), and *tricks of the trade* (procedures known within the profession).

18. For New Year's Eve 1999, chef Daniel Boulud presented her with "La Diva Renée," a mixture of chocolate, hazelnuts, and amaretto cookies in a sauce of clementines. The score of *Der Rosenkavalier,* Fleming's next opera at the Metropolitan Opera, was printed on the chocolate on top. Boulud features the dessert in his restaurant whenever Fleming is in New York.

19. Benjamin Franklin, *The Autobiography and Other Writings* (New York: Signet Classics, 1961), p. 24. Franklin spanned the eighteenth century (1706–90).

20. The same held true for the arts. Writing to his wife, Abigail, from Paris, John Adams made clear that he had no time to stroll about and admire Versailles. "It is not indeed the fine Arts, which our Country requires. . . . I must study Politicks and War that my sons may have liberty to study Mathematicks and Philosophy. My sons ought to study Mathematicks and Philosophy, Geography, natural History, Naval Architecture, navigation, Commerce and Agriculture, in order to give their Children a right to study Painting, poetry, Musick, Architecture, Statuary, Tapestry, and Porcelaine." John Adams to Abigail Adams, May 1780, in *Adams Family Correspondence*, ed. L. H. Butterfield et al. (Cambridge, Mass.: Harvard University Press, 1963–), 3:342. The higher pleasures of fine food would probably need a generation of two more, if they were even allowed.

21. He continues:

> The predominance of grease in the American kitchen, coupled with the habits of hasty eating and of constant expectoration, are the causes of the diseases of the stomach so common in America. The science of the table extends far beyond the indulgence of our appetites, as the school of manners includes health and morals, as well as that which is agreeable. Vegetable diet is almost converted into an injury in America, from an ignorance of the best modes of preparation, while even animal food is much abused, and loses half its nutriment.
>
> The same is true as respects liquours. The heating and exciting wines, the brandies, and the coarser drinks of the laboring classes, all conspire to injure the physical and the moral man, while they defeat their own ends.

James Fenimore Cooper, "On Civilization," in *The American Democrat or Hints on the Social and Civic Relations of the United States of America* (1838; reprint, New York: Vintage, 1956), pp. 162–63. Note that Cooper wrote French well enough to have a piece included in a journalistic venture of the day, *Paris, ou le livre des 101* (1831).

22. See Jacques Pépin's autobiography for a striking discussion of the changes in the American palate since the 1960s, when he first arrived in New York. Working at Howard Johnson's, he saw a positive side to Americans' lack of culinary sophistication in their openness to new preparations. "In France," he explains, "unless a dish was prepared exactly 'right,' people would know and complain. In the States, if it tasted good, then fine, the customer was happy." *The Apprentice: My Life in the Kitchen* (Boston: Houghton Mifflin, 2003), p. 164. More generally, Pépin gives a great sense of the traditional French culinary world—another world that has changed almost beyond recognition.

23. See <http://www.u-bourgogne.fr/IUVV/reglementation/histoireaoc.pdf>. Since 1935, the Institut National des Appellations d'Origine (INAO), a branch of the Ministry of Agriculture, has supervised the classifications. Currently about 400 Appellations d'origine contrôlées (AOC) exist for wines, 30 for cheese (Camembert not among them, which is why Camembert can legally come from anywhere), and 35 for other products (poulet de Bresse, for instance).

24. Escoffier practiced what he preached:

> The culinary art is perhaps one of the useful forms of diplomacy. Called upon all over the world to organize restaurants in the most sumptuous of grand hotels, I was always concerned to use French material, French products, and, above all, French staff.
>
> The development of French cuisine is due largely to the thousands of French cooks who are working in the four corners of the world. . . . It is a great satisfaction for me to have contributed to this development. I "sowed" some two thousand cooks around the world. Most of them settled in these countries, and one can say that they are so many grains of wheat sown in barren territory. France today harvests the wheat.

Souvenirs inédits—75 ans au service de l'art culinaire (Marseille: Éditions Jeanne Lafitte, 1985), pp. 192–93.

25. Elizabeth Kolbert, "Everyone Lies," pp. 84–87, *New Yorker*, August 19 and 26, 2002, pp. 84–87. Following her reportage of New York City restaurant inspectors at work, Kolbert makes this statement about dining out. But surely, it applies to ingestion of foodstuffs generally. Astonished and a bit appalled by the indifference of diners to the drama of kitchen inspection and the visible dirt (and worse), Kolbert speculates that most of us do not really want to know about food preparation, especially the dirtier and destructive aspects. See the discussion of *Babette's Feast* in the epilogue below, and the Proustian narrator's horrified reaction when he discovers that the glorious roast chicken served up for Sunday dinner depends on butchery. By dinnertime, however,

he is fully reconciled to the necessary cruelty. See Marcel Proust, *À la recherche du temps perdu*, ed. J-Y Tadié, 4 vols. (Paris: Gallimard-Pléiade, 1987–89), 1:120; and *Remembrance of Things Past*, trans. C. K. Scott Moncrieff and Terence Kilmartin, 3 vols. (New York: Vintage, 1982), 1:131.

26. Jean Anthelme Brillat-Savarin, *Physiologie du goût* (1826; Paris: Charpentier, 1839), p. 12 (aphorism 7).

27. Kyri Watson Claflin argues that the much touted eating of rats during the Prussian siege of Paris in 1870 had almost nothing to do with food shortages and everything to do with pride in a characteristic French ability to triumph over adversity, to get out of an impossible situation, in short, to "make do." Such was the power of French cuisine that it turned rat to culinary account. "Savoring the Rat," in *Situazioni d'assedio/Cities under Siege* (Milan: Clio-Polis, 2002), pp. 421–25.

28. Quotations in this and the following paragraphs are from Marcel Rouff, *La Vie et la Passion de Dodin-Bouffant-Gourmet* (1924; Paris: Le Serpent à plumes, 1994), pp. 85–87, 95, 99–101 ("Dodin-Bouffant, un *pot-au-feu* et une altesse").

29. In these same early years of the twentieth century, Proust described a similar ideal of culinary and aesthetic simplicity, again with a beef dish. His great-aunt would never dispute expert opinion on most things, "but on the things whose rules and principles had been taught to her by her mother, on the way to make certain dishes, to play Beethoven's sonatas, and of receiving guests, she was certain of having the correct idea of perfection. . . . For the three things, in any case, perfection was almost the same: it was a sort of simplicity in the means, of moderation, and of charm. . . . From the first bite, the first notes, a simple letter, she claimed to be able to tell whether she was dealing with a good cook, a true musician, a properly brought up woman. . . . 'She may be an expert cook, but she doesn't know how to do steak and potatoes.' Steak and potatoes! . . . difficult by its very simplicity, a sort of culinary Pathétique Sonata." "Journées de lecture," in *Pastiches et mélanges* (Paris: Gallimard, 1919), pp. 212–13.

30. See the discussion of Carême in chapter 2 and my article, "Le pot-au-feu: Un plat qui fait la France," in *Ces plats mythiques qui ont fait la France: Le Pot au feu* (Paris: Éditions Autrement, 1999), pp. 13–19. The entire book is devoted to the *pot au feu*, its variants and its foundational Frenchness.

31. See the discussion in chapter 4, and Allen S. Weiss, "The Ideology of the pot-au-feu," in *Taste Nostalgia*, ed. Allen S. Weiss (New York: Lusitania Press, 1997), pp. 99–110; and Lawrence R. Schehr, "Savory Writing: Marcel Rouff's *Vie et la passion de Dodin-Bouffant*," in *French Food: On the Table, on the Page, and in French Culture*, ed. Lawrence R. Schehr and Allen S. Weiss (New York: Routledge, 2001), pp 124–39.

32. There is a significant difference between the original and the translation. Where Rouff talks simply about "cuisine," the translator feels it necessary to specify "great cooking." But surely the point is that all cooking worthy of the name draws on love.

33. Takeru Kobayashi beat his own 2001 record of fifty hot dogs. Second place went to a 410-pound New Yorker, who barely made it through his twenty-sixth hot dog. The secret of the winner seems to have been his methodical, even assembly-line ap-

proach to consumption. On the contest see <http://www.ifoce.com/nathans%20his
tory.html>; and <http://www.newyorkled.com/moreNYseasonal_4th_July_HotDog
_Contest.htm>. Although Kobayashi won the contest once again in 2003, his 44 ½ hot
dogs disappointed the fans of competitive eating, ever on the outlook for new records.

34. For the French bean eater (who consumed 2.7 kilos of beans in fifteen minutes),
see Pierre Bourdieu, *Distinction: A Social Critique of the Judgement of Taste* (1979), trans.
R. Nice (Cambridge, Mass.: Harvard University Press, 1984), p. 383. More generally, see
<http://www.ifoce.com>, the official Web site for the International Federation of Com-
petitive Eaters, which presents competitive eating as a sport. The only rule is that vom-
iting eliminates the contestant.

35. Susan Gilson Miller, ed. and trans., *Disorienting Encounters: Travels of a Moroccan
Scholar in France in 1845–1846* (Berkeley and Los Angeles: University of California Press,
1992), pp. 166–67. My thanks to Jan Goldstein for passing on this gem. On the British
and French food in the same period, see Amy Trubek, *Haute Cuisine: How the French Invented the Culinary Profession* (Philadelphia: University of Pennsylvania Press, 2000),
chap. 4.

Epilogue

1. Isak Dinesen [Karen Blixen], "Babette's Feast," in *Anecdotes of Destiny* (New York:
Random House, 1958). Dinesen originally published the tale in *Ladies' Home Journal*
(1952).

2. Other celebratory works include the fantasy *Like Water for Chocolate* (1992) and *Big
Night* (1992). This listing is merely the icing on one of many cakes. While this is not the
place for a disquisition on food and film, see Daniel Rogov, "Food as Filmic Metaphor
or, 5,484 Words in Defense of Gastronomy," <http://www.stratsplace.com/rogov/
food_as_film.html>. Rogov proposes *Babette's Feast* as a breakthrough against the negative perspective on food in films such as Louis Malle's *My Dinner with André* (1981),
Luis Bruñuel's *Discreet Charm of the Bourgeoisie* (1972), Marco Ferreri's death-by-eating
comedy, *La Grande Bouffe* (1973), or Peter Greenaway's even more disgusting *The Cook,
the Thief, His Wife and Her Lover* (1989), where food is a stand-in for humans' grosser appetites. See <http://www.wsu.edu/~dehaboyd/foodfilms.html>.

3. Transcription by David Schimpf here and for the other lines quoted from the film:
<http://cw.mariancollege.edu/dschimpf/keylinesfrombabettesfeast.htm>.

4. The Café Anglais, which opened in 1815 and closed in 1913, was one of the premier restaurants in Paris, known for the magnificence of its cuisine and the cos-
mopolitanism of its clientele. It is there that the mother of Proust's narrator sends their
cook, Françoise, to sample the fare. Marcel Proust, *À la recherche du temps perdu*, ed. J-Y
Tadié, 4 vols. (Paris: Gallimard-Pléiade, 1987–89), 1:476–77; *Remembrance of Things
Past*, trans. C. K. Scott Moncrieff and Terence Kilmartin, 3 vols. (New York: Vintage,

1982), 1:523–24. Its glorious reputation notwithstanding, Françoise allows only that the restaurant serves "a good little cuisine bourgeoise."

5. To judge from the film, the quail is split, deboned, stuffed with foie gras, roasted, and placed in a puff pastry shell; its head is put back in place so that it looks like a nesting or, in this instance, entombed, bird. Just before serving, a slice of (black) truffle is added, and the pastry "sarcophagus" is surrounded by a deep red wine reduction sauce. The gastronomic critic of *Le Monde* concluded that this preparation would produce a disaster, since the quail would be overcooked. He gives instead a recipe from the *Gastronomie pratique* (1907 first edition) by Ali Bab for "ortolans en sarcophage," enveloped and cooked in parchment paper, not puff pastry. (Ortolans are exquisitely succulent diminutive game birds, whose consumption in France is now forbidden by law.) La Reynière [Robert Courtine], "Babette et les ortolans," *Le Monde*, November 12, 1988.

6. In his letter introducing Babette to the women he quit thirty-five years before, the graying, lonely Achille Papin asks, "What is fame? The grave awaits us all." At the dinner, the general, too, is taking stock of his life and the choices that he made. All the disciples worry about their fate in the hereafter. Wendy Wright reminds us that quail is a form of manna and that *sarcophagus* means "flesh-eater." Moreover, she sees an allusion to Jesus' discourse in the book of John (6:51–54), "I am the bread of life. . . . this is the manna that comes down from heaven. . . . if you do not eat of the flesh of the Son of Man you will not have life." "*Babette's Feast*: A Religious Film," *The Journal of Religion and Film* 1, no. 2 (1997). <http://www.unomaha.edu/~wwwjrf/BabetteWW.htm>.

7. Transcription by David Schimpf here and for the other lines quoted from the film. <http://cw.mariancollege.edu/dschimpf/keylinesfrombabettesfeast.htm>

8. "Jerusalem, my heart's true home / Your name is forever dear to me. / Your kindness is second to none / You keep us clothed and fed / Never would you give a stone / To the child who begs for bread." This hymn is sung on three separate occasions in the course of the film. Note, of course, that food turns up even in the hymn.

9. La Reynière, "Babette et les ortolans."

10. The duet is sung in French so that the pastor and Martine, who are listening in the next room, comprehend Philippa's peril. The duet from *Don Giovanni* brings the don together with Zerlina, a peasant girl whom he is endeavoring to seduce. Like Don Giovanni, Papin promises Philippa a vastly different life, a life of brilliance and glory. It is worth noting that Papin first appears in the film in the role of Count Almaviva from Rossini's *Barber of Seville*—another enterprise of seduction, and there successful. Like Papin with Philippa, Don Giovanni is foiled in his venture with Zerlina, though Philippa, unlike Zerlina, makes her own decision.

11. The Spanish Eugénie de Montijo (1826–1920) became empress of France when she married Napoleon III (1808–73) in 1853. After the fall of the empire, they both lived in England until their deaths. As a refugee from the Commune, very likely under sentence of death, Babette could not have returned to France until 1880, when the Third Republic declared a general amnesty for Communards.

12. General Gaston A. A. marquis de Galliffet (1830–1909) was later named Minister of War (1899–1900) and charged with persuading the army to accept a retrial of Alfred Dreyfus.

13. Dinesen is precise: in 1854, Martine and Philippa are 18 and 17 respectively. Babette arrives 17 years later, making them 35 and 34 when Babette arrives in 1871. Twelve years to the feast puts them at 47 and 46 for the end of the story. In the film, however, Papin's letter of introduction of Babette specifically recalls that he had been in Jutland 35 years previously, that is, 1836. The girls' ages are never mentioned, but this scenario would give them birthdates in the 1820s, in their fifties in 1871, and, after 14 (not 12) years, in their sixties for the celebratory dinner. The aging of the sisters produces one anachronism. Another is Papin's promise to Philippa that she will sing for the emperor, which works for Dinesen's chronology but not for the film, since 35 years before the Commune, France was a monarchy, not an empire. Though inconsequential, the anachronism shows that Axel deliberately aged the sisters.

14. Dinesen makes the disciples less restrained, mildly gluttonous, and drunk enough to stumble home, falling in the snow in a "kind of celestial second childhood." There is no final dance and hymn as in the film. Moreover, Dinesen treats the guests with an ironic distance that is much less evident in the gentler treatment given by the film. Consider the following description of the General at the dinner: "tall, broad and ruddy, in his bright uniform, his breast covered with decorations, [he] strutted and shone like an ornamental bird, a golden pheasant or a peacock, in this sedate party of black crows and jackdaws" ("Babette's Feast," pp. 50–51).

15. As Carolyn Korsmeyer notes, this is a heavily romantic view of art that places the creative genius on a lofty plane above the trivialities and the sufferings of everyday life. *Making Sense of Taste—Food and Philosophy* (Ithaca, N.Y.: Cornell University Press, 1999), p. 210. However, Korsmeyer reads the short story, with only an occasional reference to the film. See generally her chapter 6, "Narratives of Eating," in which she argues for the connection between the processual nature of narrative and of dining.

16. Dinesen specifies only one hymn, which is sung at the banquet, and Papin, in something of a melancholy funk, goes to church in order to hear music rather than, as the film shows it, being drawn in by the celestial singing as he sits on a cliff overlooking the sea. In the story, Papin appends the opening bars of the Mozart duet to his letter to the sisters; the film, of course, plays the music itself.

17. Dinesen, on the other hand, gives more color to the landscape of the Norwegian setting of her tale, which Axel moved to Denmark. The small town "looks like a child's toy-town of little wooden pieces painted gray, yellow, pink and many other colors." The two sisters live in what is referred to several times as the yellow house. The film, however, keeps to the subdued palette, the better to dramatize the dinner.

Bibliography

Primary Sources

Almanach perpétuel des Gourmands, contenant Le Code Gourmand et des applications, règles et méditations de gastronomie transcendante. 6th ed. Paris: Barba, 1830.

Athenaeus. *The Deipnosophists of Athenaeus of Naucratis.* Translated by C. B. Gulick. 7 vols. Cambridge, Mass.: Harvard University Press, Loeb Classical Library, 1969.

Balzac, Honoré de. *Oeuvres diverses.* Edited by M. Bouteron and H. Longnon. 2 vols. Paris: Conard, 1938.

——. *La Comédie humaine.* 12 vols. Paris: Gallimard-Pléiade, 1976–81.

Beauvilliers, Antoine B. *L'Art du cuisinier.* 1814. 3d ed., Paris: Pillet, 1824.

Berchoux, Joseph de. "La Gastronomie, ou l'Homme des champs à table, poème didactique en quatre chants, pour servir de suite à L'Homme des champs'" [1801]. Reprinted in *Les Classiques de la table* (3d ed., Paris: Au Dépôt de la Librairie, 1845), 1:149–77.

Briffault, Eugène. *Paris à table.* Illustrated by Bertall. Paris: Hetzel, 1846.

Brillat-Savarin, Jean Anthelme. *Physiologie du goût, ou Méditations de gastronomie transcendante, ouvrage théorique, historique, et à l'ordre du jour.* 1826. New ed., Paris: Charpentier, 1839.

——. *Physiology of Taste.* Translated by M. F. K. Fisher. 1949. Washington, D.C.: Counterpoint, 2000.

Cadet de Gassicourt, C. L. *Cours gastronomique. Les Dîners de Manant-Ville.* 1808. 2d ed., Paris: Capelle et Renand, 1809.

Les Classiques de la table. Petite bibliothèque des écrits les plus distingués publiées à Paris sur la gastronomie et la vie élégante. 1843. 2d ed., 2d printing, 2 vols., Paris: Chez Martinon, 1844; 3d ed., 2 vols., Paris: Au Dépôt de la Librairie, 1845; new ed., 2 vols., Paris: Firmin-Didot Frères, 1855.

Cooper, James Fenimore. "On Civilization." In *The American Democrat or Hints on the Social and Civic Relations of the United States of America.* 1838. New York: Vintage, 1956.

Curnonsky [Maurice Edmond Sailland]. *Souvenirs littéraires et gastronomiques.* Paris: Albin Michel, 1958.

Doussin-Delys, Louis Josey. *Vatel, tragédie (si l'on veut) ou drame burlesque par un gastronome en défaut.* Poitiers: F. A. Saurin, 1845.

Dumas, Alexandre. *Grand Dictionnaire de Cuisine.* Edited by Jean-Pierre Sigre. Paris: Alphonse Lemerre, 1873. Paris: Phébus, 2000.

———. *Propos d'art et de cuisine.* Paris: Calmann Lévy, 1877.

Encyclopédie ou Dictionnaire raisonné des sciences des arts et des métiers. 1751–80. Reprint, Stuttgart: F. Frommann Verlag, 1966.

Escoffier, Auguste. *A Guide to Modern Cookery.* 1909. Reprint, London: Studio Editions, 1994.

———. *Souvenirs inédits—75 ans au service de l'art culinaire.* Marseille: Éditions Jeanne Laffitte, 1985.

Fayot, Frédéric. "Notice sur Antoine Carême." In *Le Pâtissier royal parisien,* by Antonin Carême, 3d ed., 2 vols., 1: xxxvii–lvi. Paris: n.p., 1841.

Franklin, Alfred. *La Cuisine.* La Vie privée d'autrefois. Arts et métiers. Modes, Moeurs, usages des Parisiens du XIIe au XVIIIe siècles d'après les documents originaux et inédits. Paris: Plon, Nourrit et Cie, 1888.

Fuji Television, Inc. *Iron Chef—The Official Book.* Translated by Kaoru Hoketsu. New York: Berkley Books, 2000.

Furetière, Antoine. *Dictionnaire Universel.* La Haye: Arnout & Reinier Leers, 1690.

Grimod de La Reynière, A. B. L. *Almanach des Gourmands servant de guide dans les moyens de faire excellente chère par un vieil amateur.* 8 vols. 1803–12. Reprint, Paris: Valmer, 1984.

———. *Journal des Gourmands et des Belles, ou L'Epicurien français.* Paris: Capelle et Renaud, 1806.

———. *Manuel des Amphitryons—Contenant Un Traité de la Dissection des viandes à table, la Nomenclature des Menus les plus nouveaux pour chaque saison, et des Élémens de Politesse gourmande.* 1808. Reprint, Paris: Éditions A. M. Métaillié, 1984.

———. *Écrits gastronomiques.* Edited by Jean-Claude Bonnet. 1978. Paris: UGE/10-18, 1997.

Hall, William. Avertissement. In *French Cookery,* by M. Carême. London: John Murray, 1836.

King, Shirley. *Pampille's Table.* Boston: Faber & Faber, 1996.

Larousse, Pierre. "Gastronomie." *Grand Dictionnaire Universel du XIXe siècle,* s.v. 1866–79. Reprint, Geneva-Paris: Slatkine Reprints, 1982.

Le Cordier, Helie. *Le Pont—L'Evesque.* Paris: Chez Charles de Tunes, 1662.

Le Grand d'Aussy, P. J. B. *Histoire de la vie privée des français depuis l'origine de la nation jusqu'à nos jours.* 3 vols. 1782. 2 vols., Chilly-Mazarin: Éditions SenS, 1999–2000.

Lorenzo, Annie. *Profession? Cuisinier-restaurateur.* Paris: Charles Massin, n.d.

Maupassant, Guy de. "Amoureux et primeurs." *Le Gaulois,* March 30, 1881. <http://maupassant.free.fr/index.html>.

Melville, Herman. *Moby-Dick* [1851], edited by Harrison Hayford and Hershel Parker. New York: Norton, 1967.

Mercier, Louis-Sébastien. *Tableau de Paris.* 12 vols. 1788. 2 vols., Paris: Mercure de France, 1994.

Monselet, Charles. *Gastronomie—Récits de table,* 2d ed. Paris: Charpentier, 1874.

Montaigne, Michel de. *Essais.* 3 vols. Paris: GF-Flammarion, 1969.

Morgan, Lady (Sydney). *France in 1829–30,* 2d ed. 2 vols. London: Saunders and Otley, 1831.

Orwell, George. *Down and Out in Paris and London.* 1933. New York: Harcourt, Brace, Jovanovich, 1961.

Périgord, A. B. de [Horace Raisson]. *Nouvel Almanach des Gourmands servant de guide dans les moyens de faire excellente chère.* Paris: Baudoin Frères, 1825.

Proust, Marcel. "Journées de lecture." In *Pastiches et mélanges.* Paris: Gallimard, 1919.

———. *Remembrance of Things Past.* Translated by C. K. Scott Moncrieff and Terence Kilmartin. 3 vols. New York: Vintage, 1982.

———. *À la recherche du temps perdu.* Edited by J-Y Tadié. 4 vols. Paris: Gallimard-Pléiade, 1987–89.

Rouff, Marcel. *La Vie et la Passion de Dodin-Bouffant-Gourmet.* 1924. Paris: Le Serpent à plumes, 1994.

———. *The Passionate Epicure.* Translated by Claude. New York: The Modern Library, 2002.

Sue, Eugène. *Les Sept Péchés capitaux—La Gourmandise* (1848). Vol. 52 in *Oeuvres complètes.* Reprint, Geneva-Paris: Slatkine Reprints, 1992.

Viard, Alexandre. *Le Cuisinier impérial, ou l'art de faire la cuisine pour toutes les fortunes.* 1806. Facsimile reprint, Nîmes: C. Lacour, 1993.

———. *Le Cuisinier royal, ou l'art de faire la cuisine et la pâtisserie pour toutes les fortunes.* 9th ed. Paris: Barba, 1817.

Wenfu, Lu. *Vie et passion d'un gastronome chinois* [*Meishiija*]. Translated by A. Curien and Feng Chen. Arles: Éditions Philippe Picquier-Unesco, 1988.

Secondary Sources

À table au XIXe siècle. Paris: Flammarion, 2001.

Abad, Reynauld. *Le Grand marché: L'approvisionnement alimentaire de Paris sous l'Ancien régime.* Paris: Fayard, 2002.

Abbott, Andrew. *The System of Professions: An Essay on the Division of Expert Labor.* Chicago: University of Chicago Press, 1988.

Abramson, Julia. "Grimod's Debt to Mercier and the Emergence of Gastronomic Writing Reconsidered." *EMF: Studies in Early Modern France* 7 (2001): 141–62.

———. "Legitimacy and Nationalism in the *Almanach des Gourmands* (1803–1812)." *JEMCS* [*Journal for Early Modern Cultural Studies*] 3, no. 2 (fall–winter 2003): 105–35.

Ackerman, Diane. *A Natural History of the Senses.* New York: Vintage, 1990.

Anderson, Benedict. *Imagined Communities: Reflections on the Origin and Spread of Nationalism.* London: Verso, 1983.

Appadurai, Arjun. 1981. "Gastro-Politics in Hindu South Asia." *American Ethnologist* 8, no. 3 (1981): 494–511.

———. "How to Make a National Cuisine: Cookbooks in Contemporary India." *Comparative Studies in Society and History* 30, no. 3 (1988): 3–24.

Aron, Jean Paul. *Essai sur la Sensibilité alimentaire à Paris au 19ᵉ siècle.* Paris: Armand Colin, 1967.

———. *Le Mangeur du XIXe siècle.* Paris: Laffont, 1973.

———. *The Art of Eating in France: Manners and menus in the nineteenth century.* Translated by N. Rootes. London: Owen, 1975.

L'Art culinaire au XIXe siècle—Antonin Carême. Paris: Délégation à l'action artistique de la ville de Paris, 1984.

Aubaile-Sallenave, Françoise. "La Méditérranée: Une cuisine, des cuisines." *Information sur les sciences sociales* 35, no, 1 (1996): 139–94.

Bancquart, Marie-Claire. *Fin de siècle gourmand 1880–1900.* Paris: PUF, 2001.

Barthes, Roland. "Steak and Chips" and "The World of Wrestling." In *Mythologies* [1957], translated by A. Lavers. New York: Hill and Wang, 1972.

———. "Lecture de Brillat-Savarin," preface to J. A. Brillat-Savarin, *Physiologie du goût,* edited by Michel Guibert (Paris: Hermann, 1975).

———. "Reading Brillat-Savarin." In *On Signs,* edited by Marshall Blonsky. Baltimore: Johns Hopkins University Press, 1987.

Becker, Howard. *Art Worlds.* Berkeley and Los Angeles: University of California Press, 1982.

Beecher, Jonathan. *Fourier—The Visionary and His World.* Berkeley and Los Angeles: University of California Press, 1986.

Belasco, Warren J. "Ethnic Fast Foods: The Corporate Melting Pot." *Food and Foodways* 2, no. 1 (1987): 1–30.

Bendix, Regina. *In Search of Authenticity —The Formation of Folklore Studies.* Madison: University of Wisconsin Press, 1997.

Bensoussan, Maurice. *Le Ketchup & le gratin: Histoire(s) parallèle(s) des habitudes alimentaires françaises et américaines.* Paris: Éditions Assouline, 1999.

———. *Les particules alimentaires: Naissance de la gastronomie au XVIe siècle.* Paris: Maisonneuve & Larose, 2002.

Bernier, Georges. *Antonin Carême 1783–1833: La sensualité gourmande en Europe.* Paris: Grasset, 1989.

Bertho Lavenir, Catherine. *La roue et le stylo: Comment nous sommes devenus touristes.* Paris: Odile Jacob, 1999.

Bessière, Jacinthe. "Local Development and Heritage: Traditional Food and Cuisine as Tourist Attractions in Rural Areas." *Sociologia Ruralis* 38, no. 1 (1998): 21–34.

Billig, Michael. *Banal Nationalism.* London: Sage, 1995.

Boisard, Pierre. *Le Camembert—Mythe national.* Paris: Calmann-Lévy, 1992.

———. *Camembert—A National Myth.* Translated by Richard Miller. Berkeley and Los Angeles: University of California Press, 2003.

Boissel, Thierry. *Brillat-Savarin—Un chevalier candide.* Paris: Presses de la Renaissance, 1989.

Bonnain-Merdyck, Rolande. "Fourier, gastrosophe." In *Actualité de Fourier: Colloque d'Arc-et-Sans,* by Henri Lefebvre et al., pp. 145–80. Paris: Anthropos, 1975.

Bonnet, Jean-Claude. "Le Système de la cuisine et du repas chez Rousseau." *Poétique* 22 (1975): 244–67.

———. "Le Réseau culinaire dans l'*Encyclopédie.*" *Annales E.S.C.* 31, no. 5 (1976): 89–94.

———. "Carême ou les derniers feux de la cuisine décorative." *Romantisme* 17–18 (1977): 23–43.

———. "Carême, or the Last Sparks of Decorative Cuisine." In *Taste Nostalgia,* edited by Allen S. Weiss, pp. 155–82. New York: Lusitania Press, 1977.

———. "Présentation." In A. B. L. Grimod de la Reynière, *Écrits gastronomiques,* edited by Jean-Claude Bonnet, pp. 7–92. 1978. Paris: UGE/10-18, 1997.

Bourdain, Anthony. *Kitchen Confidential—Adventures in the Culinary Underbelly.* New York: Bloomsbury, 2000.

Bourdieu, Pierre. "Intellectual Field and Creative Project" [1966]. *Social Science Information* 8, no. 2 (1969): 89–119.

———. *Distinction: A Social Critique of the Judgement of Taste* [1979]. Translated by R. Nice. Cambridge, Mass.: Harvard University Press, 1984.

———. *The Field of Cultural Production.* New York: Columbia University Press, 1993.

———. *The Rules of Art: Genesis and Structure of the Literary Field* [1992]. Translated by S. Emanuel. Stanford, Calif.: Stanford University Press, 1996.

Braund, David, and John Wilkins, eds. *Athenaeus and His World: Reading Greek Culture in the Roman Empire.* Exeter: University of Exeter Press, 2001.

Brenner, Leslie. *The Fourth Star—Dispatches from inside Daniel Boulud's Celebrated New York Restaurant.* New York: Clarkson Potter, 2002.

Buford, Bill. "The Secret of Excess" [on Chef Mario Batali]. *New Yorker,* August 19 and 26, 2002, pp. 122–41.

Camporesi, Piero. *The Magic Harvest: Food, Folklore and Society* [1989]. Translated by J. K. Hall. Cambridge: Polity Press, 1993.

Capatti, Alberto. *Le Goût du nouveau—Origines de la modernité alimentaire*. Paris: Albin Michel, 1989.

Capatti, Alberto, and Massimo Montanari. *La Cuisine italienne—Histoire d'une culture*. Translated by Anna Colao with Mino Colao. 1999. Paris: Le Seuil, 2002.

Certeau, Michel de. *L'Invention de la vie quotidienne*. Paris: UGE/10-18, 1980.

———. *The Practice of Everyday Life*. Translated by Steven Rendell. Berkeley and Los Angeles: University of California Press, 1984.

Certeau, Michel de, Dominique Julia, and Jacques Revel. *Une politique de la langue— La Révolution française et les patois: L'enquête de Grégoire*. Paris: Gallimard, 1975.

Chang, K. C. Introduction to *Food in Chinese Culture: Anthropological and Historical Perspectives*, edited by K. C. Chang, pp. 3–21. New Haven, Conn.: Yale University Press, 1977.

Claflin, Kyri Watson. "Savoring the Rat." In *Situazioni d'assedio/Cities under Siege*, pp. 421–25. Milan: Clio-Polis, 2002.

Clark, Priscilla Parkhurst. *Literary France—The Making of a Culture*. Berkeley and Los Angeles: University of California Press, 1987.

Compagnon, Antoine. "La *Recherche du temps perdu* de Marcel Proust." In *Les Lieux de mémoire—La Nation—III—Les France*, edited by Pierre Nora, pp. 927–67. Paris: Gallimard, 1992.

Cooper, Ann. *"A Woman's Place Is in the Kitchen"—The Evolution of Women Chefs*. New York: Van Nostrand Reinhold, 1998.

Cooper, John. *Eat and Be Satisfied: A Social History of Jewish Food*. Northvale, N.J.: Jason Aronson, 1993.

Corbin, Alain, et al. *Les Usages politiques des fêtes aux XIXe et XXe siècles*. Paris: Publications de la Sorbonne, 1994.

Coulon, Christian. "La Cuisine comme objet politique." *Revue Internationale de politique comparée* 6, no. 2 (1999): 311–19.

———, ed. "Cuisine, Manières de table et politique." *Revue Française de science politique* 48, nos. 3–4 (June–August 1998).

Courtine, Robert. *Balzac à table*. Paris: Laffont, 1976.

——— [La Reynière, pseud.]. "Babette et les ortolans." *Le Monde*, November 12, 1988.

Csergo, Julia. 1997. "La Constitution de la spécialité gastronomique comme objet patrimonial en France (fin xviiie–xxe siècle)." In *L'Esprit des lieux—Le patrimoine et la cité*, edited by Daniel J. Grange and Dominique Poulot, pp. 183–93. Grenoble: Presses Universitaires de Grenoble, 1997.

———. "L'Émergence des cuisines régionales." In *Histoire de l'alimentation*, edited by Jean-Louis Flandrin and Massimo Montanari, pp. 823–41. Paris: Fayard, 1997.

———. "La modernité alimentaire au XIXe siècle." In *À table au XIXe siècle*, pp. 42–69. Paris: Flammarion, 2002.

———, ed. *Le Pot-au-feu—Ces plats mythiques qui ont fait la France*. Paris: Éditions Autrement, 1999.

D'Arms, John H. "Performing Culture: Roman Spectacle and the Banquets of the Powerful." In *The Art of the Ancient Spectacle,* edited by Bettina Bergmann and Christine Kondoleon. New Haven, Conn.: Yale University Press, 2000.

Diner, Hasia R. *Hungering for America: Italian, Irish, and Jewish Foodways in the Age of Migration.* Cambridge, Mass.: Harvard University Press, 2001.

Dornenburg, Andrew, and Karen Page. *Becoming a Chef.* New York: Van Nostrand Reinhold, 1995.

Douglas, Mary. "Deciphering a Meal" [1972]. In *Implicit Meanings: Essays in Anthropology.* London: Routledge & Kegan Paul, 1975.

Dulude, Julie. "Chowders Do Battle for Red Stocking." *Vineyard Gazette,* December 19, 1997, p. 8a.

Echikson, William. *Burgundy Stars—A Year in the Life of a Great French Restaurant.* Boston: Little, Brown & Co, 1995.

———. "Death of a Chef: The Changing Landscape of French Cooking." *New Yorker,* May 12, 2003, pp. 61–67.

Edwards, Nancy J. "The Science of Domesticity: Women, Education and National Identity in Third Republic France, 1880–1914." Ph.D. dissertation, University of California-Berkeley, 1997.

Elias, Norbert. *The Court Society.* Translated by E. Jephcott. Oxford: Blackwell, 1983.

———. *The Civilizing Process—Part 1, The History of Manners* [1939]. Translated by E. Jephcott. Oxford: Blackwell, 1994.

Ennès, Pierre. "1789–1848—Naissance de la table moderne." In *Histoire de la table,* edited by Pierre Ennès, Gérard Mabille, and Philippe Thiébaut, pp. 193–251. Paris: Flammarion, 1995.

Fantasia, Rick. "Fast Food in France." *Theory and Society* 24 (1995): 201–43.

Ferguson, Priscilla Parkhurst. *Paris as Revolution—Reading the 19th-Century City.* Berkeley and Los Angeles: University of California Press, 1994.

———. "A Cultural Field in the Making: Gastronomy in 19th-Century France." *American Journal of Sociology* 104, no. 3 (November 1998): 597–641.

———. "Paysages culinaires." In *Paysage et identité régionale, de pays rhônalpins en paysages,* edited by C. Burgard. Paris: Éditions La Passe de vent, 1999.

———. "Le pot-au-feu: Un plat qui fait la France." In *Le Pot au feu—Convivial, Familial: Histoires d'un mythe,* pp. 13–19. Paris: Éditions Autrement, 1999.

———. "Writing out of the Kitchen: Carême and the Invention of French Cuisine." *Gastronomica* (August 2003).

Ferguson, Priscilla Parkhurst, and Sharon Zukin. "What's Cooking." *Theory and Society* 24 (1995): 193–99.

———. "The Careers of Chefs: 'French' and 'American' Models of Cuisine." In *Eating Culture,* edited by Ron Scapp and Bryan Seitz, pp. 92–111. Albany: State University Press of New York, 1998.

Fine, Gary Alan. "Justifying Work: Occupational Rhetorics as Resources in Restaurant Kitchens." *Administration Science Quarterly* 41 (1996): 90–115.

———. *Kitchens: The Culture of Restaurant Work.* Berkeley and Los Angeles: University of California Press, 1996.

Fink, Beatrice. "Diderot face au manger: scénario de table et cuisine." In *Interpréter Diderot aujourd'hui.* Paris: Le Sycomore, 1984.

———. Introduction to *Les Liaisons savoureuses—Réflexions et pratiques culinaires au dix-huitième siècle.* St Étienne: Publications de l'Université de Saint-Étienne, 1995.

Fischler, Claude. *L'Homnivore—Le goût, la cuisine et le corps.* Paris: Odile Jacob, 1990.

———. "La 'Macdonaldisation' des moeurs." In *Histoire de l'Alimentation,* edited by Jean-Louis Flandrin and Massimo Montanari, pp. 859–79. Paris: Fayard, 1997.

Flandrin, Jean-Louis. "Choix alimentaires et art culinaire (xvie–xviiie siècles)." In *Histoire de l'Alimentation,* ed. Jean-Louis Flandrin and Massimo Montanari, pp. 657–81. Paris: Fayard, 1997.

———. "L'alimentation paysanne en économie de subsistance." In *Histoire de l'Alimentation,* ed. Jean-Louis Flandrin and Massimo Montanari, pp. 597–627. Paris: Fayard, 1997.

———. "De la diététique à la gastronomie, ou la libération de la gourmandise." In *Histoire de l'Alimentation,* ed. Jean-Louis Flandrin and Massimo Montanari, pp. 683–703. Paris: Fayard, 1997.

———. *L'ordre des mets.* Paris: Odile Jacob, 2002.

Flandrin, Jean-Louis, and Massimo Montanari, eds. *Histoire de l'alimentation.* Paris: Fayard, 1997.

———. *Food, A Culinary History.* New York: Columbia University Press, 1999.

Flandrin, Jean-Louis, Philip Hyman, and Mary Hyman. "La Cuisine dans la littérature de colportage." In *Le Cuisinier françois,* edited by Jean-Louis Flandrin, Philip Hyman, and Mary Hyman, pp. 11–107. Paris: Montalba, 1983.

Ford, Caroline. *Creating the Nation in Provincial France—Religion and Political Identity in Brittany.* Princeton, N.J.: Princeton University Press, 1993.

Fourier, Charles. *Oeuvres complètes.* 12 vols. Paris: Anthropos, 1966–68.

Freeman, Michael. "Sung." In *Food in Chinese Culture: Anthropological and Historical Perspectives,* edited by K. C. Chang, pp. 141–76. New Haven, Conn.: Yale University Press, 1977.

Gall, Michel. *Le Maître des Saveurs—La Vie d'Auguste Escoffier.* Paris: Éditions de Fallois, 2001.

Garval, Michael. "Grimod de la Reynière's *Almanach des gourmands:* Exploring the Gastronomic New World of Postrevolutionary France." In *French Food: On the Table, on the Page and in French Culture,* edited by Lawrence R. Schehr and Allen S. Weiss, pp. 51–70. New York: Routledge, 2001.

George, Joselyn. "Le Banquet des maires ou la Fête de la Concorde républicaine." In *Les Usages politiques des fêtes aux XIXe et XXe siècles,* by Alain Corbin et al., pp. 159–67. Paris: Publications de la Sorbonne, 1997.

Giard, Luce, and Pierre Mayol. *L'Invention du quotidien—2—Habiter, Cuisiner.* Paris: UGE, 1980.

Gillet, Philippe. *Le Goût et les Mots. Littérature et gastronomie (xive–xxe siècles)*. Paris: Éditions Payot & Rivages, 1987. 2d ed., Paris: Éditions Payot & Rivages, 1993.

Girard, Alain. "Le Triomphe de *La Cuisinière bourgeoise:* Livres culinaires, cuisine et société en France aux xviie et xviiie siècles." *Revue d'histoire moderne et contemporaine* 24 (October–December 1977): 497–523.

Goblot, Edmond. *La Barrière et le niveau—Essai sur la bourgeoisie française moderne.* 1927. Reprint, Paris: Presses Universitaires de France, 1967.

Goffman, Erving. *The Presentation of Self in Everyday Life.* New York: Doubleday, 1959.

Goldstein, Darra. "Gastronomic Reforms under Peter the Great: Toward a Cultural History of Russian Food." *Jahrbuch für Geschichte Osteuropas* 48 (2000): 481–510.

Goody, Jack. *Cooking, Cuisine and Class—A Study in Comparative Sociology.* Cambridge: Cambridge University Press, 1982.

Gopnik, Adam. "The Crisis in French Cooking." In *Paris to the Moon,* pp. 144–65. New York: Random House, 2000.

Guy, Christian. *Une histoire de la cuisine française.* Paris: Les Productions de Paris, 1962.

Hamp, Pierre. *Mes Métiers.* Paris: Gallimard-Éditions de la Nouvelle revue française, 1930.

Heinich, Nathalie. *Du peintre à l'artiste: Artisans et académiciens à l'âge classique.* Paris: Minuit, 1993.

Herpin, Nicolas. "Le Repas comme institution: Compte rendu d'une enquête exploratoire." *Revue française de sociologie* 29 (1988): 503–21.

Hobsbawm, Eric. "Inventing Traditions" and "Mass-Producing Traditions: Europe, 1870–1914." In *The Invention of Tradition,* ed. Eric Hobsbawm and Terence Ranger, pp. 1–4 and 263–307. Cambridge: Cambridge University Press, 1983.

Huetz de Lemps, Alain, and Jean-Robert Pitte, eds. *Les Restaurants dans le monde et à travers les âges.* Grenoble: Glenat, 1990.

Hyman, Mary, and Philip Hyman. "Imprimer la cuisine: Les livres de cuisine en France entre le xve et le xixe siècle." In *Histoire de l'alimentation,* edited by Jean-Louis Flandrin and Massimo Montanari, pp. 643–55. Paris: Fayard, 1997.

———. "Printing the Kitchen: French Cookbooks, 1480–1800." In *Food—A Culinary History,* edited by Jean-Louis Flandrin and Massimo Montanari, pp. 394–402. New York: Columbia University Press, 1999.

———. "Livres et cuisine au XIXe siècle." In *À table au XIXe siècle,* pp. 80–89. Paris: Flammarion, 2001.

———. "Les livres de cuisine imprimés en France du règne de Charles VIII à la fin de l'Ancien régime." In *Livres en bouche: Cinq siècles d'art culinaire français,* pp. 55–72. Paris: Bibliothèque Nationale de France-Hermann, 2001.

Hyman, Philip. "Culina mutata, Carême et l'ancienne cuisine." In *L'Art culinaire au XIXe siècle—Antonin Carême,* pp. 63–69. Paris: Délégation à l'action artistique de la ville de Paris, 1984.

———. "Culina mutata, Carême and l'ancienne cuisine." In *French Food: On the Table, on the Page, and in French Culture,* edited by Lawrence R. Schehr and Allen S. Weiss, pp. 71–82. New York and London: Routledge, 2001.

Ihl, Olivier. "De bouche à oreille: Sur les pratiques de commensalité dans la tradition républicaine du cérémonial de table." *Revue française de science politique* 48, nos. 3–4 (1998): 387–408.

Khare, R. S., ed. *The Eternal Food: Gastronomic Ideas and Experiences of Hindus and Buddhists.* Albany: State University of New York Press, 1992.

Kolbert, Elizabeth. "Everyone Lies." *New Yorker,* August 19 and 26, 2002, pp. 84–87.

Korsmeyer, Carolyn. *Making Sense of Taste—Food and Philosophy.* Ithaca, N.Y.: Cornell University Press, 1999.

Kuh, Patric. *The Last Days of Haute Cuisine—America's Culinary Revolution.* New York: Viking, 2001.

Kurlansky, Mark. *Cod—A Biography of the Fish That Changed the World.* New York: Walter & Co., 1995.

Laurendon, Gilles, and Laurence Laurendon. "Carême, ou le Palladio de la cuisine." In Antonin Carême, *L'Art de la cuisine française au dix-neuvième siècle: Traité Élémentaire et Pratique,* edited by Gilles Laurendon and Laurence Laurendon, pp. 7–19. Paris: Payot & Rivages, 1994.

———, eds. Antonin Carême, *L'Art de la cuisine française au dix-neuvième siècle: Traité Élémentaire et Pratique.* Paris: Payot & Rivages, 1994.

———. *L'Art de la cuisine française au XVIIe siècle.* Paris: Payot & Rivages, 1995.

Laurioux, Bruno. "Le règne de Taillevent." In *Livres en bouche—Cinq siècles d'art culinaire français,* pp. 31–45. Paris: Bibliothèque Nationale de France-Hermann, 2001.

Lévi-Strauss, Claude. "Social Structure" [1952]. In *Structural Anthropology.* Garden City, N.J.: Doubleday-Anchor, 1967.

———. *L'Origine des manières de table.* Paris: Plon, 1968.

Livres en bouche: Cinq siècles d'art culinaire français. Paris: Bibliothèque Nationale de France-Hermann, 2001.

Mabille, Gérard. "1690–1800—La Table à la française." In *Histoire de la table—Les arts de la table des origines à nos jours,* by Pierre Ennès, Gérard Mabille, and Philippe Thibaut, pp. 125–91. Paris: Flammarion, 1994.

MacDonogh, Giles. *Brillat-Savarin: The Judge and His Stomach.* Chicago: Ivan R. Dee, 1992.

Marchand, Bernard. *Paris, histoire d'une ville—xixe–xxe.* Paris: Seuil, 1993.

Mauss, Marcel. *The Gift* [1927]. Translated by I. Cunnison. New York: Norton, 1967.

May, Georges. "Diderot gastronome, Les recettes de cuisine de l'*Encyclopédie*." In *Quatre visages de Diderot.* Paris: Boivin, 1951.

McNamee, Thomas. "Dinner in Tuscany." *Saveur* 54 (November 2001), pp. 42–54.

Menger, Pierre-Michel. *Portrait de l'artiste en travailleur: Métamorphoses du capitalisme.* Paris: Le Seuil, 2002.

Mennell, Stephen. *All Manners of Food: Eating and Taste in England and France from the Middle Ages to the Present.* Oxford: Basil Blackwell, 1985.

Mervaud, Christiane. *Voltaire à table—Plaisir du corps, plaisir de l'esprit.* Paris: Éditions Desjonquères, 1998.

Mezner, Paul. 1998. *Crescendo of the Virtuoso: Spectacle, Skill, and Self-Promotion in Paris during the Age of Revolution.* Berkeley and Los Angeles: University of California Press, 1998.

Michel, Dominique. *Vatel et la naissance de la gastronomie.* Paris: Le Grand Livre du mois, 1999.

Miller, Susan Gilson, ed. and trans. *Disorienting Encounters: Travels of a Moroccan Scholar in France in 1845–1846.* Berkeley and Los Angeles: University of California Press, 1992.

Miller, Toby. "Screening Food: French Cuisine and the Television Palate." In *French Food: On the Table, on the Page, and in French Culture,* edited by Lawrence R. Schehr and Allen S. Weiss, pp. 221–28. New York: Routledge, 2001.

Mintz, Sidney W. *Tasting Food, Tasting Freedom—Excursions into Eating, Culture, and the Past.* Boston: Beacon Press, 1996.

Montanari, Massimo. *The Culture of Food.* Translated by C. Ipsen. Oxford: Blackwell, 1994.

Morin, Marie-Renée. "Une cuisine nouvelle." In *Livres en bouche—Cinq siècles d'art culinaire français,* pp. 179–221. Paris: Hermann, 2001.

Moulin, Leo. "Les Abats et le sacré." In *L'Imaginaire des nourritures,* edited by Simone Vierne. Grenoble: Presses Universitaires de Grenoble, 1989.

Mukerji, Chandra. *Territorial Ambitions and the Gardens of Versailles.* Cambridge: Cambridge University Press, 1997.

Neirinck, Edmond, and Jean-Pierre Poulain. *Histoire de la cuisine et des cuisiniers: Techniques culinaires et pratiques de table, en France, du Moyen-Age à nos jours.* 3d ed. Paris: Éditions Jacques Lanore, 2000.

Nora, Pierre. *Les Lieux de mémoire.* 7 vols. Paris: Gallimard, 1984–92.

Ory, Pascal. "La Gastronomie." In *Les Lieux de mémoire: La Nation—Les France—II,* edited by Pierre Nora, pp. 822–53. Paris: Gallimard, 1992.

———, ed. *Le Discours gastronomique français des origines à nos jours.* Paris: Gallimard-Julliard, 1998.

Ozouf, Jacques, and Mona Ozouf. *"Le tour de France par deux enfants:* Le livre rouge de la République." In *Les Lieux de mémoire: La République,* edited by Pierre Nora, pp. 291–321. Paris: Gallimard, 1984.

———. *"Le tour de France par deux enfants:* Le livre rouge de la République." In *Realms of Memory—The Construction of the French Past,* edited by Pierre Nora and translated by A. Goldhammer. 3 vols. New York: Columbia University Press, 1997.

Paul, Harry W. *Science, Vine and Wine, in Modern France.* Cambridge: Cambridge University Press, 1996.

Pépin, Jacques. *The Apprentice: My Life in the Kitchen.* Boston: Houghton-Mifflin, 2003.

Pitte, Jean-Robert. *Gastronomie française—Histoire et géographie d'une passion.* Paris: Fayard, 1991.

————. "Naissance et expansion des restaurants." In *Histoire de l'alimentation,* edited by Jean-Louis Flandrin and Massimo Montanari, pp. 765–78. Paris: Fayard, 1997.

————. *French Gastronomy—The History and Geography of a Passion.* New York: Columbia University Press, 2002.

Podles, Mary Elizabeth. "*Babette's Feast:* Feasting with Lutherans." *Antioch Review* 50, no. 3 (summer 1992): 551–67.

Rao, Hayagreeva, Philippe Monin, and Rodolphe Durand. "Institutional Change in Toque Ville: Nouvelle Cuisine as an Identity Movement in French Gastronomy." *American Journal of Sociology* 108, no. 4 (January 2003): 795–843.

Revel, Jean-François. *Un festin en paroles.* Paris: Pauvert, 1979.

Richard, Jean-Pierre. "Proust et l'objet alimentaire." *Littérature,* no. 6 (1972): 3–19.

Robuchon, Joël, and Elisabeth de Meurville. *Le Carnet de route d'un compagnon cuisinier.* Paris: Payot, 1995.

Rogov, Daniel. "Food as Filmic Metaphor or, 5,484 Words in Defense of Gastronomy." <http://www.stratsplace.com/rogov/food_as_film.html>.

Rotberg, Robert I., and Theodore K. Rabb, eds. *Hunger and History: The Impact of Changing Food Production and Consumption Patterns on Society.* Cambridge: Cambridge University Press [*Journal of Interdisciplinary History* 14, no. 2, (autumn 1983)].

Rowley, Anthony. *À Table! La Fête gastronomique.* Paris: Gallimard, 1994.

Ruhlman, Michael. *The Soul of a Chef—The Journey toward Perfection.* New York: Viking, 2000.

Russell, Beverly. *Women of Taste—Recipes and Profiles of Famous Women Chefs* [32 American chefs]. New York: John Wiley & Sons, 1997.

Schehr, Lawrence R. "Savory Writing: Marcel Rouff's *Vie et la passion de Dodin-Bouffant.*" In *French Food: On the Table, on the Page, and in French Culture,* edited by Lawrence R. Schehr and Allen S. Weiss, pp. 124–39. New York: Routledge, 2001.

Schehr, Lawrence R., and Allen S. Weiss, eds. *French Food: On the Table, on the Page, and in French Culture.* New York: Routledge, 2001.

Schimpf, David. "Keylines from *Babette's Feast.*" <http://cw.mariancollege.edu/dschimpf/keylinesfrombabettesfeast.htm>.

Schivelbusch, Wolfgang. *Disenchanting the Night: The Industrialization of Light in the 19th Century.* Berkeley and Los Angeles: University of California Press, 1988.

Schrambley, Regina. "That New Brightness of the Plate: Chefs Translate the Classics." *New York Times,* October 10, 2001, pp. F1, F4.

Schuler, Jean. "Kierkegaard at *Babette's Feast:* The Return to the Finite." *The Journal of Religion and Film* 1, no. 2 (1997). <http://www.unomaha.edu/~wwwjrf/BabetteWW.htm>

Serventi, Silvano. "La table dressée ou la mise en ordre de l'abondance." In *Livres en bouche—Cinq siècles d'art culinaire français*, pp. 167–77. Paris: Hermann, 2001.

Shaw, Timothy. *The World of Escoffier*. London: Zwemmer, 1994.

Simmel, Georg. "The Metropolis and Mental Life," "The Stranger," and "Sociology of the Meal." In *Simmel on Culture*, edited by David Frisby and M. Featherstone. London: Sage, 1998.

Sokolov, Raymond. *Why We Eat What We Eat*. New York: Simon & Schuster, 1991.

Soler, Jean. "Sémiotique de la nourriture dans la Bible." *Annales E.S.C.*, no. 4 (1973): 943–55.

Spang, Rebecca. *The Invention of the Restaurant: Paris and Modern Gastronomic Culture*. Cambridge, Mass.: Harvard University Press, 2000.

Stevens, Kimberly. "A 24-Karat Wedding Cake with Diamonds You Eat." *New York Times*, March 23, 2003, sec. 9, col. 1, p. 15.

Tannahill, R. *Food in History*. New York: Stein and Day, 1973.

Terrio, Susan J. *Crafting the Culture and History of French Chocolate*. Berkeley and Los Angeles: University of California Press, 2001.

Teti, Vito. "L'Invention d'une cuisine régionale—Le cas de la cuisine calabraise." In *Alimentation et Régions*, edited by Jean Peltre and Claude Thouvenot, pp. 413–21. Nancy: Presses Universitaires de Nancy, 1989.

Teulon, Fabrice. "Gastronomy, *Gourmandise* and Political Economy in Brillat-Savarin's *Physiology of Taste*." *The European Studies Journal* 15, no. 1 (1998): 41–53.

———. "Le Voluptueux et le Gourmand: Économie de la jouissance chez La Mettrie et Brillat-Savarin." *Symposium* 52, no. 3 (fall 1998): 176–92.

Teuteberg, Hans-Jurgen, and Jean-Louis Flandrin, 1997. "Transformations de la consommation alimentaire." In *Histoire de l'alimentation*, edited by Jean-Louis Flandrin and Massimo Montanari, pp. 725–46. Paris: Fayard, 1997.

Tobin, Ronald, ed. *Littérature et gastronomie*. Paris: Biblio 17 Papers on French Seventeenth Century Literature, 1985.

Toussaint-Samat, Maguelonne. *Histoire de la cuisine bourgeoise du moyen âge à nos jours*. Paris: Albin Michel, 2001.

Trubek, Amy. *Haute Cuisine—How the French Invented the Culinary Profession*. Philadelphia: University of Pennsylvania Press, 2000.

———. "Terroir: From Local Knowledge to National Discourse." Paper delivered at the meetings of the Society for French Historical Studies, Milwaukee, April 2003.

Veblen, Thorstein. *The Theory of the Leisure Class*. 1899. Reprint, New York: Viking-Penguin, 1979.

Vicaire, Georges. *Bibliographie gastronomique*. 1890. Reprint, Geneva: Slatkine, 1978.

Vierne, Simone, ed. *L'Imaginaire des nourritures*. Grenoble: Presses Universitaires de Grenoble, 1987.

Watson, James L., ed. *Golden Arches East—McDonald's in East Asia*. Stanford, Calif.: Stanford University Press, 1997.

Weber, Eugen. *From Peasants to Frenchmen.* Stanford, Calif.: Stanford University Press, 1976.

Weiss, Allen S. *Feast and Folly: Cuisine, Intoxication, and the Poetics of the Sublime.* Albany: State University of New York Press, 2002.

Wheaton, Barbara Ketchum. *Savoring the Past: The French Kitchen and Table from 1300 to 1789.* Philadelphia: University of Pennsylvania Press, 1983.

Wilkins, John, David Harvey, and Mike Dobson, eds. *Food in Antiquity.* Exeter: University of Exeter Press, 1995.

Wilson, C. Anne. *"The Appetite and the Eye"—Visual Aspects of Food and Its Presentation within Their Historic Context.* Edinburgh: Edinburgh University Press, 1991.

Wright, Wendy M. *"Babette's Feast:* A Religious Film." *The Journal of Religion & Film* 1, no. 2 (1997). <http://www.unomaha.edu/~wwwjrf/BabetteWW.htm>

Zukin, Sharon. *Landscapes of Power: From Detroit to Disney World.* Berkeley and Los Angeles: University of California Press, 1991.

———. *The Cultures of Cities.* Oxford: Blackwell, 1995.

Index

as calling, 133; versus chefing, 131–
47, 150, 192–93; definition of, 215;
in England, 132, 134–35, 139, 159–
60, 185; versus gastronomy and cuisine, 3, 20–21; home, 20, 22–23,
131, 143, 164; as modern spectacle,
160
cooks, 141; as *bricoleur*, 144; Mercier
on, 135; Escoffier on, 144–45; negative opinions on, 131, 140; Sophie
(cook to D. Véron), 133
Cooper, James Fenimore, 1, 171–72,
233n21
cordon-bleu (female cook), 141, 230n29
cuisine, American, lack of, 9, 106
cuisine, aristocratic, 25, 42, 132, 135
cuisine, bourgeoise, 42–43, 116,
131–32, 237n4
cuisines, peasant, 25
cuisines, regional, 23, 129–30
Cuisinière bourgeoise (Menon), 40–43,
143, 153, 218n22; English translation of, 41–43
culinarity, 2, 8
culinary contract, 179, 181–85
culinary culture, 3, 17, 167; versus
restaurant world and gastronomic
field, 108
culinary discourse, 18, 33
culinary geography, 46–47, 81–82,
129–31, 158, 170
culinary journals, 124, 140, 159, 223n8
culinary nationalism, xiv, 81, 126,
172–73, 185; of Dodin-Bouffant,
176–79
culinary pantheon, xiv, 6, 129
culinary place, versus cultural space,
21, 44
culinary polemics, 20, 37–38, 75
culinary sociolects, 173
culinary texts, 17, 22, 83, 132, 183
cultural field, 104–5, 225n19

Curnonsky (Maurice Sailland). *See*
La France gastronomique

De Certeau, Michel, 142, 144, 176, 192
democratization of dining, 167. *See also*
restaurants
Discourse on Method (Descartes), versus
cuisine, 37, 50
distinction, strategy of, 125, 139,
154–55
Dodin-Bouffant (protagonist of *La Vie et
la pasion de Dodin-Bouffan-Gourmet*),
121, 176–81; on cooking as love,
181; and redefinition of culinary
couple, 179–80
Down and Out in Paris and London (Orwell), 156–57
Dumas, Alexandre, on Carême, 51, 56,
59, 60, 76

Elias, Norbert, 12, 29–30; on civilizing
process, 29–30, 39; on dance as
model for relationship between
structure and freedom, 29
Encyclopédie, 90
Escoffier, Auguste, 51, 72; as author,
157; on Carême, 51; celebrity of,
157; on cuisine as diplomacy, 7,
157, 174, 234n24; dishes invented
by, 157, 170; influence of, 145; Legion of Honor awarded to, 174;
partnership of, with César Ritz, 157;
on sociability, 184; street named for,
173; on women cooking, 144–45

fast food, 106, 149, 166
food: versus cooking and cuisine, 15–
22; ephemerality of, 3, 151; fears
raised by, 15, 35, 174–75, 234n25;
negative attitudes toward, 89–92;
religious proscriptions and, 35,
89; versus sex, 16; as total sensory